AF531748

INTERNATIONAL ENVIRONMENTAL ECONOMICS

MANAGEMENT AND POLICY ISSUES

Edited by

Dr. Ram Krishna Mandal

Associate Professor of Economics
Dera Natung Govt. College
Itanagar – 791 113
Arunachal Pradesh
(India)
e-mail: rkm_1966@yahoo.co.in

DISCOVERY PUBLISHING HOUSE PVT. LTD.

NEW DELHI-110 002

Published by:
Tilak Wasan
DISCOVERY PUBLISHING HOUSE PVT. LTD.
4383/4A, Ansari Road, Darya Ganj
New Delhi-110 002 (India)
Phone : +91-11-23279245, 43596064-65
Fax : +91-11-23253475
E-mail : parul.wasan@gmail.com
discoverypublishinghouse@gmail.com
web : www.discoverypublishinggroup.com

***First Edition:* 2012**
ISBN: 978-93-5056-151-5

Management and Policy Issues

Printed at:
Shree Balaji Art Press
Delhi

Dedicated

to

Elder Sisters

Mrs. Mita Mandal (School Mistress)

Mrs. Sandhya Mandal (Custom Officer)

Miss Malati Mandal (School Mistress)

Dr. Deepali Mandal (Principal)

With Reverence and Affection

PREFACE

The present study is an attempt at a comprehensive and critical analysis for the role of *Management and Policy Issues* for the Protection of Natural Resources in the world. Environmental Degradation has been the most remarkable realization of the last century and it is likely to of increasing significance for the present century and beyond for the sake of healthy living of human being and all living things on this very live planet of the universe. The ignorance as well as prolonged disregard with respect, to the nature and on the contrary its cumulative impact at the advent of rapid industrialization that has occurred, misuse as well as overuse of natural resources due to the rising of standards of living and population explosion has very much resulted in a severe backlash which has ultimately affected the Environment by way of its severe effect resulting in soil degradation, global warming, depletion of stratospheric ozone, environmental pollution, loss of bio-diversity thus resulting in economic disparities in our own country passing through the critical phase of industrialisation and international trade. The people's participation in the management of *common property resources can increase the productivity of privately owned assets such as agricultural holdings and milch cattle. The study also provides an analytical model of cooperative programmes for the optimal sharing of resource management between governmental agencies and people's organizations*. ISO 14001: 2004 is an environmental management standard. It defines a set of environmental management requirements for environmental management systems. The purpose of this standard is to help all kinds of organizations to protect the environment, to prevent pollution, and to improve their overall environmental performance. This new ISO 14001 standards was officially published on November 15, 2004. It cancels and replaces the old ISO 14001 1996 standard. ISO 14001 1996 expired on May 15, 2006. Since it was first published in 1996, ISO 14001 has rapidly become the most important environmental standard in the world. Thousands of organizations use it, environmentalists support it, and governments actively encourage its use. ISO 14001 applies to all types of organizations. It doesn't matter what size they are or what they do.

The present volume is a collection of papers contributed by eminent scholars, academicians, policy makers, bureaucrats and thinkers from different parts of the world. The publication of this book would not have been possible without their contributions. Their work is based on diverse source materials which consist of official reports, published journals, books and findings of field work. Most of their writings are based either on the social structural aspects or on the social dynamism and rapid regional socio-economic transformation. I have felt the need to put some of their writings together so as to enable the readers to get an overall idea about the aspect. Some of their writings have been updated, revised and edited for the purpose. I hope that the readers will find it relevant for understanding the present problem raised by globalization. I hope, this book will benefit immensely the students, researchers, teachers, young scholars, planners and administrators in the area of sustainable rural development and common property resources. I am conscious of the bulk of the work which becomes largely inevitable on account of the intrinsic sweep of the subject. I acknowledge my gratitude to all contributors, whose works are consulted in the preparation of this volume.

I would be falling in my duty if I do not extend my gratitude to my Principal, Shri Tomar Ete, Dera Natung Government College, Itanagar, Arunachal Pradesh, India for generating in me an interest to edit this book.

I also acknowledge the inspiration received from my beloved teacher and guide, Prof. Chandan Kumar Mukhopadyaya, Department of Economics, University of North Bengal, West Bengal. I extend my gratitude to him.

I have received support and cooperation from my colleagues Dr. A.I. Singh and Mrs. Madhuparna Bhattacharjee, I acknowledge a deep sense of gratitude to them.

I am also taking the opportunity to thank profusely to Discovery Publishing House Pvt. Ltd., New Delhi, for publication this book.

Lastly, I am grateful to the members of my family: Mrs. Archana Mandal (wife) and Miss Anusree Krishna Mandal (Daughter) and Master Avinandan Krishna Mandal (son) for their untiring support and patience during the work of this volume.

Dr. Ram Krishna Mandal

CONTENTS

LIST OF CONTRIBUTORS

Prof. G. Manachala, Head of P G Studies, Mahaveer Institute of Science & Technology, Hyderabad, Andhra Pradesh, India

Prof. U. Padmavathi, Vishwa Vishwani Institute of Systems & Management, Hyderabad-, 500078, Andhra Pradesh, India

Dr. Nursadh Ali, Principal, Chandidas Mahavidyalaya, Khujutipara, Birbhum, West Bengal, India

Prof. Pradeep K Vaid, Department of Public Administration(ICDEOL), and Director, Institute of Tribal Studies, Himachal Pradesh University, Summerhill, Shimla, Himachal Pradesh, Pin Code-171005,

Prof. Pavan Mishra, Professor & Director, Rajeev Gandhi Management Institute, Bhopal, M.P., India

Mrs. Swati Mathur, Assistant Professor, Rajeev Gandhi Management Institute, Bhopal, M.P., India

Mr. Bhupendra Singh Jina, Faculty, Department of Botany, DSB Campus, Kumaun University, Nainital, Uttarakhand, India

Mr. Kala Jina, Facult, Department of Geography, DSB Campus, Kumaun University, Nainital, Uttarakhand, India

Mr. Pankaj Sah, Faculty, Department of Applied Sciences, Higher College of Technology, Al-Khuwair, PO Box 74, PC 133 Muscat (Sultanate of Oman)

Mr. Chandrapal Singh Bohra, Faculty, Department of Forestry, SSJ Campus Almora, Kumaun University Nainital, Uttarakhand, India

Dr. R. Ganapathi, Assistant Professor in Commerce and Directorate of Distance Education, Alagappa University, Karaikudi. Pin Code – 630 003, Tamil Nadu, India

Mr. S. Sannasi, Senior Faculty, Department of Commerce, Park's College (Autonomous), Tirupur. Pin Code – 641 605, Tamil Nadu, India

Mr. Francis Kuriakose, Assistant Professor of Commerce & Management, University of Kerala, Thiruvananthapuram, Kerala, India

Ms. Deepa Kylasam Iyer, writer, researcher, freelance journalist and Editor, 3rd Floor, 22 A, Manakular Vinayakar Koil Street, Puducherry- 605001, India

Dr. N. V. Kavitha, Faculty of Commerce, St. Ann's College for Women, Santosh Nagar Colony, Mehdipatnam, Hyderabad-500028, India

Ms. Usha Rani, Faculty of Commerce, St. Ann's College for Women, Santosh Nagar Colony, Mehdipatnam, Hyderabad-500028, India

Dr. N. Sivakumar, Assistant Professor, Department of Commerce, Sri Sathya Sai University, Brindavan Campus, Kadugodi, Bangalore 560067, India

Dr. T. Ravikumar, Associate Professor, Department of Chemistry, Sri Sathya Sai University, Brindavan Campus, Kadugodi, Bangalore 560067, India

Dr. A. Abdul Raheem, Assistant Professor (SS), Dept of Economics, The New College, Chennai-14, Tamil Nadu, India

Md. Tapan Mahmud, Lecturer, Dept. of Business Administration, ASA University, Dhaka, Bangladesh

Mohammad Tariq Hasan, Senior Lecturer, Dept. of Business Administration, East-West University, Dhaka, Bangladesh.

Mrs. N. V. Kavita, Faculty of Commerce, St. Ann's College for Women, Santosh Nagar Colony, Mehdipatnam, Hyderabad-500028, India

Mrs. Anuradha, Faculty of Commerce, St.Ann's College for Women, Santosh Nagar Colony, Mehdipatnam, Hyderabad-500028, India

Mrs. Swena Shanti Mathur, Faculty of Commerce, St. Ann's College for Women, Santosh Nagar Colony, Mehdipatnam, Hyderabad-500028, India

Dr. Santosh Singh Bais, Assistant Professor, Dept. of Commerce and Management, Govt. First Grade College, Chimcholi -585307, Dist: Gulbarga, Karnataka, India

Mr. Sangappa Hosmani, Associate Professor & HOD, Dept. of Political Science, Smt. Channamma Basappa Patil College, Chincholi–585307, Dist: Gulbarga, Karnataka, India

Mr. Rajiv Mili, G.B. Pant Institute of Himalayan Environment & Development, N.E. Unit, Vivek Vihar, Itanagar-791 113, Arunachal Pradesh, India

Mr. L. Jitendro Singh, G.B. Pant Institute of Himalayan Environment & Development, N.E. Unit, Vivek Vihar, Itanagar-791 113, Arunachal Pradesh, India

Mr. Prasanna. K. Samal, G.B. Pant Institute of Himalayan Environment & Development, N.E. Unit, Vivek Vihar, Itanagar-791 113, Arunachal Pradesh, India

Mr. Mihin Dollo, G.B. Pant Institute of Himalayan Environment & Development, N.E. Unit, Vivek Vihar, Itanagar-791 113, Arunachal Pradesh, India

Mr. Bipul Kumar Rabha, Ph. D. Research Scholar, Department of Economics, University of Hyderabad, Hyderabad-500046, Andhra Pradesh, India

Mr. Bhaskar Sarmah, Academic Consultant in Economics, Krishna Kanta Handiqui State Open University, Housefed Complex, Dispur, Guwahati-781006, Assam, India

Dr. Ram Krishna Mandal, Associate Professor of Economics, Dera Natung Govt. College, Itanagar-791 113, Arunachal Pradesh, India, Email: rkm_1966@yahoo.co.in, Mobile-+91-96 477 582 09 / +91-943 6633 120

1

Environmental Governance
Value Creation

— Prof. G. Manachala & Prof. U. Padmavathi

Introduction

The concept of Governance expresses the relationship between Rules-ruled and Ruler, that are referred as regime features. Good governance depends upon ability to exercise power and to make sound decisions over time across Economic, Human and Environmental resources, that in turn depends on Resources allocation, implementation and maintenance of key relations. A good governance can be featured as:

1. Technical and Managerial competencies;
2. Organizational capacity;
3. Reliability, Predictability and the rule of law;
4. Accountability;
5. Transparency and open information systems; and
6. Effective participation

Deterioration of natural resources may effect the livelyhood of rural dwellers and make them to leave their homes into urban centres resulting in urban decay. Governmental policies such as Land tenure systems, Credit policies, Taxation policies Animal husbandry, Mining, Forestry etc, will effect the environment. Hence environmental governance needs to be reviewed in a broader perspective as many cross sectional issues are involved in national and global environment.

The roots of environmental regulations is UK. Over the last two decades, these roots have become entwined with the growth of ideas, often emanating from Brussels, that the environment itself is deserving of protection. A multitude of laws have been designed specially to control environmental degradation. In spite UK has roots, USA has made a commendable progress in environmental issues.

Environmental Legislations in India

The concern for environmental protection had started in 1970s in India. Right to a wholesome environment is a fundamental right. Article 48A of the constitution entrusts upon the state to take the measure to protect and improve environment and to safeguard forests and wildlife in the country. Article 51G (g) makes it a fundamental duty of every citizen to protect and improve the natural environment including lakes, rivers, forests and wild life. To provide a structure in this direction The National Committee on Environmental Planning and Coordination (NCEPC)was brought into existence in 1972. Government of India has set up a 'Department of Environment' under Ministry of Science and Technology, in November, 1980, to act as a nodal agency for protection of Environment, Eco-development work and development of projects and their appraisals. Finally, Environment (Protection) Act,1986, was passed to provide an integrated approach to tackle environmental pollution problems.

Legislative framework on Environmental Protection

Water	Air	Wastes Handling & Management
1. Water Pollution Act, 1974 2. The Water Prevention and Control Pollution) Cess Act,1977	1. Air Pollution(Prevention & Control) Act, 1981 2. Bhopal Gas Tragedy (December 2/3), 1984 3. The Air (Prevention & Control of Pollution) Act, 1988	1. The Hazardous Wastes (Management and Handling) Rules, 1989 2. Manufacture, Storage and Import of Hazardous Chemicals Rules, 1989 3. The Public Liability Insurance Act, 1991 4. The National Environment Tribunal Act,1995 5. The Bio-Chemical Waste (Management)

Environmental Acts Applicable to any Manufacturing Unit:

1. Water Pollution Act, 1974 (Amended in 1988)
2. The Air (Prevention and Control of Pollution)Act, 1981 (Amended in 1988)

3. The Environmental Protection Act, 1986 (With Rules 1986 & 1987) (EPA)
4. The Forest (Conservation) Act, 1980 (Amended in 1988)
5. The Wild Life Protection Act, 1972 (Amended in 1991)
6. Mines and Mineral (Development and Regulation) Act,1957

The issues of pollution are not simple legislative or administrative actions, but matter of culture frailties, social acceptance and issues of governance. 1. In India, people are culturally in sensitive towards their rights and liabilities; so the political parties use the personal properties of households for painting several slogans and advertisements for their personal campaign; 2. The use of plastic bags for own advertisement by business people and throwing of these bags by users at neighborhood and eco-sensitive places; and 3. The business people consider environmental governance is an extra cost to them. Now the question is how the governance approach towards pollution will contribute environment protection. This is possible only through internalization of corporate governance as a part of daily routine and to develop respect towards human environment and with introduction of comprehensive legislation on Environmental Governance in place of existing several anti-pollution legislations.

Basic Structure of Effective Environment Governance Model

To be responsive to the complex challenges of Environmental Management, the structure of effective corporate governance shall comprise the following dimensions:

1. *Legislative and Policy Making*—To be the Responsibility of MoFE
2. *Regulation, Monitoring and Enforcement*—To be the responsibility of—to be the responsibility of National Environment Protection Authority (NEPA)
3. *Adjudication*: To be the responsibility of National Green Tribunal (NGT), A bill for this has been introduced in the Parliament. This will support the constitutional support of High Courts.

The state Pollution Control Boards (SPCBs) will continue to play their respective roles in Environmental Management. Central Pollution Control Board (CPCB) requires some functional adjustments by taking into account of role of NEPA

Environmental Clearance Process

- Identifying the location for proposed plant
- Compliance of laws and guidelines relating to the proposed plant location and to verify whether the project requires environmental clearance

- If the proposed project requires clearance, the proponent has to conduct an Environment Impact Assessment (EIA) either directly or through consultant.
- Based on EIA, Verify the project under category of the project, If it comes under 'B' category, is referred to state Government for clearance. If the project comes under B1, a detailed report on EIA is to be prepared. Otherwise, In case of B2, preparation reports on EIA is not required.
- In case of projects, other than B2, The promoter approaches State Pollution Control Board and State Forest Department (If the project is proposed on forest land) and submits EIA report.
- SPCB evaluates and assesses EIA report and measures quality of effluents generated from proposed unit.
- Public hearing is mandatory in the process of environmental clearance for certain projects (Manufacturing). It facilitates a legal space for public of that area and Public hearing committee, formed by Government, to press their views and objections, and submits its report to Ministry of Forests and Environment, for the next stage of approval.
- If SPCB satisfies with prescribed effluent and emission standards set/ proposed by the project, It issues 'No object Certificate (NOC).
- If the falls under Category 'A', Submission of an application to the Ministry of Forests and Environment for Environmental Clearance. If the Project falls under category 'B', an application is to be submitted to State Government, Along with EIA Report, details of Public hearing and NOC.
- Multi-disciplinary staff working under Ministry of Environmental and Forests, Scrutinizes applications and take site- visits and consults with promoters and places the proposals before Environmental Appraisal Committee, specially constituted for respective sector. Special committees are constituted for each sector such as Mining, industry, River Valley etc.
- The said committee meets regularly in the Ministry, to appraise the proposals.
- The Committee arranges Public hearing in case of controversial projects, where Public interest gets effected. Announcements for such Public hearings shall be given 30 days before through News-papers.
- Based on the appraisals and public hearing, Appraisal Committee makes their recommendations for approval or rejection of proposed project.

- Based on the recommendations of the committee, Ministry of Environment and Forests, approves or rejects projects.
- Where the project requires Environmental clearance and approval under Forest (Conservation Act 1980, Proposals for the both are to be processed simultaneously for approval or rejection.
- Once requisite documents are received from the authorities and Public hearing hearings are held, assessment and evaluation from environmental angle is completed within 90 days and the decision of the Ministry shall be conveved within 30 days thereafter.
- The clearance granted is valid for a period of five years from commencement of construction/operation of the project.

Environmental Legislations—Business Practices

It is imperative to the business units to make adequate arrangements for compliance of environmental legislations. It is estimated that 70 per cent of waste material could be eliminated through better design decisions, reuse and alternative use of materials. Vedanta Mining is trying to bring Aluminum as an alternative to wood by mining more mica and processing it locally. With adoption of this alternative, many trees are saved and will contribute to environmental protection. Inhabitants voice is otherwise as we are going to loose lots of medical plants of rare quality, as it is a hilly area (Niyamgiri Hills).It is creating a dilemma between State and Central Governments whether to go for Mining activity.

Organizations shall chalk out such Environmental governance that encourage to implement the best available technology which is economically viable to them to achieve the environmental objectives. According to Environmental Management system model for International Standards, ISO 14001 requirements, include Structural policy covering the existing legislations applicable to Environment, Environmental policy, Environmental Planning, Technology, implementation and operation, controlling, Management Review and Continual improvement.

Environmental Activities—Value Creation

A well designed and integrated EMS will reduce operating costs through effective and optimal utilization of resources, Business processes, appropriate waste management policy and compliance of existing environmental laws. It also influences profitability of organizations both in tangible and intangible ways in the form of enhanced productivity, morale motivation, relationships with external agencies, protecting brand names and image, identifying new products etc. The proper environmental management gives the following benefits:

1. The effective environmental system strengthens broader competitiveness related goals
2. It enhances goodwill, in turn, organizations may identify new products/projects under the same roof.
3. The compliance of environmental Laws will result into
   - Avoidance of punishment—both prosecution and fines
   - No liability on environmental taxes
   - With the increase in brand value, sales will enhance
   - Minimises contingent liabilities
   - Compliance of CSR improves corporate image
   - Safeguards and gives pollution free environment for future generations
4. Every corporate will realize its responsibility in safeguarding environment in which they operate and identifies Implements an effective environmental management system in their organization.
5. Increases Resources Utilisation rates and efficiency of processes bt reducing wastes.
6. Value addition to the economy as a whole.

Environmental Governance in Auto Industry

The Auto industry plays a key role in the transport sector posing the environmental issues that evolved due to inferior quality of fuel, traffic planning, structure of roads etc. causing air pollution. The implementation of Environmental Management Policy (EMS) even on voluntary basis by the industry, environmental accidents and disasters can be minimized and many lives can be saved, in addition, other benefits such as reduced pressure on environment, reduced cost of enforcement etc.

A Case study

Case—EHT Coils Technology

The study was conducted by Icon International Limited, Mumbai, India

Operation/activity taken up-Installation of Pitch lines by avoiding boiler operation in its carbon plant.

Operation—Carbon plant was producing carbon electrolytic paste by mixing calcinated petroleum coke and pitch. Molten Pitch at 180° C is transferred from pitch process tank to the mixer.

Earlier operation—Seam was generated from a boiler o 3000kg/hr capacity and and a working pressure of 7 kg/cm. The average furnace oil consumption was from 10-15 litres/Ton of carbon paste production.

Existing—Steam is passed in the outer jacket of pitch pipe line, that avoids loss of heat from pitch during transfer. For the purpose of containing heat in the jacketed pipelines, strainer, NRV and PRV were replaced by plain stainless steel material. Electrical heat tracer was rapped around the pipe line and synthetic wool insulation with aluminum cladding was done. The heat tracer oil cal generate 180° C temperature within 24 hours. Electric Heat Tracer consumes only 32 watts of electrical energy per meter length which is much lower than electricity consumed earlier.

Result—The operation gives the following benefits:

1. Avoids the operation of boiler
2. Reduces oil consumption in carbon paste preparation

Proactive Environmental player value Creation

Value creation with new technology in 1st year	
Total investment (US $)	45000
Energy cost savings	190000
Additional savings beyond energy (Water, Raw material etc.) (US$)	40000
Electricity Savings, (MWh)	15
Oil savings (Kl)	540
CO_2 Mitigated (Tons)	1644
Pay back period of Capital investment for this technological upgradation	<3 Months

Conclusion

Pollution in India is a major problem in India. The Indian Government is turning its attention to environmental problems and focuses how to address them. One of the important activities to be taken up is, to strengthen environmental governance. Organizations are required to have cultural internalization of environmental governance in their daily routine activities and concern and respect for human environment. This is possible only through good governance approach. The Environmental Management may influence performance of companies, in the form of reduction in costs, enhances revenues through value creation and strengths competitive advantage. The authors believe that effective environmental governance will create value addition to the corporate monetarily as well as non-monetarily and protects Natural resources and environment for future generations.

REFERENCES

Mofe.nic.in

www.indiaenvironmentalportal.org.in

Jose PD (1999), Environment: The Next Source of Competitive Advantage, The EHS Magazine, 5th Issue, March, pp-5-9

The Financial Express, dated 17th January, 2011, pp. 1 & 2.

Case—The Study is Conducted by Icon International Limited, Mumbai, India.

2

Community-based Forest Management Policy in Thailand

— Dr. Nursadh Ali

Introduction

Forest management policy has undergone a paradigm shift in most of the countries in Southeast Asian countries. Based on the strategy of devolution of power to the local communities through decentralization policies and laws, government espoused national forest management policy for a greater cause like more sustainable system of natural resource stewardship. It is argued that devolution of resource management and access rights to local communities has to be an important policy tool as rural people have a significant role to play in managing and protecting forest lands including those presumably under state jurisdiction. This transformation at policy level is well documented by Poffenberger (1996) when he remarks "Each year more nations are approving initiatives that provide forest users groups with greater rights and responsibilities in the care of protected areas, upland watershed forests, protection forests and timber concession" that clearly imply the nature and status of community forest management at official level. However, the apparent change in policy from the traditional state managed top-down approach to the community level was never a spontaneous step from government side but a result of struggles in many places and stirred by the acknowledgement of the limits of government agencies in managing forest resources (and pressure from the donor countries as well) which had supposedly resulted in massive deforestation and substantial degradation of these resources in preceding years. However, as follow up action government of Thailand and its agency started implementing the participatory management policy during last decade of the previous century by Community Forest Management (CFM) or more recently Community Forest Bill (CFB).

Review of Literature

Studies on participation in resource management have shown that poor communities not only have significant incentives to management their resources sustainable but they also have often been able to develop a variety of effective and adaptable means to do so. Numerous studies on common property resource management have been conducted and worldwide evidences show that local people dependent on forest resources collectively involve designing rules and regulations for sustainable resource governance on which their welfare depends (Ostrom, 1990; Baland and Platteau, 1996; Ghate and Jhoda, 2006). These studies report that under certain conditions local people of their own can manage common resources like forest successfully. In Thailand studies reveal that local communities have long managed and used forests by developing a set of community laws that indicate how local forest is to be used (Hafner, 1990; Pragtong and Thomas, 1990). A national inventory conducted by Royal Forestry Department (RDF) documents overall 12,000 rural community groups protecting forest patches ranging from 1 to 4,000 hectares for a variety of religious, ecological, and economic purposes.

The mountainous region of northern Thailand is the habitat of many ethnic groups proven to be knowledge forest managers. Community Forestry has been practiced in many regions of Thailand for centuries. Increasing conflicts and competition over forest resources between community members, between neighbouring villages, and between state agencies and local people have posed serious challenges to Community Forest ideology to prove itself as a viable system of resource management (Santasombat, 2003). During the past two decades, there has been a steady increase in the number of community-based projects in biodiversity management. Some of the most critical issues that still need to be tackled are the unequal power relations in ownership of, and access to, natural resources, and the recognition of indigenous people and local communities' rights, and their traditional knowledge and customary use. A much more active approach is needed in order to respond to indigenous people and communities' efforts, initiatives and demands as well as to fulfill governments' obligation under international law (Ferrari, 2006).

In fact many studies report that local communities in general and indigenous tribal in particular traditionally have long history of forest use and management systems where they themselves develop sets of communal institutions that indicate how local forest to be used sustainably (Hafner, 1990; Ghate and Jhoda, 2006) subject to customary rights on forest lands. But unfortunately these indigenous patterns of stewardship of natural resource conservation remain in the shadows because they are given little or no recognition under the land laws and national forest management policies in most Asian nations and hence the new policy only rarely result in the strengthening the locally constituted resource management institutional arrangements (Agrawal and Ostrom, 2001; Ribot, 2002,2004). There are plans and policy of CFM in Thailand but there is no serious discussion of legal recognition of minorities' rights to live in forest (Anan, 1998).

People may be deprived of access to the resources on which they depend, their traditional tenure rights and rights to exclude outsiders may be abrogated, or their ability to make their own decisions regarding resource management may be curtailed. The struggles for greater participation are essential elements of the foundation of an endurable basis for sustainable development (Vivian, 1995). Perhaps the most serious problems that face the indigenous forms of local level institutions are government policy designed to protect forest without recognizing the local level institutional arrangements. The history of forest tenure in Thailand is very complex and a survey of different regions of it clearly shows the failure of state led programmes because state has not recognized or allowed local participation in natural resource management (Shiniichi, 2000). The problem lies in property right as the modern Thai land tenure system acknowledges individual ownership, whereas in the low land peasant society of North Thailand known as ***khon muang*** land was customarily possessed by matrilineal kin groups demonstrates that self-sufficient peasant society based on unity of kinship or community has been destroyed by modern institutions which promote individuals and cash economy. In Thailand, Community Forest Management (CFM) is not recognized by the legal system; however, there are *de facto* CFM practices under common property resource regimes. CFM has in essence been practiced here for hundred of years by local people, and represents an important aspect of Thai culture. The various hindrances to achieve sustainable CFM: (*i*) legal support for CFM is absent; (*ii*) the Royal Forest Department (RFD) can not transfer appropriate technology to community people due to legal support; (*iii*) scope for developing effective strategies for sustainable CFM by combining traditional knowledge with existing scientific knowledge is limited; (*iv*) a formal institutional arrangement for CFM does not exist. Therefore, in addition to legalizing CFM, a formal institutional framework for elaboration, implementation and control of CFM is essential to achieve sustainable CFM in Thailand (Salam, et al. 2006).

Community-based Forest Management Institutions in Thailand

It is interesting to note that the map of inhibition of tribal in South and Southeast Asia almost overlaps the forest map of the region and the relationship between forests and indigenous communities is found to be very close, intrinsic and multifaceted. In fact from prehistoric era many ethnic group of this region are found to live in harmony with nature by developing a long term relationship with the forest ecosystem. They are historically inhabitants of forest ecology and their socio-cultural, religious and economic life is strongly associated and highly dependent on forest resource. Because of their dependency and practice of Swidden cultivation it is generally believed particularly in government circle that these indigenous communities are responsible for forest degradation, at least at recent times, though serious works on deforestation do not support and ecological studies have also questioned the extent to which upland agriculture in Thailand actually impacts on alleged problems such as soil erosion, water shortages and biodiversity loss (Schmidt-Vogt, 1998). In contrary to government claims, many studies reveal primitive communities instrumental in conserving the forests for generations after centuries, traditional methods of forest use by communities have resulted in valuable indigenous knowledge concerning patterns and processes of biologically diverse forests.

Traditional Belief and Indigenous Practice of Forest Conservation

From the prehistoric period indigenous communities have developed close relationship with forest with regard to religion, culture and common faith. They have system of natural resource management that are "centered on traditional knowledge which, hey have developed, tested and passed down from generation to generation for hundred of years" (Kamonphan, 2005). For all indigenous communities, natural resource management always has a spiritual component to it. This belief is manifested in the ceremonies and rituals they perform. The tribesmen consider many forest areas as abode of spirits and deities. The most famous communal forests of this type are the 'sacred groves' which are protected for local deities and contain great biodiversity and many rare floras in small forest regions. Taboos, ceremonies and rituals which express respect and devotion to the spirits that are believed to guard different natural resources not only serves an important ceremonial role but also ensures the rules for resources use are adhered to by community members. Such practices over time have been institutionalized through the ceremonies and rituals of indigenous people. For example, Karen tribe classifies forest according to various criteria-topography, altitude, climate, belief, and use. They conserve forests for sources of water, burial sites, ritual sites, etc. These forests are absolutely forbidden to be disturbed; there can be no activity of any kind within them. All indigenous communities have beliefs and taboos against disturbing any watershed areas or springs. It is no coincidence but an indication of the knowledge of indigenous communities about the importance of such forest areas for the sustenance of plant and animal forms that depend on it.

Indigenous Institutional Set-up for Forest Management

In recent years it has become increasingly well recognized that people living in and near forests often have quite sophisticated knowledge and techniques for forest use and arrangements for regulated access to and use of forests. These systems can be described as indigenous forest management systems, defining management as 'regulated use'. For studying the institutional aspects of natural resources management by the local communities it needs to analyze in terms of the communities or to stake holders, the resources itself, and the type of property rights the community enjoy as all these factors are crucial to evolve and sustain the institutional arrangements or their breaking down. The history of community forestry in Thailand is very old. Oral histories and field investigations reveal different types of communal forest management, including varieties of sacred forests, watershed forests, and village woodlots (Shalardchai, et al., 1993). Our field experiences as well as the relevant literature suggest that forms of common property regimes or communal management regarding the use of land are found frequently in the villages, even though communal rights on land do not have a legal base in Thailand. These rules and regulations concerning the use of 'communal land' in some villages are legitimized traditionally while in others new institutions have been created, for example the context of the management of community forests. The ethnic communities of Thailand have strong kinship and community wise settlement. They also follow some type of social and customary practices in social governance.

Resource Condition

The forest biodiversity in Chiang Mai is not that rich as the vegetation cover is found to be thin and the valley is comparatively flat and well communicated area. Forest of Thailand can be classified as: (*i*) evergreen forests with three sub-types-tropical rainforests, semi evergreen forests and hill evergreen forests, dominated by species of the genera Dipterocarpus, Hopea, Shorea, Lagerstoemia, Diospyros, Terminalia, and Artocarpus; (*ii*) pine forests, mainly of Pinus merkusii; (*iii*) mixed deciduous forest, the dominant species being Tectona grandis, Pterocarpus macro carpus, etc; and (*iv*) dry dipterocarp forests. But the watershed forest of the region is in very good condition in comparison to other forests.

Structure of Property Rights

Like many parts of the world, forests and forest land in Thailand are owned by the State as by law all the forests are state Property. The property rights on forest lands have been in a wobbly position everywhere though it plays a crucial role in the management of forest by the villagers as community. Indigenous hill tribes of Thailand do not enjoy such rights on forests in their localities as community forests in this country are not recognized by the Thailand legal system although there are *de facto* practices under common property resource regime. This has resulted struggles and conflicts between the forest dwelling communities and government agency. There is very strong sense of State ownership of forests in Thailand which began with the creation of the Royal Forest Department (RFD) in 1896. The forest Act of 1941 further strengthened State ownership by declaring that any land not acquired or possessed under the land law would be considered as forest. A provision which has direct consequence for indigenous land use and natural resource management is Sec. 54 which prohibits the clearing, burning, occupying or possession of any forest land. The Land Code of 1954 of the country stipulates that all mountain land and land within 40 m of the foot of a mountain must not be damaged, destroyed or taken possession of. The hill tribe population therefore has no legal right to the land in the mountains. The rights of local people over forests are often claimed for customary and historical reasons, whereas the rights of national governments are claimed through policies and imposed upon society at large. Thus in Thailand as a whole, and particularly in the north, local villagers have been alienated from their resources base, first as a result of concessions for timber extraction, and second as the government has increasingly recognized the need for habitat protection and established state protected areas, largely national parks and wildlife sanctuaries. In Thailand the forests available for community forestry must reside outside protected areas or protected watersheds, which include national parks, wildlife sanctuaries, headwaters and critical watersheds. Whereas there are more than 9,000 community forests in Thailand (Asia Forest Network, 2006), many forest that rural people access are situated in the mountainous regions of northern and western Thailand, that is, in protected watersheds. Hence, many of those forests do not qualify for community forestry status and are under state control. The question of citizenship is another problem as many of the hill tribes do not enjoy Thai citizenship status.

Institutional Issues

In Thailand we find a well organized institution for forest management. Local people have developed use and management rules for sustainable use of nearby as well as watershed forests. They organized themselves under the leadership of village headman. They call meeting at least once in a month to discuss about the resource condition, the importance of these resources and need for their conservation. They have also formulated various rules regarding how and when and how much to use, who will use, how to protect, how to exclude the non-members, and how to punish the rules violators in the meeting. It shows that they have very well crafted operational rules of forest use and management but they are lacking collective choice rules and constitutional choice rules. The group discussion and the personal interview established the fact of emergence of institution in the wake of government more aggressive control on the hill forests. They opined that it was the need of the hour to control it because of its scarcity and to keep away others from occupying the forest. In Thailand it is found that the recent revitalization of community forests is motivated by the need to guard resource against outsider invasion, such as commercial logging, enclosure of the forestland by business, and degradation of the watershed forests by hill people's cultivation. In the wake of government accession local people normally try to transform their customary rules into written regulations and organize patrol groups to safeguard their forest against outside intruders. The main reasons for the formalization of customary practices are to gain legal recognition from the government and to obtain official assistance in protecting their forests from encroachment by influential political and business interest (Anan, 1992).

National Forestry Policy

The problem of deforestation in Thailand during 1980s was alarming and in the wake of such a problem national government introduced National Forest Policy. But a close analysis reveals that the basic focus of the policy was to check the rapid ongoing problem of deforestation. It seems that the National Forest Policy of Thailand (TNFP) adopted in 1985 " to achieve a long term and coordinated national forest administration and development.. " is an attempt to unify forest policy in the country and to place forestry within the context of overall national development ((Jantakad and Gilmour, 1999).The key aims of TNFP are: the establishment of guidelines of maximizing national social economic benefits and national security; promotion of shared roles and responsibility between government and private sector in forest management and development; recognition of national forest administration; maintaining 40 per cent of the country area under forests; development of a forestry management plan; improved efficiency in timber production; establishment of National Forest Policy Committee; undertaking awareness programmes on positive forest resources use; encouraging reforestation and export of wood and wood products and community forestry such as reforestation on public land by private sector, tree planting on marginal agricultural land and establishment of forest woodlot for household consumption; encouraging integrated wood use; amendment of forest laws; substituting fossil fuels with wood use through energy plantations; designation of land with a slope of 35 per cent or more as forest land; formulate guidelines to deal with forest degradation problems e.g. shifting agriculture, forest fires, forest clearing by the hill tribe minorities etc; incentive for reforestation by the private sector; and rural settlement planning to conform with national natural resource management and conservation plans.

It seems that TNFP covers a vast area of economic, private sector, supply of forest products but unfortunately it does not include any design that encourages community participation in forest management nor there do any provision for conservation of forest. The policy in Thailand encourages the private sector to become involved in tree planting projects for both domestic and exports supply and there is an emphasis on partnership with the private sector. Hence the national forest policy emphasizes the roles of government and the private sector and cooperation between the two, but little is said about the people's participation (Makarabhirom, 2002). However, the issue of community forestry in Thailand comes later in 1990s with the policy of decentralization and devolution of power of forest management at grass-roots level.

Community Forestry in Thailand

Though in the TNFP (1995) community-based forest management and people's involvement ha not been explicitly stated but the term 'community forestry', without proper meaning of the term, for the first time appeared in the cabinet resolution of 1985. The resolution stated "community forestry such as reforestation on public land by private sector, tree planting on marginal agricultural land and establishment of forest woodlots for household consumption shall be promoted". This led to sharp rise in the number of area of industrial tree plantations (mainly eucalyptus) in the northeast. The question of community forestry with private plantation in 'degraded forest' (actually agricultural lands) provoked a wave of resistance by farmers, who demanded a different kind of 'community forestry'. Afterwards, a national meeting of NGOs called on the government to issue a community forestry bill after a Member of Parliament's (MP) wife encroached on community-based forest to start 'reforestation', the RDF was forced to concede the community's right to manage the forest for the first time. In 1990, the pressure led to a draft of a community forest bill being proposed by the RDF for the first time, at least in paper.

The importance of CFB consist four choices that all sides agree to one another as the following:

1. This bill is one of the tools in environmental protection and development. It has not meant to be used to define and grant land rights.
2. It is a framework for utilizing natural resources sustainable in order to protect the forest eco-system.
3. To underline and support the roles of communities that protects, used and develops forests in traditional ways.
4. To promote the process hereby the state and the community operate in supporting the state's development process.

There are a number of laws and legislations for CBFM in Thailand. The following are bills and legislated policies relating to CFM:

1. Community Forest Bill (started in 1994)
2. Tambon Administration Organization (TAO) Act (1994) which strengthens the role of village governments in forest use, planning and decision making.
3. National Constitution (Article 45 on Decentralization Policy) in 1997 providing traditional communities to right and duties to manage resources in their areas.
4. Decentralization Act of 1998 providing guidelines for the election of community representatives to the Tambon Council.
5. National Park Act.
6. Environment Act.
7. National Forest Reserve Act.
8. Forestry Act

The Community Forestry Bill (CFB) in Thailand is the documented context of community forestry in the country. Brenner et al (1999) divide its history in four phases: emergent phase (1985-91), the hot phase (1991-92), the submerging phase (1993-96), and the Bill agenda (1996-2007). The first phase of the struggle for community forestry started when the RFD conceded the community rights over forests and when it proposed a draft of the Community Forestry Bill for the first time in 1990. In this first phase, the State advanced a forestry policy that advanced private economic plantations and conservation areas at the expense of communities living in the national forest reserves. The second phase began when the Internal Security Operations Command (ISOC) launched an ambitious plan to relocate thousand of households from national forest reserve to a 'community forestry' area which was barely arable land. The third phase buried the bill under the ground after the introduction of Thai Forestry Sector Master Plan in 1993, which was based on the private plantation system in more legitimate way but due to protest the plan failed.

The final phase is the drafting and redrafting of various versions of the bill and discussion and debate in the parliament, passed in cabinet and then rejected in senate and finally get through in November, 2007. Throughout this period the three contested points in the draft with respect to the moving of the people from the national reserve forests were the issue of community forest area (settlement for villagers), the activities and residence of people (locals' ability to manage and protect forests), and management and monitoring (evaluation procedures). While pro-people NGOs and academics proposed evidence that people are able to protect and use the forest in a sustainable way, the dark green NGOs and conservationists, including the conservative members of the RDF strongly oppose these idea. At last, communities have obtained their customary rights over forests within the National Reserve Forests at the cost of about 20,000 indigenous peoples' exclusion.

It should be noted that the community forestry issues of Thailand largely affect by other related acts such as Reserve Forest Act. Both the National Reserve Forest Act 1964 and National Park Act 1961 form the basis for the determination, control and use of national Reserved Forest under the law. The NRFA had direct negative impacts on highland indigenous communities because within the National Reserved Forests, no person shall occupy, posses, exploit and inhabit the land, develop, clean, burn the forest, collect the forest products nor cause by any other means whatsoever may damage to the nature of the National Forest Reserve (Sec.14). But interestingly, logging or collection of forest products and logging of reserved timber species may be done after obtaining permission from the Director General (Secs. 15 & 16). Similarly under the NPA, a national park may be created from "any area of land which is of interest and maintained with a view to reserving it for the benefit of public education and pleasure.... (such) land shall not be owned or legally possessed by any person other than a public body (Sec. 6)". It is clear that the purpose of creating parks under the law is not for conservation or preservation of resources, and that 'education and pleasure' superseded the emphasis on sustainable use of resources. As such it impinges directly on the use rights of forest resources for indigenous peoples and hence finales the possibility of participatory forest management.

In short, the NFP of Thailand has been a policy of disclaiming the claim of forest dwellers and the question of involving those does not arise. In such a situation the function of CBFM is almost impossible because people living near to the forests are to get involved in the management. In 1989 following the disastrous floods in the country resulted in a national logging ban. This ban marked an important policy shift towards greater emphasis on the involvement of communities in forest management activities. But subsequent policies, however, have been consistent regarding community rights in natural forest areas. Neither the National Forest Policy of 1985 nor the Land Reform Act included any specific provisions to transfer forest management rights and responsibilities to communities.

In the mean time while CFM legislation was yet to be approved , the concept gained legal support under the new constitution of 1997 and decentralization laws such as Tambon Administration Organization (TAO). The 1992 as a measure of democratic decentralization the Tambon Administrative Organization Act was promulgated to strengthen the role of village governments in forest use and planning decision making which is rightly considered as an effort to enhance popular participation in resource stewardship and formally institutionalize it within a governance framework (Ribot, 2002). Under this act, TAOs have responsibility for managing all natural resources within their boundaries. The 1997 constitution recognizes the rights and duty of traditional and other local communities to participate in natural resource management but unfortunately no policies or laws have implemented these objectives and they are not reflected in national policy, which aims to achieve long-term sustainable management of forest decentralization policy gives the right to the local people that seems inconsistence as other laws prevent them from the rights.

In Thailand the RDF holds legal responsibility and authority in management decision making, national forestry planning, and budget allocation and approves registered CF's and their operational plans. The Provincial Environment and Natural Resource Office provide technical support, monitors and reviews implemented programmes to ensure forest sustainability. TAO obtains responsibility without legal authority for the implementation of CF activities. Villagers and households obtain usufruct rights tot the resources without legal ownership over the land and must follow the forestry law decree 15 of 1964. Community benefits include some harvesting of forest products in CF outside the national forest whereas costs are born in collective activities requiring time, labour and financial contribution. Within a CF various forest products represent spectral property rights regimes. For example, open access: NTFPs e.g., mushrooms, wild vegetables, bamboo shoots insects, and some medicinal plants; common property: fuel wood, some medicinal plants and wild vegetables; state property: forestland, timber products. Steps involved in planning for CF include the following: Identification of community groups to which the Community Forest will be allocated or transferred. There is no clear identification process for the CF group to which CFs will be allocated or transferred. CFs in the protected areas will be allowed on condition that communities prove they have settled in the area before 1993 and demonstrated their ability to protect forests. A local group in agreement and with support of at least 50 local residents who are at least eighteen years old is eligible to establish and organize a CF. It shows that in all the three levels of decision making, the stakeholders play very insignificant role in the CBFM in Thailand. In spite of all the efforts the areas under such forestry is not very high. The area under CF management (in both NFR and outside it) accounts for about 1.16% of total forest area (RDF's 2003 record) or 0.38% of the total country land area involving 5,331 villages.

Conclusion

Since the last decade of the previous century only when forest resource rightly considered as an environmental good besides its economic value it received attention for conservation. It also rightly contemplated that decentralization and devolution of power to the local people is crucial as without involvement of the local people in the management it is very difficult to have a long term success. The successful decentralization forest management policy depends on many contesting issues. The most important factor that associated with it is the property rights and that right is not only the use right but management and ownership right what is meant that collective and constitutional choice level involvement of the local actors. When government involve villagers in the management as CBFM, the incentive of the stakeholders plays the crucial roles and the interest is in the benefit they derive including the property rights of the forests. Therefore decentralization can be said to have occurred only when governments devolve property rights over resources that conform to the collective and constitutional choice levels.

The local resource management institutions developed without taking the question of property rights explicitly because the community had the absolute right to use and conserve the resource. It is obvious that due to lack of ownership of property rights tribes in Northern Thailand had but no option to join with the Forest Department for conservation of forest. This finding shows that property rights plays- it may be customary rights an important role in continuing the locally crafted forest management institutions though they may be under pressure because of other reasons like market pressure and political change. Thus it is government policy that can alienate local villagers from their resources base, first by giving concessions for timber extraction to the timber merchants and second increasingly recognition of the need for habitat protection and established state protected areas, largely national parks and wildlife sanctuaries.

REFERENCES

Agrawal, A and E. Ostrom (2001). Collective Action, Property Rights and Decentralization in Resource Use in India and Nepal. Politics and Society, 29(4).

Anan Ganjanapan (1998). The Politics and Conservation and Complexity of Local Control of Forests in the Northern Thai Highlands. Mountain Research and Development 18(1).

Asia Forest Network (2006). Community Forest Management in Thailand. http://www.asiaforestnetwork.org

Baland, J.M. and J.P. Platteau (1996). Halting Degradation of Natural Resources: Is There a Role for Rural Communities? Oxford: Clarendon Press.

Brenner, V., R. Buergin, C. Kessler, O. Pye, R. Schwarzmeier and R. Sprung (1999). Thailand's Community Forest Bill: U-turn or Roundabout in Forest Policy? SEFUT Working Paper No.3, Freiburg: Albert-Ludwig Universitat.

Ferrari, M.F (2006). Rediscovering Community Conserved Areas in South-East Asia: Peoples' Initiative to Reserve Biodiversity Loss, Parks, 16(1).

Ghate, R and N. Jodha (2006). Promise, Trust and Evolution: Managing the Commons of South Asia, Oxford University Press.

Hafner, J.A. (1990). Forces and Policy Issues Affecting Forest Use in Southern Thailand, in Keeper of the Forest: Land Management Alternative in Southeast Asia (ed) M. Poffenberger, Kumarian Press.

Jantakad, P and D. Gilmour (1999). Annex II: Forest Rehabilitation Policy in Practice in Thailand. Workshop Proceedings on Rehabilitation of Degraded Forest Ecosystems in the Lower Mekong Basin: Assessments of Rehabilitation Policy and Practice in Thailand. November 24-25, 1999, Chiang Mai, Thailand.

Makarabhirom, P. (2002). Constraints on People's Participation in Forest Management in Thailand. The Southeast Asia Sustainable Forest Management Network.

Ostrom, E (1990). Governing the Commons: The Evolution of Institutions for Collective Action. Cambridge University Press, New York.

Poffenberger, M. (1996). The Struggle for Forest Control in the Jungle Mahals of West Bengal 1750-1990, in M. Poffenberger and B. McGean (eds) Village Voices, Forest Choice: JFM in India, Delhi: Oxford University Press.

Pragtong, K. and D. Thomas (1996). Evolving Management System in Thailand. In Mark Poffenberger (ed.), Keeper of the Forest, Land Management Alternatives in Southeast Asia, Kumarian Press.

Ribot, J.C.(2002). Democratic Decentralization of Natural Resources: Institutionalizing Popular Inclusion, Washington DC: World Resource Institute.

——— (2004). Waiting for Democracy: The Politics of Choice in Natural Resource Decentralization, Washington DC: World Resource Institute.

Salam, M.A, T. Noguchi, and R. Pothitan (2006). Community Forest Management in Thailand: Current Situation and Dynamics in the Context of Sustainable Development, New Forests, 31(20).

Santasobat, Y. (2003). Biodiversity Local Knowledge and Sustainable Development, Chiang Mai: Regional Centre for Social Science and Sustainable Development, Chiang Mai University.

Schmidt-Vogt, D (1998). Defining Degradation: The Impact of Swidden on Forests in Northern Thailand, Mountain Research and Development, 18(2).

Shalardchai, R, A. Ganjanapan, and S. Ganjanapan (1993). Community Forest in Thailand: Development Alternatives, Community Forests in Northern Thailand (Vol. 2). Bangkok: Local Development Institute.

Shiniichi, S. (2000). Cooperation and Community in Rural Thailand: An Organizational Analysis of Participatory Rural Development.

Vivian, J.M. (1995). Foundation of Sustainable Development: Participation, Empowerment and Local Resource Management in Ghai, D and Vivian, J.M. (eds), Grassroot Environment Action: People's Participation in Sustainable Development, London: Routledge.

3

Integrated Strategies for Sustainable Forest Management in the State of Himachal Pradesh

Issues and Options

— **Prof. Pradeep K. Vaid**

The Problem

Forest conservation development programmes cannot be implemented and achieved without appropriate practices, structure and active people's participation, in particular human capacities for achieving the goal of eco-development. India is facing an acute shortage of forests and the problem is accentuating every year. Forests are among the basic life form by which biotic communities may be classified. There is probably no other area of India's environment that has been more viciously attacked and destroyed in the last century than the country's forests. Today India has just an area of 670 lakhs hectares (67 million hectares) of forests which represents around 20 per cent of its total geographical area. The Forest Act envisaged that 60 per cent of the land area in the hills should be under forest cover as against 33 per cent of the country as a whole. But the fact remains that neither in the hills nor in the plains has this Act achieved the target. While the dense forest cover for the country is around 12 per cent, for the Himalayan region the figure is about 22 per cent, and this present situation calls for serious introspection and management of forest sector policy and strategy.

Himachal Pradesh State Forest Policy is essential to the proper running of the permanent forest estate. To be effective a forest policy needs to be on a national basis with clear perception of specific reasons for maintaining and improving the forests. Because of these constraints, conserving forests in the

State has given key priority to achieve harmonized relations between people and environment by the State Government.

It seeks to address the aspirations of the people by making forestry a vibrant sector contributing towards livelihood enhancement of forest dependent communities through the department working on natural resources management. Forests and other ecosystems of the State, which constitute two-third of the geographical area, are crucial for its environmental, ecological and economic well-being and that the influence of the state's forests transcends well beyond its boundaries, significantly impacting on the ecology of Indo-Gangetic plains. The forests of the state are rich in biodiversity and play a vital role in preserving the fragile Himalayan ecosystem while also being a primary livelihood source for the rural population. Realizing that there has been a paradigm shift in the objectives and management practices of forestry at the state level from the first forest policy which was adopted during 1980 in furtherance of the National Forest Policy resolution of 1952 to the coming into force of the Forest Conservation Act 1980 and National Forest Policy of 1988 and a constitutional development of power to the Panchayati Raj Institutions to user in a democratic decentralization process through the Constitutional (73rd Amendment) Act, 1992. Keeping in view the National Forest Policy (1988) with a principal aim 'to ensure environmental stability and ecological balance' the State Department of Forest take the initiative to involve the village communities and voluntary agencies for regeneration of forest land through the concept of Joint Forest Management (JFM) in 1993 and subsequently Participatory Forest Management(PFM)Rules in 2001.

The Forest Sector Policy and Strategy 2005 of the state also reflect various conservation and development emphasis on forest in future in Himachal Pradesh and includes the entire biophysical and environmental components comprising lands, soil, water and biological resources (flora and fauna) under the control and management of Himachal Pradesh Forest department. The various issues and trends are taking place in Himachal Pradesh for the development of forest sector such as:

- The decision-making process is progressively being opened up to allow increased public participation through programmes JFM/ PFM.
- An increasing awareness and sensitivity about issues concerning local people and their rights on forest and forest resources.
- A shift towards a more decentralized and people oriented forestry, including community control and management of community resources.

State Forests and Options

Himachal Pradesh was formed in 1948 by the integration of some 30 princely states. The forests are the principal source of livelihood for the vast majority of rural population of the state and forests not only provide number of valuable products but also play an important role in maintaining ecological balance. In 1966 more areas from Punjab were merged in the state at the time of re-organization of states. Consequently, the area under forests increased from 9.000 sq. kms; in 1950-51 to about 21,000 sq. km; in 1966-67. The total forest area of the State is 37,033 km. (legally defined) this consists 66.52% of geographical area of the state. The area comes under tree cover is 14,353kms.and cover 25.78% of geographical area along with crown density above 8,976kms, with 16.12% of geographical area of the state. Further, the area leads to open forest crown density 1040% is 5.377kms and having 9.66% of geographical area and cover 14.52% of forest area in Himachal Pradesh. This is due to physiographic conditions of the state which is characterized by lofty mountains, innumerable snow-clad peaks, glaciers, deep gorges and glens, roaring water falls and narrow valleys of the state. Keeping in view—the better figures for Himachal certain conservation and development policy and programmes are taken in order to improve upon and remove difficulties of various projects on forestry especially their economic viability and institutional sustainability. The State Government gave effect to PRI's through the Himachal Pradesh Panchayati Raj Act, 1994 to strengthening the working and improving the local institutions actively for the promotion and sustainable development of Forest Sector Policy in the State.

The Forest Sector Policy seeks to achieve sustainable forest management in Himachal Pradesh i.e. forests, watersheds, wildlife, biodiversity and habitats for the maintenance and rehabilitation of its environment and strive for enhanced livelihood of the people of State, especially women and other resource poor groups. The guiding principles of the State Forest Policy of Himachal Pradesh are:

- Sustainable Development of Natural Resources and improving the quality of life in the State.
- Integrated Natural Resources Management of natural resources that incorporates economic, social and environmental values and involves the community. Decentralized governance reduces costs and increase efficiency through good governance-transparency, rationality, accountability in time and costs at the local level. Gender and equity refers to both equity in entitlement and participation of all stakeholders in process of decision-making over management and control of forest resources.

Integrated Strategies

The Himachal Pradesh Forest Sector Reforms Projects (HPFSRP) is being implemented by the H.P. Forest Department. The purpose of the project is to establish and implement an integrated and cost effective strategy for sustainable forest management and enhance livelihoods of the poorest forest-dependant women and men in Himachal Pradesh. The project is based on convergence of developmental agencies through the PRI's participatory planning and capacity building to sustain livelihood of forest dependent. For institutional strengthening in the changing scenario and to undertake a comprehensive programme of functional review on change management strategy, four special units have been constituted in H.P. Forest Department: (*i*) Human Resource Development (HRD); (*ii*) Planning and Management Information System (PMIS); (*iii*) Research and Extension (R& T); and (*iv*) Monitoring and Evaluation (M&E). The main function of these units is to support structural change and strengthen functioning of the State Forest Department for developing sustainable livelihoods and sustainable forest management mechanism at the community level; Panchayats across the state have been selected to the implementation of micro-plans at community level. The project is providing funds for a limited period for local level activities relating to the conservation and development of forests.

The institutional framework for the administration of forest lands and resources in Himachal Pradesh dates back to the 19th century when forest settlements were carried out. These legal settlements were made at the end of 19th century and the first two decades of the 20th century, these still provides the basis institutional framework for administering forest resources. The legal provisions on control, use and management of forests, have developed over a period of time. At different times, legal instruments were introduced to deal with administrative agencies. As a result, the legislation and laws are not a coherent body of provisions, but are a contradictory body of conflicting objectives, modalities and provisions. While, the Indian Forest Act of 1927, remains a pervasive Act for the Constitution, management and protection of forests, various laws, acts and rules enacted by the state of Himachal Pradesh such as: (*i*) Himachal Pradesh River Rules, 1971; (*ii*) Forest Produce Transit (Land routes) Rules, 1978; (*iii*) Mandi and Chamba Minor Forest Produce Extraction and Export Act of 1937; (*iv*) Wildlife(Protection) Act, 1972, as amend in 1990; (*v*) Himachal Pradesh Land Preservation Act, 1978; (*vi*) Himachal Forest Produce (Regulation of Trade) Act, 1994; (*vii*) The Himachal Pradesh Resin and Resin Products (Regulation of Trade) Act, 1981; and (*viii*) The Forest Conservation Act, 1970 as amended in 1988; (*xi*) Indian Forest (H.P second Amended) Act, 1911.

Policy Implications

Sustainable management of sources like forests, require a through knowledge of the eco-system, in particular the role played by the different elements, sectors, agencies and departments. On the face value Himachal Pradesh seems to be comparatively in happier position in context of national averages.

But deeper thought makes this position not so comfortable. Himachal Pradesh consists of hills terrain criss-crossed by big and small rivers, rivulets, nulls. glaciers and deep gorges. The one-third of the state is snowbound making any vegetation on that area impossible. Being a state studded with the responsibility of sitting a large number of irrigation and hydroelectric dams, Himachal needs a bigger forest cover for their conservation. Thus, the better figures for the state are no consolation. These are rather the 'danger signal to improve the condition and bring the forest ratio to stipulated 50 per cent of geographical area without any further loss of state. However, there seems to be a clear realization of the importance of forests in the context of their socio-economic and all the more their ecological balance. There is no denying the fact that this fact has duly been recognized by the society as well as administration that the existence of human race depends on the existence of balanced ecological system. State forest sector policies and its administration are showing awareness about ecological balance and its importance in present scenario. The forest policy of the state, the various schemes, planned and undertaken, the financial provisions envisaged in various plans by the state government, the co-operation and active involvement of local level agencies for various sectors indicate an awareness of the utility. of the forests not only as a big reservoir of economic resources but also as the highest single factor responsible for maintenance of the ecological balance, better understanding and benefits to the state in particular and nation in general.

Importance of law making, particularly in the field of environmental management is extremely high. Judicial approach to environmental law will bring in to light the shortcomings of our social system and would inspire us to think of the ways of redeeming them. Duty of legislature would be to procedure the required medicine to the society in the forms of laws. No doubt, efforts of the State Government to protect its forests through various legislative provisions are encouraging but still unable to control the menace of environmental protection for sustainability. To ensure full implementation and effective enforcement of laws, it is essential to impart meaningful and worthwhile education of the subject so as to make the society fully aware of the dynamics of law in this area.

REFERENCES

State of Environment Report, Himachal Pradesh, 2000.

Annual Administrative Reports of Forest Department, Govt. of Himachal Pradesh.

Himachal Pradesh Forest Sector Review, 2000.

H.P. Panchayati Raj Act. 1994.

H.P. Forest Department, FSR 2005.

Knowledge Management

Issues and Challenges in Context to Indian Economy

— Prof. Pavan Mishra and Mrs. Swati Mathur

ABSTRACT

In this age the only constant is change. The ability of an organization to stay current and stay relevant needs a core competence in knowledge Management. The purpose of this article is to highlight issues, challenges and answer how and why Knowledge Management (KM) can be used to create competitive advantage of an organization. This chapter outlines the perspectives of knowledge management and examines the way it characterizes knowledge sharing process and role of information technology in creating a vital organization for knowledge sharing purposes, This KM study will help other organization as they embark on their KM Journey. It is the interaction between technology, people and techniques which can lead to effective knowledge management in an organization A nurturing and learn by experience and new approaches concept can help an organization to sustain its competitive advantages.

Key Words : *Knowledge Management, Knowledge Sharing, Interaction, Sustained Competitive Advantage, Issues and Challenges, Research Barriers.*

Introduction

The key to the knowledge-based economy today is not knowledge infused products but tacit knowledge that provides the capacity for there knowledge infused products and for non-codified knowledge services (Sveiby 1997). Advances in research and theory are needed in 21st century organizations which deals the issues like conceptualizing knowledge as the central organizational asset, incorporating knowledge capital into strategic management process and designing organizations to facilitate knowledge utilization.

The importance of knowledge and the means by which it is utilized to add economic value varies from industry to industry and even between firms. To allow for planning and investment in knowledge, a new way of conceptualization capital is needed so that they can use it economically like economic capital.

The basic economic research the means of production is no longer capital, nor natural resources, nor labor it is and will be knowledge. Knowledge management is continually disconcerting what an organization knows. It includes—codifying tacit knowledge, data mining and business intelligence, increasing organizational learning and communities of practical and organizing and disseminating explicit knowledge for use our research includes the knowledge management emerging perspectives and knowledge sharing process in organization, it includes the interaction and knowledge works and barriers in an organization along with the best practices used. It also covers the sustained competitive advantages and barriers in the KM journey of any firm. Then finally we will draw some implication for KM.

Knowledge Management

Knowledge and its applications are the means by which creativity can be promoted (Nonaka and Neshiguchi, 2006) innovation facilitated and competencies pulled in such a way as to advance overall organizational performance whether in the public, private or not for profit sectors (pitt and Clarke, 1999) KM is crucial to organizational survival. It induces drivers like competition, customer foes, challenges of a workforce, and the global imperative (Macintosh, 1998).

Knowledge Management has objectives of mailing the organizations to act as intelligently as overall success and realize the best value of KM. Knowledge Management's purpose, thus, is to leverage organizations intellectual assets in sustaining competitive advantage.

Knowledge Management systems address both the past and the future they focus on problem solving, they support both tacit and explicit knowledge they should. Support both objective and subjective aspects, they are highly dependent on internet based technologies and they enable the sharing of knowledge throughout the organization (Wicleramasinghe, 2003)

Knowledge Management Framework

The knowledge management framework we use was originally based on work by van der Spek and de Hoog. It covers identifying what knowledge assets a company possesses

- Where is the knowledge asset?
- What does it contain?
- What is its use?
- What form is it in?
- How accessible is it?

analyzing how the knowledge can add value

- What are the opportunities for using the knowledge asset?
- What would be the effect of its use?
- What are the current obstacles to its use?
- What would be its increased value to the company?

specifying what actions are necessary to achieve better usability and added value

- How to plan the actions to use the knowledge asset?
- How to enact actions?
- How to monitor actions?

reviewing the use of the knowledge to ensure added value

- Did the use of it produce the desired added value?
- How can the knowledge asset be maintained for this use?
- Did the use create new opportunities?

Techniques to Manage Knowledge

We believe that the knowledge modelling techniques that exist to support the use of the knowledge, along with traditional business management techniques, provide a starting point to manage the knowledge assets within a company. Therefore the techniques we employ for managing knowledge within the organization are drawn from these two distinct areas:

- the techniques that have been used previously from business management, for example, SWOT (Strengths Weaknesses Opportunities Threats) analysis, balanced scorecards (Kaplan, Robert S.; Norton, David P. (1996)), modelling languages such as: IDEF (Process Flow and Object State Description Capture Method, Mayer, R., Cullinane, T., de Witte, P., Knappernberger, W., Perakath, B., & Wells, S. (1992)) and RADs (Role Activity Diagrams, Ould, M. (1993));

- the knowledge techniques that have been used previously for the disciplined development of knowledge-based applications (Benus, B. (1993) and Schreiber, A. T., Akkermans, J. M., Anjewierden, A. A., De Hoog, R., Van De Velde, W., & Wielinga, B. J. (1998)).

Our recommended approach is a multi-perspective modelling approach. Several models need to be developed, each of which represents a different perspective on the organization which can be characterized as "How, What, Who, Where, When and Why"

- How the organization carries out its business—modelling the business processes
- What the processes manipulate—modelling the resources
- Who carries out the processes—modelling capabilities, roles and authority
- Where a process is carried out—modelling of the communication between agents
- When a process is carried out—this specifies the control over processes

Knowledge Management Sharing and Interacting

Knowledge Management is the discipline of enabling individuals teams and entire organization to collectively and systematically create, share and apply knowledge to better achieve their objective (Ron young, CEO Knowledge Associates International) knowledge management will deliver outstanding collaboration and partnership working. it will ensure the region maximizes the value of its information and knowledge assets and it will help its citizens to use their creativity and skills better leading to improved effectiveness and greater innovation (West midlands regional observatory UK) KM is about encouraging individuals to communicate their knowledge by creating environment and systems for capturing, organization and sharing knowledge throughout the company (Martinez, 1998-89)

KM is clearly the capturing, retention and reutilizing of the foundation for imparting an understanding of how all these pieces fit together and how to convey them meaningfully to some other person.

Knowledge sharing is done through communities of practice in literature, They have two complementary views. One view reflects cops as channels in which knowledge sharing takes place through the process of learning. Other view considers, Co Ps as channels is which knowledge sharing can take place on demand. A cop operating with the underlying principles of the above two views will not only serve the members of an organization but will also serve external members on demand. A cop act like a kind of gene pool within which lies the ability to evolve future solutions. These help in addressing the issues of trust and motivation essential to ensure knowledge sharing and continuity to KM.

Knowledge Management : Issues Challenge and Sustained Competitive Advantage

Knowledge Management is essential for a economy may be old or new. Due to influence of various technologies and the globalization of world trends the KM is must in order to create and maintain competitive advantage in turbulent economics.

In the new economy we have the speed for data capturing, processing and disseminating. Today in our economy varied demanding issues prevails. As customers demand and receive more customization at even diminishing

7 K.M. PROCESS

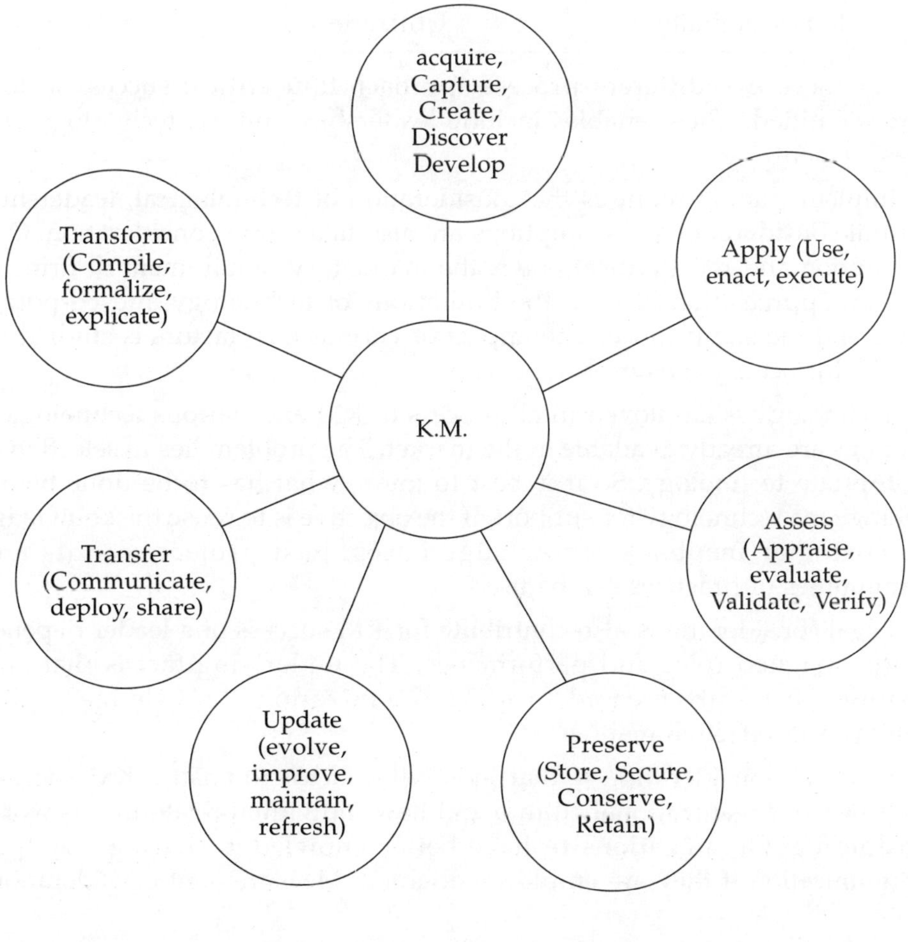

costs from knowledge oriented private sector firms expect similar benefits from the public sector. Knowledge about its customer and their tastes is an asset that assists the company in learning how to adjust product quality and quantity so as to create and maintain a loyal customer base.

The concept of KM has been in practice for a long time and mostly in an informal manner. Creating new knowledge is a complex process and it requires establishing links with existing or prior knowledge. Unlike physical goods that are giving decreasing returns, knowledge appreciates and yields increasing returns.

KM implementation presents the greatest challenges. The implementation is a challenge as the nature of knowledge is complex and it involves seven processes (*See diagram on page 33*)

The 4 KM Process later on proposed was :

Identification	Elicitation
Dissemination	Utilization

For these two different process approach four critical success factors were identified. These enables include leadership, culture, technology and measurement.

Implementation requires the consideration of technological, leadership. cultural considerations. Assumptions are also taken into consideration. One assumption and most critical one is the mandatory requirement of firms to have an appreciation of both the limitations of technology and corporate sector and the significance. The impact of various CFS factors is studied on each KM Process to ensure KM Success.

Technology is employed in all process of KM and various technological solutions are already available in the market. The problem lies in selection of appropriate technology. So it is best to know what has to be done before looking for a technology for support. If the objective is to reuse the knowledge the customer feedback, knowledge bases, past project records and communities of practices can be used.

Legal considerations also contribute for KM success of a leader depends on the assigned roles and performance. The underlying fact is that new positions/titles are created to make organizations knowledge capital employed in effective manner.

Cultural consideration is that most vital factor to ensure KM success. Dynamics of organizational culture and how individual relate to it is worth considering. Organizations to have better knowledge sharing use open communication if they are employee oriented. Measurement considerations are not much essential requirement being not such practical aspect. As of yet there are no generally accepted accounting methods for measuring such intangible assets.

Key Issues and Application of KM in Context to Indian Economy may be Traced as

(1) Role of organizations dealing with the areas intelligent agents, ontology and computer mediated collaborations. Corporate memories are used for enhanced decision-making. Artificial Intelligent has merged as the core technology for knowledge and representation and is the way to discover knowledge and collaboration around competencies to the new practice of KM.

(2) Insight into the measurement of intellectual capital, methods and instruments of knowledge and epistemology, knowledge action dynamics, actualizing learning and social sciences in organizational learning is seen.

(3) In our economy challenges prevails. These include elements concerned with delivery to customers who achieve growth and profitability through partners in an industry.

The major challenges include implementation. The various challenges in business cover aspects of following terms:

Aspect	Terms
A. Delivery	Value added services Variety of products
B. Customer	Innovation Global Execution
C. Industry	Larger and dispersed organization Hundreds of partners
D. Industry	Growth Sustained Profitability

Knowledge management draws from a wide range of disciplines and technologies like Document Management, Technical Writing, Cognitive Science, Data Warehouse and Network Database, Case-based Reasoning

Intellectual Assets Management and Performance Support Systems. Peter Senge (1990) defines a learning organization as :

> "A learning organization is a particular vision of an enterprise that has the capacity to continually enhance its capabilities to shape the future."

The concept of a learning organization is where learning is a continuous and cyclic interactive process and actionable knowledge is turned is to innovative product and process to achieve global competitiveness. This whole process is a learning organization acts as a framework towards organizing Indian firms for global competitiveness.

How knowledge in a learning organization leads to global competitiveness.

An effective KM should help the company to :

(*a*) Improve customer service by streamlining the time factor;

(*b*) Reduce cost by elimination of unnecessary process;

(*c*) Increase and session to market at taster rate;

(*d*) Help in innovation and certainty enhancement by free flow of ideas;

(*e*) Improved efficiency, higher productivity and increase revenues in any business function practically.

Conceptual and Research Barriers to the Utilization of Knowledge

Which taking knowledge into effective account firms address barriers and operating level barriers.

Strategic Level Management Barriers

There include measurement and accountability. Traditionally the rely on things which were measurable and accountable. But it possessed limitations as such revisions might be based on illusionary facts and hence were unjustified.

To allow for planning and investment in knowledge a new way of conceptualizing capital is required and initial efforts in this direction have already that capital might take a conceptual framework has not been made till date. It is really difficult to evaluate the alternative forms of capital. It we take the case of social capital at national level it refers to issues like moral character crime and trust. On the other hand at the time or societal level it refers to connection with the outside parties that give the knowledge to individuals.

The categories of measures are constant across major units in a concept like human focus renewal and development focus but the exact variables tracked are tied to their strategic importance in particulars units of a concern. The measurement of non-economic forms of capital is difficult. So a sustained period of practice and theory evaluation is required before concepts and measures can be used in a common pattern across firms. In order to lower barriers at strategic level for planning and investment in knowledge.

Operational Barriers

As like the strategic Barriers operational barriers are also prevailing in acquiring knowledge operational barriers in traditional approaches put owners of economic capital in charge of a hierarchical system that seeks to maximize the return on the economic capital while minimizing risk it tends at direct control and manipulation. Organizational from and a set of processes is required for flow and transfer of knowledge. Adaptation of new forms and processes requires descriptions of what successful firms are doing coupled with the conceptual framework in order to explain success and generalize the principles being used. It also requires thc description of work teams with and across firms and forms like networks contributing the development and utilization of knowledge many a times it is really difficult for economic capital to hire knowledgeable members. Members contrarily increasingly expect full financial recognition of the value of their knowledge and know-how.

Graham and Pizzo (1990) developed a framework to help companies position and manage knowledge for competitive advantage. The process of configuring for knowledge has four independent and dynamic elements that always focuses on the balance between institutional domains and fluid to get operational efficiencies and strategic flexibility. In the institutional domains, work is structured controlled and measured. In the fluid domain, knowledge originates and groups from individual and improvisation the elements are :

1. Applying Jed (just-enough-discipline) which deigns with focus on culture and consideration of variables used for dissemination.
2. Identifying the drivers required for strategic business.
3. Establishing the knowledge core and interrelationships which includes both intangible and tangible, technology, business capabilities and people.
4. Determination of business critical knowledge existence and creating a knowledge value chain to trace the patterns of knowledge use and movement through format and informal sides of the organization.
5. Rebalancing and monitoring.

Spender (1996) identified four heuristics that managers could use to help them define the form as a knowledge based activity system and to understand their relationship to it. These include :

(*a*) Interpretive flexibility;

(*b*) Boundary management;

(*c*) Identification of institutional influences;

(*d*) The distraction between systemic and component features.

A firms current and desired knowledge strategy includes tow dimensions which are similar to the traditional strengths-weaknesses-opportunities-threats include :

(1) The extent to which the firms is mainly a creator, rather than a user of knowledge.

(2) Whether the primary sources of knowledge are internal or external.

Knowledge-based SWOT analysis can lead to mapping knowledge resources and capabilities against to clear understand advantage and weakness for doing so the organization should express the intent of the strategy and after word should identify the knowledge required in executing it.

Strengths

1. Good reputation in research
2. gives company access to outstanding students
3. Multi disciplinary, wide range of competence

Weaknesses

1. Strong boundaries between research groups
2. Reward system not geared toward goal
3. Insufficient knowledge about market
4. Lack of overview of exploitable knowledge
5. Physical layout of building hampers knowledge exchange

Opportunities

1. Additional funds can boost research
2. Current courses can be interesting for people outside the university
3. Better planning in research
4. Advice and counselling are frequently requested
5. Shift toward applied research in funding bodies

Threats

1. Competition of other universities, they all go in the same direction
2. Other parties in the market are stronger
3. Financing of projects may make them less profitable
4. Meet the goal the university has set in 1999.
5. Doubts about the usefulness of the discipline, lack of cohesion and direction, no major societal problems.

Core competencies also relates the internal capabilities of organizations Three tests are applied to identify a core competence:

(1) It should posses leverage potential;

(2) It should be relevant to the customer's key buying criteria; and

(3) It should be difficult for competitors to imitate for competitive viability the application of invisible assets, innovation leadership and knowledge is required.

KM is thus clearly an approach to solving current problems such as competitiveness and the need to innovate. In our research we also include the answer to the question how and why the KM can yield the competitive advantage.

Advantage comes from using knowledge management systems to support what is well and to add value to resources not readily available to competitors it should have properties like rarity, volubility, imperfectly substitutable and non-imitable.

Implementation of KM requires understanding and development of infrastructural elements required to support the acquisition management and transfer of tacit and explicit organizational knowledge. Innovations that explicit a firms assets are likely to add value to the resources and the competitive advantage that results is likely to be sustainable.

As far as the empirical investigations are required there are four variable used between knowledge management systems usage and the firms competitive edge "from the theories on organization system usage three precursors are drawn they are strategy, learning and innovations.

A research model from the electronic Journal of Knowledge Management seems to be a good approach for both research and practitioners. The model is a research work which has empirical aspects to support the measurement of KM to some extent.

Research Model : KM Quality Construct

General Environment

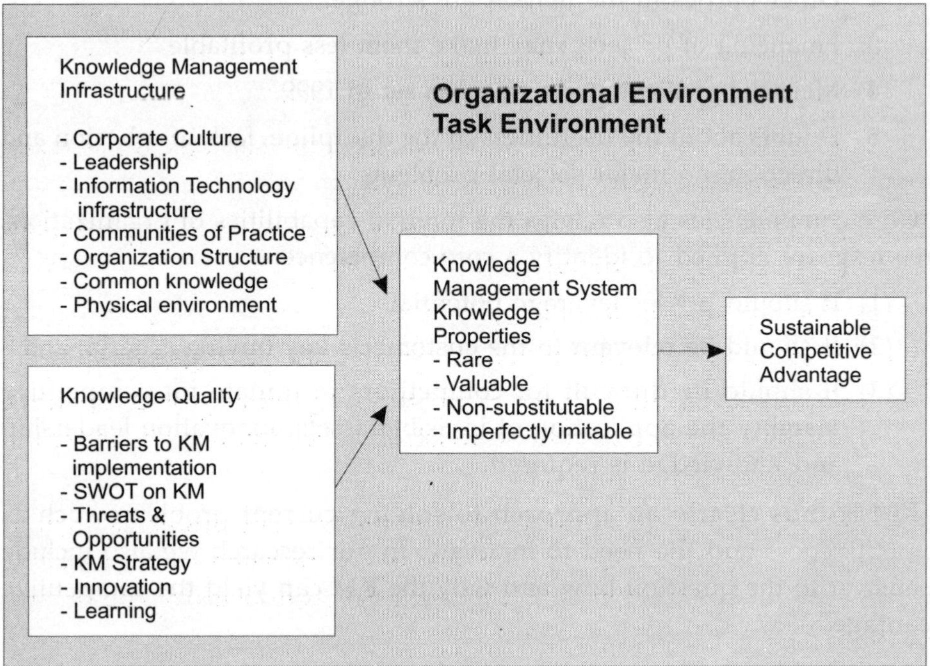

Three environment are incorporated in our modal. The organizational environment includes all internal variables that exist within the organizational boundaries. The middle frame or task environment includes the external variables with immediate relevance an d direct interactions with the organization. The outer frame, or general environment includes the external variables with potential relevance and no direct interaction with the organization. Our modal has several important constructs, namely the knowledge management infrastructure construct the knowledge quality, the knowledge management system and sustainable competitive advantage. The knowledge management infrastructure block defines the KM infrastructure in terms of the following five constructs: corporate culture, leadership, information technology infrastructure communities of practice and common knowledge. The knowledge quality block defines the knowledge quality in terms of six constructs: barriers to implementation, SWOT analysis, identification of threats and opportunities, KM strategy, innovation and learning.

This elusive measure is readily understandable in the strategic management literature, yet few have truly defined it empirically or even come close to attempting to measure its dimensions.

Despite growing interest about the strategic perspective on knowledge management (KM) there is no published or available procedure or a measurement instrument. A large number of knowledge management instruments both organizational, information and communication instrument have been proposed but none of them measured competitive advantage.

For researchers the model suggests the types of the variables that need to be included in future empirical tests of the relationship between KM and competitive advantage. Consequently, the model extends explaining of what is becoming an increasingly important issue in knowledge management, the relationship between KM and competitive advantage practitioners, on the other hand can use the model to refine their thinking about KM and their firms strategic resources.

Conclusions and Recommendations

In this chapter we have tried to develop an understanding of the conceptual framework for KM and the various processes associated with KM and issues and areas of research used in KM. Various business challenges and opportunities associated and the barriers persisting are also discussed. In this chapter the various techniques and tools or practices should be used and a new model to measure the competitive advantage in the empirical way has also been given. Our work will definitely contribute to progress being made by a business in philosophical and broad theoretical levels.

KM has assumed greater urgency in Indian context as millions of baby boomers prepare to retire over the coming decade. And when the punch out for the last time, the knowledge they gained above their jobs companies and industries over the course of their long careers walks out with them, unless companies take measure to retain their insight. All information is not valuable it is up to individual companies to determine what information qualifies as intellectual and knowledge based assets. i.e. explicit or tacit.

Knowledge utilization is a collaborative process. In collaboration the individual efforts are voluntary combined to produce outcomes that would not be achieved alone—receives scant support from either of the two views. First is full collaboration of the workers working together and achieving a level of production that could not be reached by either party individually. Second is the newer organizational forms designed to generate and utilize knowledge, such as advanced networks, alliances and the cellular design which require provoking managers and theorists to provide legitimating for collaborative behaviours. The leading edge knowledge industry firms will increasingly be 'owned' in one form or another by their own members and network partnerships will be based on maximizing resource utilization subject to equitable distributions of returns rather than on individual firm maximization of profits. This determines how fast knowledge will be utilized in the 21st century depending upon how fast and how completely collaboration takes place.

The tools and techniques used in the knowledge used in the knowledge management process support effective knowledge sharing and interaction and results in sustained competitive advantage. The selection of methods is done according to conceptual framework including sequential four activities. These are Review, Conceptualize, Reflect and Act. There is a comprehensive set of support methods available but for some peculiar aspects of knowledge assets there are still gaps.

The research model given is also a step ahead in measuring KM in empirical terms, but yet several models need to be developed.

The purpose of KM in the new economy is to provide access to knowledge information and date throughout and to its customers in a particular order Governments must compete with private sector organizations in the quality of services rendered to customers. The KM initiative includes—management, employees, partners, customers and their roles include participation, learning and collaboration in all stages of KM.

Knowledge sharing networks and especially cops provide enemas benefits at entry point in KM. They readily overcome the most crucial cultural barriers to knowledge sharing act as pool for provision of future solutions projects for KM should be at a scale manageable and in small phases where reinvention must be avoided at all cost state organizations which act as enablers and catalysts for innovative application and technology should be transferred to Government knowledge centres. This will help government agencies to implement KM effectively in an organization.

REFRENCES

Alavi, M., and Leidner, D.E. (1999) "Knowledge Management Systems: Issues, Challenges and Benefits", *Communications of the Association for Information Systems*, Vol. 1, No. 7, pp. 2-36

Alberthal, Les. Remark of the Financial Executives Institute, October 23, 1995, Dallas, TX.

Argyis, C. and Schon, D.C.(1996). Organizational Learning II—Theory, Method and Practice,. Addission Wesley Publishing.

Barney, J.B.(1991)' Firm Resources and Sustained Competitive Advantage'. Journal of Management, Vol. 17, No. 1, pp. 99-120

Bogner, W.C.., Thomas, H., and MacGee, J.(1999) 'Competence and Competitive Advantage Towards a Dynamic Mode', British Academy of Management', Vol. 10, pp.275-290.

Choi, Y.S. (2000) An Empirical Study of Factors Affecting Successful Implementation of Knowledge Management. Doctoral Dissertation, Graduate College at the University of Nebraska, University of Nebraska, Lincoln, NB.

Conner, K.R.,& Prahalad, C.K.(1996)." A Resource-based Theory of the Firm Knowledge *versus* Opportinitism".

E. Penrose, The Theory of Growth of the Firm, 3rd Edition (New York,NY, Oxford University Press,1995).

Bateson, Gregory, Mind and Nature: A Necessary Unity, Bantam. 1988.

Davidson, Mike, The Transfirmation of Management, Butterworth- Heinemann, 1996.

Drucker, P.F., "The Age of Social Transformation". The Analytic Monthly, November, 1994.

Senge, Peter. The Fifth Discipline: The Art and Practioce of the Learning Organization, Doubleday-Currency, 1990.

http: / /www.aiai.ed.ac.uk/

http: / /www.ndu.edu/irmc/Publication/MilitaryEngineer.pdf.

http: / /www.outsights.com/systems/dikw/dikw.htm

www.projectsparadise.com

www.informaworld.com

www.indianjournals.com

www.bee-india.nic.in

www.indianjobtalks.com

www.ibscdc.org

www.imrmi.com

www.knowledgeboard.com

5

The Importance of Van Panchayats (Forest Councils) for Carbon Trading in Uttarakhand Himalayas of India

— Bhupendra Singh Jina, Kala Jina, Pankaj Sah and Chandrapal Singh Bohra

Introduction

The countries of the world are seeking international commitment to reduce the emissions of CO_2 and other greenhouse gases globally. The Kyoto Protocol is an attempt to set-up an international process to address the problem of increase in the atmospheric CO_2. It provides an economic process that puts a value on not emitting CO_2 and enables countries to trade carbon emission. Europe has already created an emission trading market, expected to be operative by the year 2005. Under the Kyoto Protocol, there is a provision (under the Clean Development Mechanism, CDM) to derive monitory benefits from developed countries to support certain forestry operations in developing countries, such as carbon sequestration through afforestation and reforestation. In a way, this is a mechanism to get payment for providing an ecosystem service. Such a concept can be applied on a regional or country-scale, to compensate the regions sequestering carbon.

Deleterious Effects of Global Warming

If the global warming process is not stopped then the world will witness a mass extinction. Global warming will cause biotic impoverishment; species will be lost, specific ecotype-specific combinations of genes accumulated for each location by selection through many generations will also be lost. Forests will be replaced by savannah shrub land or grassland (IPCC, Climate change, 2001).

The Central Himalayan Region

In Central Himalaya forest is the potential vegetation up to 3500-4000 m elevations (Singh & Singh, 1987). However, as data collected from satellite imageries indicate, right now about 40 per cent of the reported area (51,000 km^2) is forested, and good forests (with more than 60% crown cover) occur in much smaller area (Singh *et al.*, 2006). The carrying capacities of fodder and firewood production systems have far exceeded in most areas (Singh *et al.*, 1988). Consequently, the Himalayan region has become a net releaser of carbon. Next to combustion of fossil fuels, forest harvesting is regarded as the biggest source of net release of CO_2 to the atmosphere (Hoghton *et al.*, 1983).

Poor Conditions of Himalayan Villagers

In Himalayan mountain regions people are among the poorest. The communities in Uttaranchal consist of small holders (generally less than 1 ha per household of 5-6 persons) who depend critically on community forests for subsistence living. Around 90 per cent of their crop fields are rain fed with food grain yield sufficient only to fulfil their need for 6-7 months in a year. Almost nothing has been done to provide training on silvicultural practices to manage community forests on sustainable basis. Though the forest cover of Uttaranchal, India is about 40 per cent, the threat of degrading forces continues to be high largely because of poverty of the people and lack of any alternative strategies for development. Forest stands in general have a lower biomass and productivity than their potentials (Singh and Singh 1992) Some species, like *Quercus semecarpifolia,* are failing to regenerate because of excessive lopping, livestock grazing, frequent fires, poaching and the spread of invasive/exotic plant species (Phartiyal and Tewari, 2006).

Kyoto Protocol and Eligibility for Carbon Credits

Though in Kyoto protocol, afforestation and reforestation are eligible for carbon credits, in the present context of immediate threat of climate change they are important mainly because they can prevent deforestation of natural forests, such as those managed by VP's. It may be pointed out that what matters is Carbon pool size, not the rate at which carbon cycles through this pool (Steffer *et al.* 1998). The slow refilling (through raising plantations) of carbon gap created by previous logging is a small counter-weight to the release of carbon by ongoing logging. With regard to efficiency, a dollars '$ value' per unit of preventing forest clearing would be far greater than the gains from a dollar invested in raising a plantations (Körner, 2001). Activities which lead to the maintenance of existing mature forests need to be given priority for carbon saving. They may include: assisting natural regeneration in existing forests; preventing forest fires; cultivating trees next to crop fields and homesteads so that pressure on VP forests remains within the sustainable limits, and restoring forest sites still with adequate remains of old stands.

Uttaranchal's Van Panchayat (Forest Council or Forest Committee)

Van Panchayat (Forest Council or Forest Committee) were introduced to Kumaun region of Uttaranchal (erstwhile United Provinces, UP) in 1920's following agitation against British expansion of control over forest areas. The landmark Van Panchayat Act 1931 handed over control of designated community forests to elected Van Panchayat (VP) members in place of the State Forest Department. The Van Panchayat probably represents one of the largest experiments in common property management in collaboration with the state (both State Forest Department and State Revenue Department). It has a legal backing, and has an elected body, called forest committee or forest council which holds responsibility of using and managing village forest resources. However, the various activities are undertaken under the control and supervision of the rules of the Revenue Department, and the State Forest Department is supposed to provide technical inputs. In a way, the village forest is a kind of natural resources, used by a definite user group (the village people) and is liable to degradation due to over use. Though called village property, the land in legally belongs to the state. The village people however, consider it as their property and resent government interferences. Most community forests were initiated on degraded sites, officially on a kind of Civil/Soyam forests (forests managed by the Gram Panchayat on behalf of the revenue department) falling under administration of the Revenue Department. But unlike Civil Soyam forests the community forests are not open-access forests.

Depending on the number of households in a village, there are generally 5-9 elected members in a Van Panchayat, who elect a 'Sar Panch' from among themselves. The Sar Panch is the elected head of the village forest committee or VP and has the following responsibilities:

(*a*) To convene and preside over all meetings of VP

(*b*) Keep watch over the finances and bring any irregularity in finance in notice of VP

(*c*) Look after the legal matters

(*d*) Supervise and control the staff and establishments maintained by VPs. Elections are held after 5 years. At least one schedule caste and/or woman member should be elected to the committee (Singh *et al*, 2003). Recently the government of the new state, Uttaranchal (Now Uttarakhand) has taken initiatives to include more villages under VPs.

Current State of Van Panchayats in Uttaranchal

The total geographical area of Uttaranchal (UA) is 5,563,174 ha, of this agricultural land is 792,000 ha (about 13% of the total area) and forest area 3,671,695 ha (about 66%) and others about 21 per cent. At present there are more than 12064 Van Panchayats (VPs) in UA occupying nearly 5,23,289 ha of the total forest area. The Van Panchayats are located only in the hill districts of UA. The average forest area under the control of one VP is close to 44 ha (Table 5.1). Variations are common in size of VP forest, for example, the Makku VP in Garhwal region has about 2500 ha forest area. The total population of UA is 8,879,562 of which 4,316,401 are males and 4,163,161 females as per 2001 census. The literacy level in UA is 72.28% in which the male % being higher (84.01%) than females (60.26%). The female ratio in UA is 964 per 1000 male.

Table 5.1 : District-wise distribution of VPs in Uttaranchal covering more than 0.5 million ha area

Sl. No.	District	No. of Van Panchayats	Area covered by VP forests (ha)
1.	Almora	2,199	69,854
2.	Nainital	496	28,068
3.	Pithoragarh	1,661	87,054
4.	Champawat	629	31,233
5.	Udham Singh Nagar	0	0
6.	Bageshwar	822	38,783
7.	Pauri Garhwal	2,430	52,184
8.	Haridwar	0	0
9.	Chamoli	1,073	1,67,310
10.	Rudraprayag	574	20,702
11.	Uttarkashi	643	5,510
12	Dehradun	205	7,659
13.	Tehri Garhwal	1,332	14,932
	Total	**12,064**	**5,23,289**

Source: Uttaranchal Forests Department, July, 2005.

Responsibilities of Van Panchayats (VPs)

The responsibilities are laid out in the law as following:

1. To ensure that only those trees that have been considered silviculturally fit for cutting by the State Forest Department (SFD) would be cut.
2. To ensure that the village forest land is not diverted to any other use.
3. To erect and maintain boundary pillars.
4. To carry out the directions and execute the orders given to it by the state Revenue Department (on the advice of SFD) to maintain, improve and utilize the trees.
5. To utilise the forest produce to the best advantage of village community and of the right holders (A right holder is a person who owns land in the village where a Panchayati Forest has been constituted or a person who has been given rights to graze cattle, collect fodder, fuel and timber in a Panchayati Forest under law or any order of the court) recognised by established customs or permitted by the State Revenue Department.
6. To close generally at least 1/5 of the grazing area to promote conservation.
7. To protect the forest from fire, illicit felling and damage to trees due to lopping.

Functioning of Van Panchayats

A watchman is appointed to guard the forest, and his salary is paid by the community. The watchman's services can also be taken on voluntary basis. He is authorised to take action against offenders. In some villages, households watch the forest on a rotational basis. The VP may grant permission for cutting grass, grazing and collection of fallen wood, and may charge fees for these provisions with the permission of the government. The other rights include extraction of pine resin for domestic and medicinal purpose and disposing of trees with the permission of State Revenue Department (on advice of State Forest Department). The trespassers can be fined up to Rs. 50 and up to Rs. 500 with the permission of State Revenue Department. If rules for grazing are violated cattle can be detained up to 48 hours, and the Van Panchayat has the right to disallow the use of privilege of any person found guilty. The Van Panchayat rules are framed by the State Government in consultation with the local people. However, within a certain framework, each Van Panchayat makes its own local rules and regulations i.e. imposition of fines, making micro plans etc. as per needs and wisdom. The technical support to the VP is provided by the State Forest Department (DFO at the Division level) and the State Revenue Department has the responsibility for the creation of VP.

Motives for forest management are founded upon expectations of immediate product returns as well as to make sacrifices for forest conservation (e.g. foregoing community forest use). Desire to prevent outsiders from using forest and to become self-sufficient in firewood, leaf litter (for manuring) and fodder is said to be the driving force for the development of community forests in some villages with a high level of success.

Biomass Extraction and Conservation

The VP forests are used to sustain the subsistence living, involving biomass extraction almost each day. The biomass extraction involves collection of firewood, fodder and ground floor litter, grazing/browsing by domestic animals and occasional cutting of 'whole trees' for timber. Rotational grazing and collection of biomass are followed to allow a forest stand to get time to recover. Another effective way then to save these VP forests is to find alternatives. Some NGOs have been popularising biogas as a means to save fuel wood and also improve lives of the hill women who spend several hours every day collecting wood. Biogas generation is a biochemical process where organic mater such as cow dung is digested anaerobically by microbes (in the absence of oxygen) to yield a mixture of Methane (65%) and carbon dioxide (about 35%). Methane is a highly combustible gas and can be used for cooking heating and lighting applications.

Role of Non-Government Organisations (NGOs)

NGOs in certain cases have made useful contributions. For example, CHIRAG, of Almora district while working in Kilmora and Katural Van Panchayats of Nainital districts redefined the forest guards as 'forest maintainer' and were trained to improve the growth conditions of tree seedlings and saplings, repair boundary walls and protect trees from excessive lopping.

At Makku Van Panchayat, the NGO AT-India, Rudraprayag has made an attempt to establish NTFP's based enterprise by involving village individuals as shareholders. The NGO is also undertaking activities relating to sustainable harvest of resources and monitoring of bodies.

Gender Issues in Van Panchayats

At least one woman representative is required to be in every Van Panchayat; however, her forced inclusion has not lead to genuine representation at least in above mentioned Van Panchayats of Nainital district. The female representatives either send their son or husband; they are reluctant to attend the Van Panchayat meetings themselves. The most obvious constraint is the heavy workload mostly involving childcare, collection of fuel wood, litter for mulch, fodder for animals, water, cooking and other household and agricultural activities. Also it is felt by women that they are not encouraged by men to attend the meetings. In the VPs of Lamgarha block in Almora district the women position have been lying vacant in 3 of the 4 VPs studied while in the remaining one VP the women members have never attended the meetings. In recent years this issue has been raised repeatedly and men in some cases welcome women participation, but not much progress has yet been made.

Success and failure of Van Panchayats

At present there are more then 12064 Van Panchayats in Uttaranchal occupying nearly a quarter of the forest area. The district-wise number of Van Panchayats and the area covered is as following:

Typically, the Van Panchayats become dysfunctional where the village forest area is inadequate to meet the community needs (at least 1 ha of forest is required per household) or the community is very large (over 100 households) or where out-migration is high or where the government official are insensitive or where members are busy along with other occupations like maintaining shops and jobs in nearby areas. The fact that in many areas Van Panchayats have been successful in conserving forests clearly indicates their importance. Apart from this, village forest in a way represents: (*i*) a kind of empowerment to the people; and (*ii*) people's participatory role in the functioning of the nation. It represents an important social institution in which more creative activities can be initiated.

Inventory of Existing Community Forestry Policies

As far as the rules and regulations concerning the management of the Van Panchayat forests, they remained almost unchanged until recently, when forest administrators gave some attention to their plight. In recent years an attempt has been made to improve the gender equity in the constitution of Van Panchayat, utilisation of money generated through Van Panchayat forests, and in attitude of the forest official towards community. Environment based NGOs have taken active part in activities of community forest management.

Some of the steps indicating the above policy changes are as following:

- The Forest Policy of 1988 facilitated involvement of local communities and voluntary agencies in the development of degraded lands.
- The Van Panchayats evolved because of protests by the locals. Communities against centralised tendencies of State Governments, which looked at the forests as an economic resource.

- Till date, it is the only JFM mechanism, which has full and legal backing of the Forest Act 1925 (Tolia, 1996).
- For the creation of new Van Panchayats no permission is required under the Forest Conservation Act, 1980, as creation of Van Panchayat is a 100 per cent 'forestry activity' (Tolia, 1996).
- The Forestry Training Institute, at Haldwani was re-named as Forestry and Van Panchayat Training Institute by an order of Forest Department of the new state of Uttaranchal.
- *Training to VP officials:* A budget-head for the training of Van Panchayat office bearers was opened in the Uttaranchal Development Department.
- *The Government took some initiatives to develop cooperation between the corporate sector and Van Panchayat:* For example, Century Paper and Pulp Mills, Lalkuan helped a few Van Panchayats in establishing bamboo nurseries with 50 per cent subsidy in saplings purchased by Van Panchayat in addition to local employment.
- *More freedom for Van Panchayat to use money generated from the forest:* The cumbersome process of taking out money from the state exchequer which existed in previous policies has been mitigated to some extent by the Van Panchayat Rules 2001.
- *Enhanced coordination between Van Panchayat inspectors and Van Panchayat functioning:* In Van Panchayat rules of 1976, Forest Panchayat Inspector (FPI) was responsible for various activities in Van Panchayat but in new rules of 2001 the role of FPI is negligible.
- *Women representation:* Representation has been provided to women in Van Panchayat rules 2001.

As per 2001 census the total population of Almora district is 630,446, of which male and female numbers are 293,576 and 336,870, respectively. The total literacy rate in Almora district is 74.53 per cent, with male and female literacy percent being 90.15 and 61.43 per cent, respectively. There are 1147 females per 1000 males in Almora district. Almora district has 2199 Van Panchayats covering about 69,854 ha (that is approximately 31.78 ha per Van Panchayat).

We studied three Van Panchayats in Lamgarha Development block of Almora district; these are in the villages of Dhaili, Toli and Guna. These Van Panchayats are situated between 79°41.44′-79°41.2′ E longitudes and 29°32.98′-29°34.32′ latitudes.

Dhaili Van Panchayat (VP)

Introduction to Social Aspects

The Dhaili VPs are situated between 29°32.98′ N latitude and 79°-44.2′ E longitude, located at an altitude of about 1830 m. The area under VP forest is about 60 ha, of which 48 ha is good forest (58% crown cover) (Fig 5.1). Of the 956 villagers in Dhaili, 503 are males and 453 females, which form 116 families. The average literacy % of Dhaili Village is 50.0%, with male and female literacy being 70.0 and 30.0%, respectively. The female ratio at Dhaili VP is 1044 per 1000 male (Table 5.2). The VP has 7 members. All the members are males. The VP meetings are generally held once a month. Women folk also attend these meetings.

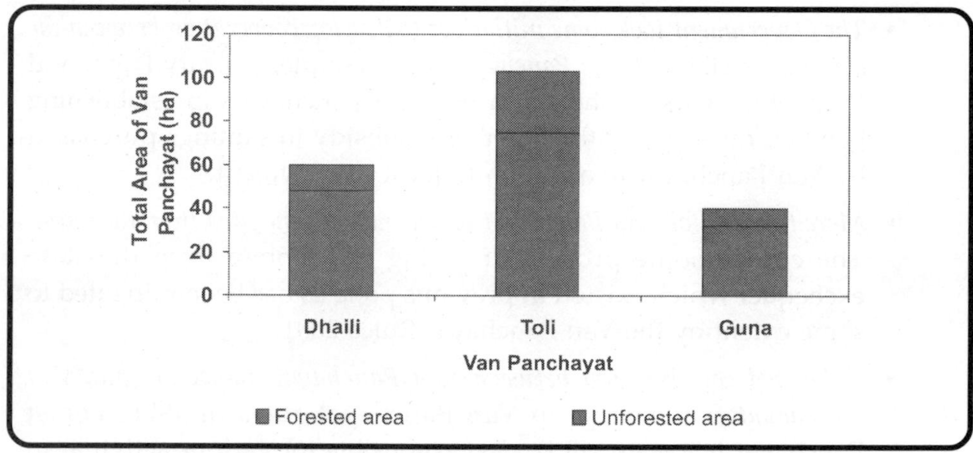

Fig. 5.1 : Forested and unforested area (ha) of Dhaili, Toli and Guna Van Panchayats

Table 5.2 : Brief socio-economic and ecological information about the studied Van Panchayats in Lamgarha block of Almora district

Van Panchayat	Dhaili	Toli	Guna
1	2	3	4
Block	Lamgarha	Lamgarha	Lamgarha
District	Almora	Almora	Almora
Physical Information			
Area of Van Panchayat	60 ha	103 ha	40 ha
Total village Population	956	1030	240
Total number of Families	116	132	22

(Contd...)

1	2	3	4
Number of Males	503	540	122
Number of Females	453	490	118
Literacy % in Males	70%	80%	80%
Literacy % in Females	30%	49%	56%
Year of formation of Van Panchayat	1999	1955	1937
Member number in Van Panchayat	07	09	07
Number of Males in Van Panchayat	07	07	06
Number of Females in Van Panchayat	0	02	01
Frequency of meeting	Every month	Once in two months	Once in two months
—Do—Female members attend meetings	NA	No	Yes
Source of Income of Van Panchayat			
• Govt. Grants	No Grant	Rs. 4 lac have been given under JFM by Govt. in 2000	No grant
• Sale of NTFP's	Rs. 10 family^{-1} for dry leaf collection Rs.30 family^{-1} for green leaf collection Dry wood 10 Rs per annual head load	Rs.10 family^{-1} for grass collection (yearly collection Rs.1000-2000) Rs.2 lakhs are present in Van Panchayat account from sale of resin.	Rs. 5 family^{-1} for grass collection (yearly collection Rs.1000-2000) Dry wood Rs.6-8 per annual head load
• Any other Source	No	No	No

(Contd...)

1	2	3	4
Silviculture/ Ecological information			
Dominant tree species of Van Panchayat Forests	-Banj (*Q. leucotricho-phora*) **60%** -Burans (*R. arboreum*) **15%**- Kaphal (*M. nagi*) **10%**-Chir (*P. roxburghii*) **15%**	-Chir **50%** -Banj approx **30%** -Kaphal **10%**- Burans **10%**	-Chir **55%** -Banj approx **35%** - Kaphal **5%** -Burans **5%**
Condition of trees	Healthy trees with moderate lopping	oak trees severely lopped but chir pine, burans, kaphal growing well.	oak trees moderate lopping but chir pine, burans, kaphal growing well.
Regeneration of species	Forest is regenerating saplings of all dominant species present	saplings of chir pine, rhododendron and kaphal present. banj oak absent	saplings of chir pine, rhododendron present. and kaphal banj oak absent
Van Panchayat	Dhaili	Toli	Guna
Afforestation/ reforestation in Van Panchayat (last 5 years)	Done in 6 ha by community	Yes, done in 2 ha of pine, cedar and acacia	No
Fire Protection done	Yes	Yes	Yes
Frequency of fire in Forest	No fire since last 5 years	Fire had occurred in May 2002	Fire had occurred in June 2003
Fire lines made	Yes	Yes	Yes
Fire line cleared regularly	Yes	Yes	Yes
Canopy/crown cover	58%	30%	42%
Ground litter cover	40%	57%	50%

(Contd...)

1	2	3	4
Growth even/uneven	Even-aged banj oak forest with under canopy to kaphal and rhododendron	Uneven aged forest of chirpine.	Uneven aged forest of chir-pine.
Grazing control	None	Yes	Yes
Other information			
Is extraction of fuel wood, fodder rotational	Green leaf fodder extraction-seasonally periodic (Spring)	Fodder extraction in seasonally periodic (Spring)	Fodder extraction in seasonally periodic (Spring)
Other NTFP's extracted			
Resin	No	No (Extraction closed for last 13 years)	No
Medicinal Plant	No	No	No
Lichens etc.	No	Yes (2% of sale money given to village)	No
Salary of Forest Guard if appointed	Rs.600 month^{-1} appointed for 12 months	Rs.1000 month^{-1} (From JFM fund) appointment for 12 months.	Rs.800 month^{-1} appointed for 12 months
Source of salary			
Horticulture	12445.50	10500.00	7850.00
Floriculture	2500.00	1000.00	800.00
Milk production	4500.00	5200.00	3800.00
As Labour @ 65 Rs/day	2575.00	2000.00	2520.00
Other NTFP's extracted as Resin, Medicinal plant, Lichens, Mushrooms	No	No	no
Total Annual income	22020.50	18700.00	14970.00
Number of people using LPG/ Biogas	3-4	4-6	3-4
Number of people fined	Rigorously followed	Mildly followed	Mildly followed

(Contd...)

1	2	3	4
• 2000-2001	12	05	08
• 2001-2002	16	09	05
• 2002-2003	30	04	08
• 2003-2004	20	11	14
• 2004-2005	34	05	06
Van Panchayat	**Dhaili**	**Toli**	**Guna**
Amount generated from fines in last 5 years	Approx. Rs.10,700	Approx. Rs.2600	Approx. Rs.2000
Perceptible change in Panchayat Van after the creation of Van Panchayat	Condition has improved	Condition of forest has improved	Condition of forest has improved
Has there been any change in distance travelled for fuel wood, fodder and drinking water collection before and after the creation of Van Panchayat	No	Distance travelled for drinking water has reduced, moderately	Distance travelled for drinking water has reduced, moderately
Water source Protection	Yes, they are cleaned regularly, and have been covered	Yes, regularly cleaned and base covered with concrete	Yes, regularly cleaned and base covered with concrete
Check dams made and their number	Stone check dams 06 Temporary ponds 150	Stone check dams 02 Temporary water ponds 50	Stone check dams 02 Temporary water ponds 20

(**Source:** data collected from Lamgarha block office)

In Dhaili Village all the families are using fuel wood for cooking and heating purposes. Though LPG is available in the area only 3-4 families are using LPG and that also occasionally. The daily requirement of fuel wood is about 6-7 kg of dry fuel wood (by field checks) per family. Pattern of collection of fuel wood shows that about 75% is from VP forest, 10% from trees on private areas and 15% from government or reserved forest. Other non-timber product, for example, resin, medicinal plants, and lichens are rarely extracted from VP forest.

Forest Condition in VPs

The year of the formation of VP is 1999. The VP forest comprises of even-aged banj oak (*Q. leucotrichophora*) forest with under canopy of *M. nagi* and *R. arboreum* (Fig 5.2). The condition of the VP forest is good; trees are in healthy condition with moderate lopping. Regeneration is also good as saplings of all species are present in the forest. The average canopy cover of Dhaili VP forest is close to 60% and the ground litter cover about 40%. After the creation of VP the people of Dhaili accepted that the condition of their forest has improved, as indicated by the reduction of distance travelled for collection of fuel wood, fodder and drinking water. About 150 small earthen ponds dug during 2003-2004 in the catchments of 4 major springs have increased water in them during the lean summer month. The VP of Dhaili also arranges a forest guard every year and pays his salary of about Rs. 600/ month from the income generated. In Dhaili VP many people have been fined in last 5 years. In the VP plantation of bamboo, bhimal (*Grewia optiva*), utis (*Alnus nepalensis*) species was done in 2004-2005 in about 6 ha with the help of villagers. The villagers also clear fire lines for the protection of forest during the dry summer season. The livestock numbers in Dhaili VP were: 180 buffalos, 50 cows, 445 goats and 200 oxen (Fig 5.3). However, there was no control of grazing in Dhaili VP (See Table 5.2).

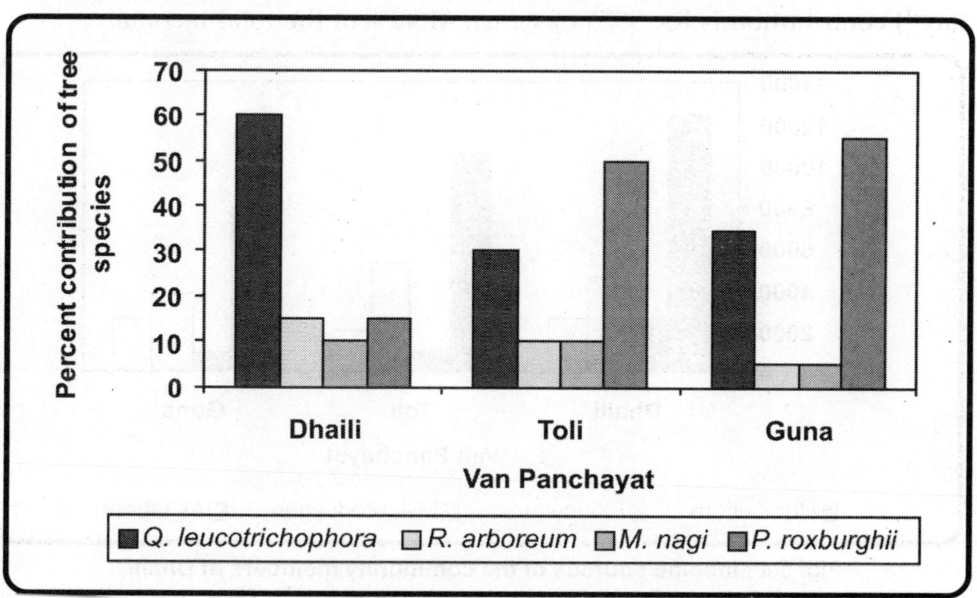

Fig. 5.2 : Per cent contribution of different tree species in VP forest of Dhaili, Toli and Guna

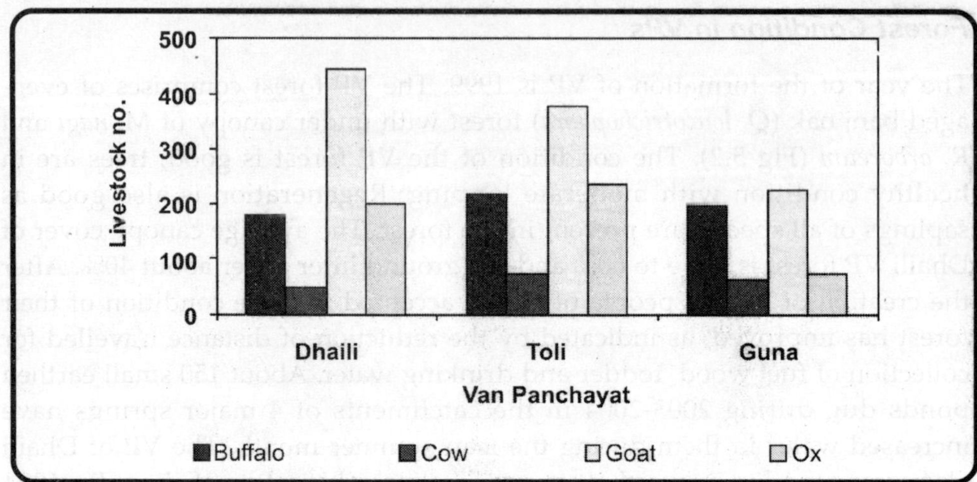

Fig. 5.3 : Livestock population in the VPs of Dhaili, Toli and Guna

Income Sources

The total income of Dhaili Village is Rs. 22,020 yr^{-1} $family^{-1}$ (Fig 5.4). The cropping pattern in Dhaili village is mainly rice, maduaa, millet and wheat. Annually agriculture income in Dhaili village is Rs. 12,445.50, which is 56.52% of the total income. Floriculture, milk production and as daily labour (@Rs.65 day^{-1}) contribution is Rs. 9575 of which 41.48% of the total income.

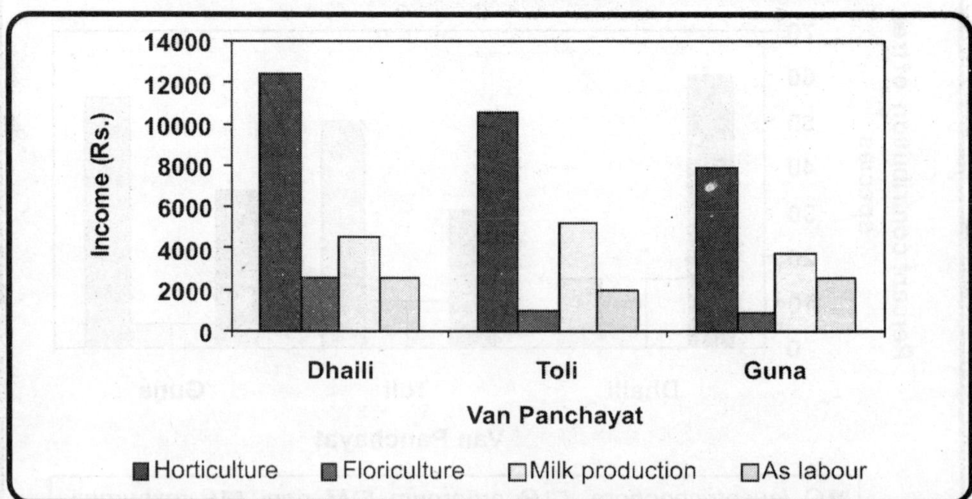

Fig. 5.4 : Income sources of the community members of Dhaili, Toli and Guna. There was no income from NTFPs

The main source of the income of VP is from the sale dry fodder @ Rs.10 per family, green fodder @ Rs.30 per family or Rs.10 per head load, besides these the imposition of fines also generates some income for the VP (Table 1.2). Thus, the total income generated by the Van Panchayat was Rs 9,500 from the sale of permits and fines in year 2005 (Fig 5.5).

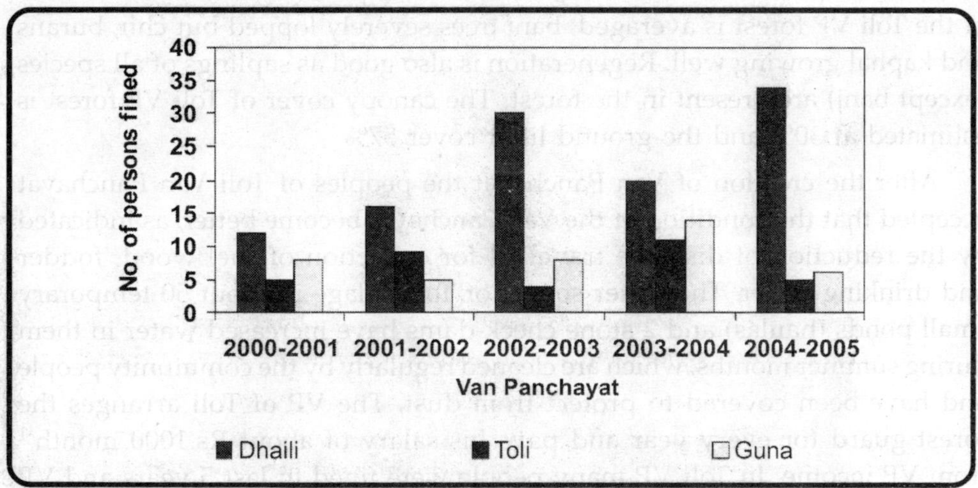

Fig. 5.5 : Fines imposed on individuals for committing forest crimes in Dhaili, Toli and Guna Van Panchayats

Toli Van Panchayat (VP)

Introduction to Social Aspects

The Toli VPs are situated are between 29° 33.04′ N latitude and 79°-41.19′ E longitude, located at an altitude of about 1839 m. The area under VP forest is about 103 ha, of which 75 ha is good forest (See Fig. 5.1). The total number of families is 132 while the population of Toli is 1030 comprising of 540 males and 490 females. The total literacy rate of Toli VP is about 65.0%, with male and female literacy at 80.0 and 49.0%, respectively. The female ratio at Toli is 1120 per 1000 males. The present number of VP members is 9 and is composed of 7 males and 2 females (Table 5.2). The VP meetings are generally held once in about two months. These meetings are attending sometimes by women-folk also.

In Toli VP all the families are using fuel wood for cooking and heating purposes. Though LPG is available in the area only 4-6 families (shopkeepers in Lamgarha market) were found to use LPG. The daily requirement of fuel wood is about 5-8 kg. Pattern of collection of fuel wood is about 60% from Van Panchayat forest, 15% from Private forest and 25% from government or reserved forest. Any other non-timber product, for example, resin, medicinal plants, lichens was some times extracted from Toli VP (Table 5.2).

Forest Condition in VP

The year of the formation of VP was 1955. The VP forest is uneven-aged forest of chir pine mixed with banj, burans and kaphal (Fig 5.2). The condition of the Toli VP forest is averaged, banj trees severely lopped but chir, burans and kaphal growing well. Regeneration is also good as saplings of all species (except banj) are present in the forest. The canopy cover of Toli VP forest is estimated at 30% and the ground litter cover 57%.

After the creation of Van Panchayat the peoples of Toli Van Panchayat accepted that the condition of the Van Panchayat become better, as indicated by the reduction of distance travelled for collection of fuel wood, fodder and drinking water. The water source of Toli village is about 50 temporary small ponds (naulas) and 2 stone check-dams have increased water in them during summer months, which are cleaned regularly by the community people and have been covered to protect from dust. The VP of Toli arranges the forest guard for every year and pays his salary of about Rs.1000 month^{-1} from VP income. In Toli VP many people were fined in last 5 years and VP generated fines about Rs. 2600. In Toli VP plantation of pine, cedar, bamboo and acacia species was done in 2004-2005 about in 3 ha by the help of community members. Community members also made the fire lines and clear them regularly for protection of forest in summer season. The livestock numbers in Toli VP were: 220 buffalos, 75 cows, 375 goats and 235 oxen (Fig 5.3). However, there was no control of grazing in Toli VP (Table 5.2).

Income Sources

The total income of Toli Villager is Rs.18700.0 yr^{-1} family^{-1}. The cropping pattern in Toli Village related that the rice, maduaa, millet, wheat, and potato are the main sources of agricultural income. The dependency on agricultural sources in Toli VP is about 65%. Annually agriculture income in Toli village is Rs. 10500.0 yr^{-1} family^{-1}, which is about 56.15% of the total income per family. The other main source of the village is milk production which is about 27.81% (Rs. 5200.0). As daily labour basis and floriculture income are Rs. 2000.0 (10.69%) and Rs. 1000.0 (5.35%) family^{-1} yr^{-1}, respectively (Fig 5.4).

The source of the income of VP is from the sale of NTFPs which is Rs.10 per family for dry fodder collection, Rs.30 per family for green fodder collection and Rs.10 per head load, besides these the imposition of fines also generates by the VP (Table 5.2). Thus, the total income generated by the VP was Rs. 4500 from the sale of permits and fines in the year 2005 (Fig 5.5).

Guna Van Panchayat (VP)

Introduction to Social Aspects

The Guna VP is located at about 1843 m. The area under VP forest is about 40 ha, of which 32 ha is good forest (Fig 5.1). The total number of families is 22 while the population of Guna is 240 comprising of 122 males and 118 females. The total literacy rate of Guna VP is 68%, with male and female literacy at 80.0 and 56.0%, respectively. The male female ratio at Guna VP is 1000:1180 (Table 5.2).

The present number of VP members is 7 and is composed of 6 males and 1 female. The VP meetings are generally held once in about two months. These meetings are attended from time to time by women-folk also.

In Guna VP all the families are using fuel wood for cooking and heating purposes. Though LPG is available in the area only 3-4 families (shopkeepers in Lamgarha market) were found to use LPG. The daily requirement of fuel wood is about 5-9 kg. Pattern of collection of fuel wood is about 65% from Van Panchayat forest, 15% from Private forest and 20% from government or reserved forest. Any other non-timber product, for example, resin, medicinal plants, and lichens were rarely extracted from Guna VP. In Guna VP the extraction of fodder is done on rotational basis. After 3 days interval the members of the family visit the forest for collection of fuel wood and fodder. The weight of one fuel wood head load is approx. 25-30 kg (by field checks) and green leaves (fodder/grass) head load is 18-22 kg (by field checks).

Forest Condition

The year of the formation of Van Panchayat was 1937. The VP forest is even-aged banj-oak forest with under canopy tree species of kaphal (*M. nagi*) and burans (*R. arboreum*) (Fig 5.2). The dominant tree species of Guna VP are banj (*Q. leucotrichophora*) 60%, burans 15%, kaphal 15% and chir 10% (*P. roxburghii*). The condition of the Guna VP forest is good, oak trees are in healthy condition with moderate lopping. The trees of chir, burans and kaphal are growing well in this forest. Regeneration is also good as saplings of all species are present in the forest except banj oak species. The canopy cover of Guna VP forest is estimated at 42% and the ground litter cover 50%.

After the creation of VP the peoples of Guna VP accepted that the condition of the VP has improved, as indicated by the reduction of distance travelled for collection of fuel wood, fodder and drinking water. The water source of Guna village is about 20 temporary small ponds (naulas) dug during 2001-2002 in the catchment of two major springs have increased water in them during lean summer months. Ponds are cleaned regularly after 3 months and have been covered to protect from dust. The VP of Guna arranged the forest guard for every year and arranged their salary about Rs.800 per month from Van Panchayats income. In Guna VP many peoples were fined in last 5 years and VP generated from fines about Rs. 2000. In Guna VP plantation was not done in past two years (Table 5.2). Community members also made fire lines for protection of forest in summer season, and regularly cleared these lines every six months. The livestock numbers in Guna VP were: 195 buffalos, 64 cows, 225 goats and 75 oxen (Fig. 5.3). However, there was no control of grazing in Guna VP.

Income Sources

The total income of Guna Village is Rs. 14970.0 family^{-1} yr^{-1} (Table 5.2). The cropping pattern in Guna village is similar with that of Toli VP (wheat, rice, millet, maduaa, and potato). Annually agriculture income in Guna village is Rs. 7850.0, which is 52.44% of the total income. Floriculture, milk production and as daily labour (@Rs.65 day^{-1}) contribution is Rs. 7120.0 which is 47.56% of the total income (Fig. 5.4).

The main source of VP income is from the sale of NTFPs which is Rs.5 per family for dry wood collection, Rs.10 per family for green fodder collection besides these the imposition of fines also generate money by the VP. Thus the total income generated by the VP was Rs. 6500 from the sale of permits and fines in the year 2005 (Fig 5.5).

Conclusion

The local communities VPs of Uttaranchal (UA) are extremely poor and depend critically on the forests for their fodder and fuel wood requirements. These communities have been conserving their forests for many years (without external financial support on a regular basis), and thus play an important role in promoting ecosystem services like carbon sink, without any financial motivation (Singh, 2004). In contrast, in another area of about 2865 ha in UA where communities were not involved in forest management, Rathore *et al.* (1997) found depletion in carbon stock biomass at the rate of about 5 t yr^{-1} over a period of 16 years, though there was only a small reduction in forest areas. This is a good example of the amount of carbon that can be saved by local people by managing their forests effectively. However, the general size of a VP forest should be close to 150 ha as smaller VP forests (below 50 ha) are not able to sustain the dependent pressure.

Carbon is now being traded internationally at the rate of US$ 13 t^{-1} C. Van Panchayats (VPs) of Uttaranchal are conserving these forests for a long time. It is important to link conservation with economic benefits. The studied VPs forests sequester carbon at the rate of 4-5 t ha^{-1}yr^{-1}. As the mean area of a VP is 60 ha, sequesters a total of 240 t carbon ha^{-1} yr^{-1} worth US $3120 annually at the rate of US$ 13 per ton. Once the people start realizing that the carbon of their forests is saleable they will be motivated to conserve them.

REFERENCES

IPCC, Climate Change (2001). The Scientific Basis. Contributions of Working Group I to the III Assessment Report of the Intergovernmental Panel on Climate Change (Eds. Houghton, J. et al.), Cambridge University Press, Cambridge, U.K.

Singh, J. S. and S.P. Singh (1987). Forest Vegetation of the Himalayan. Bot. Rev.53 (1): 82-192.

Singh, V., A. Tewari, M. Gupta and J. Ram (2006). The Prelogged Stocks of Carbon in *Shorea robusta* and *Q. semecarpifolia* Forests of Uttaranchal and Their C Sequestration Rates-A Tradable NTFP. Int. J.For. Usnf. Mngt., 7(1):1-5.

Singh S. P., G. S. Mer and P. K. Ralhan (1988). Carbon Balance for a Central Himalayan Crop Field Soil. Pedobiologia 32:187-191p.

Houghton, R.A. J.E. Hobbie, J.M. Melillo, G.R. Shaver and G.M. Woodwell (1983). Changes in the Carbon Content of Terrestrial Biota and Soil Between 1860 and 1980: A Net Release of CO_2 to the Atmosphere Ecological Monographs. 53(3): 235-262.

Singh, J. S. and S. P. Singh (1992). Forests of Himalaya-structure, Functioning and Input of Man. Gyanodaya Prakashan, Nainital, India.

Phartiyal, P. and A. Tewari (2006). Challenges Before Marginalized Hill Communities for Managing Community Dorests, Status of the Village forest Councils in Uttaranchal, India. 11th Biennial Conference of International Association for the Study of Common Property, Bali, Indonesia. (In press).

Steffer, W., I. Nobel, and J. Canadell (1998). The Terrestrial Carbon Cycle: Implications for the Kyoto Protocol. Science 280:1393-1394.

Körner, Ch. (2001). Experimental Plant Ecology: Some Lessons from Global Change Research, 227-247p.

Singh, S.P., R. Thandani and M. Kumaiyan (2003). Eds. National Biodiversity Strategy and Action Plan for Western Himalayas India Final Report.

Tolia, R.S. (1996). British Kumaun Garhwal: An Administrative History of a Non-regulation Hill Province 1836-1856 (Vol. 2), Indus International, New Delhi.

Singh, S.P. (2004). A Case for Incorporating Values of Ecosystems Services of Uttaranchal and Other Himalayan States in National Accounting Systems Submitted as Supplementary Memorandum to 12th Finance Commission, Government of India by the Government of Uttaranchal.

Rathore, S.K.S., S.P. Singh, J.S. Singh and A.K. Tewari (1997). Changes in Forest Cover in Central Himalayan Catchment: Indequacy of Assessment based on Forest Areas Alone. Journal of Environment Management. 49:265-276.

6

Forest Fires

Role and Initiatives of Panchayati Raj Institutions for the Prevention and Control in India

— **Prof. Pradeep K Vaid**

Introduction

The problem of environmental conservation and development has in recent times engaged the attention of various organisations, agencies and face various types of problems in the form of disasters, such as affect the whole world.

India is a vast country with geographical area of 3287,263 km. The variety in its climate and rich biodiversity it posses made India one of their mega biodiversity regions of the world. It has 22.20 of its geographical area per cent forests are prone to fire damage. Loss of timber, loss of bio-diversity, loss of wildlife habitat, global warming, soil erosion, loss of food and fodder, damage to water and other resources, estimate average tangible annual loss due to forest fires in country is Rs. 440 crore.

Traditionally Indian forests have been affected by fires. The menace has been aggravated with rising human and cattle population and consequent increase in demand for forest products by individual and communities. The reasons of forest fires are based on two major categories: (*i*) Environmental (which are beyond control); (*ii*) Human Related (which are controllable). Environmental causes are largely related to climate conditions such as temperature, wind speed and direction, level of moisture in soil and atmosphere and duration of dry spells. Human related causes result from human activity as well as methods of forest management.

The forests of the country are under tremendous pressure. Forest fires are a major degradation of India's forests. It is estimated that proportion of forest area prone to forest fires annually ranges from 33 per cent in some states to over 90 per cent in other. The following table gives an idea about estimated forest area affected by forest fires in India particularly to the states having suffered major losses.

Table 6.1 : Estimated Forest Area Affected by Forest Fires in India

(In lakhs)

Sl. No.	State	Released		Total
1	Chhatisgarh	44.000	105.000	149.000
2.	Himachal Pradesh	31.975	101.300	133.275
3.	Madhya Pradesh	41,750	155.100	196.850
4.	Maharashtra	191.290	—	191.290
5.	Uttarakhand	56.400	74.500	130.900
6.	West Bengal	34.850	72.650	107.500

Source: Forest and Wildlife Statistic, India, 2004.

The vulnerability of forests to fires varies from place to place depending upon the type of vegetation and climatic conditions. If we take the examples of Himalayan regions then we see that Himalayan regions of India are full of natural resources like soil, mineral, water, valleys, rivulets and forests. Forest as the backbone of the Himalayan economy, is rich in biodiversity. But the time is this that these resources are in danger due to environmental problems such as overgrazing, deforestation and forest fires.

The involvement of PRIs as the watch-dog of environment protection at the grass roots level needs to be duly recognized. The constitution (73rd Amendment) Act 1992 provides these institutions an opportunity to play their legitimate role for better results. The problem of forest fires also becoming a serious threat in forest based areas in India because of interacting effects of increasing population density, industrialization and urbanization and poor environmental management practices. The role of viable community-based institutions for environmental protection is important with full legal, administrative and technical support. These institutions should be empowered to plan, to work out the modality and implement the various measures.

The 73rd Constitutional Amendment Act in 1992 has cast constitutional imperative on all the state government to come up with appropriate Panchayati Raj Acts detailing meaningful democratic devolution of functions, functionaries and funds. The 73rd Amendment to Constitution in 1992 mandating establishment of PRIs in rural India and its subsequent Extension to Schedule Areas Act, 1996 clearly mandated the PRIs in the overall village development, including and significantly the management of natural resources. The 29 functions recommended for decentralization of PRIs include management of forests for better environment, policies and programmes. As far as forestry in India is concerned, the National Forest Policy (NFP), 1988, and the subsequent circular on Joint Forest Management (JFM) in 1990 created the space for community participation in management of forest resources. Both JFM and Panchayati Raj (PR) represent major steps towards conservation and development of natural resources through participatory governance especially in participatory forest management. Thus, while PRIs are elected representatives of the village population as mandated by the constitution to be empowered on certain aspects of forest management.

Forest Fires Prevention and PRIs

Forest fires are a major cause of degradation of India's forest. The subject of forest is in the concurrent list of Constitution of India. The field administration of the forests is the responsibility of the various state governments. The state Governments thus has the direct responsibility of the management of forest resources of the country. Each state and Union Deputy Inspector General of Forests, the Ministry is implementing a plan control. The Panchayati Raj Institution of grassroots has become.

(*i*) To determine their own destiny and take decisions relating to problems at local level;

(*ii*) To ensure the sustainable utilization of species and ecosystems which support rural communities;

(*iii*) To decentralize execution of all kinds of environmental conservation and development activities with effective participation of the people; and

(*iv*) To alter the administrative methods for environment protection and improvement point of view.

The Panchayati Raj Institutions have an effective role in the implementation of various policies and programmes contribute to environment protection and improvement, formulated by the state and Central governments. Each tier is involved in the process of local planning about their jurisdiction the plans including environmental protection are made at Village Panchayat and the examined by the Panchayat Samiti and considered by the Zila Parishad. The PRIs also provide necessary assistance to the other agencies engaged in environment protection and forest fires. The role of PRIs are also important in forest fire conservation:

(*i*) To create will and to motivate rural people to the conservation of forest fire;

(*ii*) To understand the problem and situation and to share the information about this problem;

(*iii*) To achieve integrated approach by co-ordinating the activities of various agencies involved in forest fire protection in rural areas.

(*iv*) To give guidance and training to rural community to handle this problem in rural areas; and

(*v*) To restrain the people from those activities which are prone to forest fires.

Panchayati Raj is institutionalization of public participation in planning and decision-making is rural India. The success or failure of the objectives of environment protection through PRIs would largely depend on administrative ability, leadership and motivation of personnel. The administrative capability involves the ability to mobilize, allocate and combine the actions that needs to achieve the objectives of environment protection.

The situation of forest fire in India is very different from other countries like the USA and Canada, which also have extensive area, population density is very low and there is no 'direct human pressure on forests, Forest departments in such countries have sophisticated equipment and are not dependent on the local population for the implementation of fire fighting measures. In our country, on other hand, there is a close interrelationship between the human population and the forests, both in terms the physical proximity of villages to the forests and livelihood dependence. The application of modern techniques alone is not cost effective, funds allocated under the scheme are not sufficient to equip all areas in any case. So active involvement of local people was essential to combat this problem. People participation through Panchayati Raj Institution is necessary to overcome or prevent this problem.

As the Panchayati Raj Institutions are the main functioning body of the local government, forest fire is also issue relating to the welfare of the community. To combat forest fire active involvement of people through Panchayat leadership is essential. There is a need of the contribution of Panchayati Raj Institutions and voluntary organizations like (Self Help Group) SHGs, NG0s, NSS, NCC to come and involve themselves to tackle this problem of forest fire.

JFM—Issues and Initiatives

Joint Forest Management is a management intervention under which local communities co-manage forest with the forest department within a 'care and share' principle. The National Forest Policy 1988 envisages community involvement in development and protection of forests and accords the highest priority to ecological balance and sustainable utilization of forest resources. It aims at creating a massive peoples involvement with the involvement of women and village youth, for achieving the aims and objectives of policy (which includes prevention and control of forest fires). In June 1990 the Government of India, issued guidelines to the state govt. for involving local communities in protection and development of degraded forests, followed by a new set of guidelines in February 2000 to incorporate newly emerging issues. Based on these guidelines, the JFM Programme was adopted by state government, and at present 63,618 Joint Forest Management Committees (JFMCs) are co-managing with the forest Department an area of around 14 million hectares in India.

Conclusion

Forest fire is a calamity for forests. Therefore the problem of controlling forest fires is the main issue in our forest economy. Although it is the duty of forest department to manage and do all forest related functions, but it is seen that functions done by forest department are not sufficient. It is necessary to involve other agencies to deal with the forest problems such as overgrazing, deforestation and forest fires. It is found from the previous researches on forest fires that most of forest fires are due to human beings. To eradicate this problem the Panchayati Raj Institutions can play an effective role because people participation or involvement is only possible at grassroot levels where local people can be awarded through awareness campaigns about forest fire management activities. Joint Forest Management (JFM) at the grassroot level are working very well throughout the country. Active involvement of these Joint Forest Management Committees is very essential in order to protect the forest from fires, therefore meetings of these committees should be convened at Panchayat levels to spread the message for obtaining maximum cooperation from people of that area. In this way Panchayati Raj Institutions can be effective for solving this problem of forest fires throughout the country.

REFRENCES

Report of the Committee on Panchayati Raj Institutions, New Delhi, Government of India, 1978.

T.N. Khoshoo (1988) Environmental Concerns and Strategies, New Delhi.

V.K. Bahuguna, Forest Fires, Prevention and Control Strategies in India, March 1999.

B.M. Chitlangi, Gram Panchayat and Environment Management in Rajasthan, 1990.

V.K. Bahuguna and Upadhayay, Forest Fires in India — Policy Initiatives for Community Participation, International Forestry Review, 2002.

7

Role of Academia in Imparting Environment Education

— Dr. R. Ganapathi and Mr. S. Sannasi

Introduction

Environment nowadays is considered as one of the serious issues in the society. Both the government and non-governmental organisations throughout India take much effort to conserve the society from environment pollution. Public are exposed to several environmental problems. Many are affected due to environmental pollution, which may cause to death. For example during the last week at the time of heavy rain three members in a car died due to the consumption of Carbon monoxide inside the car. Further we face many types of pollution like air pollution, noise pollution, water pollution and pollution due to lack of cleanliness in the street as well as in public places like Bus stand, Railway station, etc. The very emerging problems faced by all of us at present are Chikungunia fever in which almost 30 per cent of the population is affected. Further a strange type of viral fever is also spreading nowadays. These are all due to environmental problems prevailing in the society. Sometimes we have to consume bad odour when we are travelling in bus, when we cross a particular street. Though the government and NGOs and some public welfare organisations conduct awareness programme in various places both in urban and rural areas, we have failed to maintain good environmental condition in the society. If it goes with the same condition, in future will have to pay huge sums to control the environmental pollution. In olden days the literacy rate was very poor. But nowadays in India almost in all states the literacy rate has been increased considerably. Still the awareness about the cause of environment has not reached well to the society. Educating about the causes of pollution from environment is an emerging one. The academicians have more responsibility in this regard. Further educational institutions are the right channels to create awareness about the environment problems through educating the students.

Types of Pollution

The types of pollution may be categorised for the sake of convenience into air, land, water, radioactive and noise pollution etc.

1. Atmospheric (Air) Pollution

A healthy person takes in 16-20kg. of air daily. So the impact of polluted air on human being can be realised. The natural proportion of oxygen in the air changes with release of other gases in excess. Moreover various types of solid particles, aerosol, smoke etc. move freely in the air. Depending upon the source the pollutants may be different in different places. Air pollution is one of the most dangerous and common kind of environmental pollution reported in big cities, particularly in industrial cities. The following are the important sources of air pollution.

(*i*) Carbon monoxide
(*ii*) Sulphur compounds
(*iii*) Nitrogen oxide
(*iv*) Hydrocarbon
(*v*) Photo chemicals
(*vi*) Smoking

B. Solid Particles as Pollutants

(*i*) Lead
(*ii*) Cement and other dust
(*iii*) Fluorides, salts and agricultural chemicals

Water Pollution

Water is very much essential for maintenance of life of plants and animals. Water is essential for irrigation, navigation and for industrial purpose. Quality of water is important for all purposes. It is a great solvent and therefore various elements are found dissolved in it. It is very difficult to get water in its pure form. The standard of quality differs for different purposes for which it is used. When water contains substances more than wanted or it contains harmful elements, germs or particles, it is called polluted.

Sources of Water Pollution

1. Sewage
2. Agricultural pollution
3. Industrial pollution
4. Oil pollution
5. Thermal pollution; and
6. Marine pollution

Noise Pollution

When sound becomes undesirable it is termed as noise. To define noise for practical purposes, it means unwanted sound—sound not desired by the recipient. Nature is full of various kinds of sounds. Animals and man use sound as a means of communication. A sound may become noise depending upon its intensity, pitch and resonance. Intensity depends on the wavelength whereas pitch depends upon the rapid propagation of these wavelengths. When propagation becomes uniform the sound becomes melodious, but when haphazard it becomes noise.

Types of Noise Pollution

1. Natural sound due to thunder, rain, wind etc.
2. Man-made sound originates in factories in urban areas, railways, airport, market etc.

Soil Pollution

"Unfavourable alteration of soil by addition or removal of substances and factors which decrease soil productivity, quality of plants and ground water is called soil pollution". Soil pollutants are many natural or synthetic substances that reduce the productivity of the soil and adversely affect the physical, chemical and biological properties of the soil. Pollutants in the air and water also reach the soil and cause its pollution.

Sources of Soil Pollution

1. Pesticides and Weedicides
2. Chemicals
3. Fertilizers and Manures
4. Animal Excreta, Faecal Matter, Dead Animals, Garbage Digested Sewage Sludge and Discarded Food

5. Discarded Materials
6. Radioactive Wastes; and
7. Other Pollutants

Role of an Individual in Prevention of Pollution

Awareness regarding environment and its protection forms the basis of healthy environment. Environmental awareness changes the attitude of man towards the nature. Role of citizens is of paramount importance in controlling the pollution. Their role is not important only at the level of town/ state/ country but it is understood at international level also. Total human civilisation on the earth has the responsibility to protect the flora and fauna all around. Any step in this direction will be quite useful to conserve the environment. It is very important that our life style should be favourable towards the environment.

Role of Academicians in Imparting Awareness about the Environmental Pollution

Though the government and NGOs take more effort in creating awareness about the pollutions, the academicians are considered as the most correct channel for imparting knowledge about the danger of environmental pollution to the society as a whole. Nowadays almost in all family the children are sent to school for education. All the parents irrespective of the class, colour, race and financial soundness prefer education to their children rather than any other work without education.

In India the literacy rate is considerably increased every year. The society has more value on the academicians because of their sincere effort to impart knowledge to the students. Due to the development of consciousness among the public in every majority of the members are educated. When education about the pollution is created among the students and educated, automatically it reaches all the individuals of the society, which will help to safeguard the society from pollution to the maximum possible extent. Under this situation it is the duty of every academician to take much effort in imparting knowledge about the environmental pollution from school level. Apart from the duty of the school, at college level some more hours need to be spent by all the teachers to create awareness about the pollution. Any message is informed by teachers, most of the students follow without any change. So it is possible to create awareness about the causes of pollution to each individual with the help of academicians. Surely the academicians can make any change in the society to safeguard all the citizens from the pollution.

Conclusion

Today we should learn and understand all the aspects of environment. Every citizen should have the knowledge of environment. To create awareness among the people about the environment, we should use various methods. To create awareness about the environment amongst the students, we should give the priority from school level. Hon'ble Supreme Court of India has given directions about the environmental education at school/college level, which is an appreciable step. Awareness regarding environment should be created among masses through media. Write ups, plays, and various paintings etc. may be used for this purpose. Various programmes on T.V. and radio should be used to enlighten the masses about the environment. Knowledge regarding the environment can be imparted through special seminars, workshops and group discussions in the society.

8

Land Use and Agrarian Relations

Issues and Prospects in the Indian Context

— Mr. Francis Kuriakose and Ms. Deepa Kylasam Iyer

In India, agriculture is a way of life, tradition, the epicentre of outlook and culture and the backbone of economy. It is central to all strategies for planned socio-economic development of the country. Indian agriculture contributes to 29.3 per cent of the Gross Domestic Product (1998-99), 2.7 per cent of the world's agricultural production (ranked sixth in the world) and employs 64.90 per cent of the total work force in the country (1990-91). Due to the constant attention that agriculture received in the successive five-year plans, the momentum of agriculture increased along with the resilience of the Indian food security transforming the status from a food to mouth existence to food self sufficiency and even food surplus. This Olympian change that revolutionised Indian agriculture began with the Green revolution that resulted in a four-fold increase in food production in the last four decades helping Indians to overcome droughts and failure of monsoon. In the decade that followed the Green revolution agriculture grew by 1.15 per cent (1972-82). In two decades, the primary sector in India that includes agriculture, forestry and logging, fishery, mining and quarrying contributed to 29 per cent of the Gross Domestic Product (1998-99). From the statistics available, it is safe to assume that the limiting factors of agriculture in India can choke the sustainability of the sector seriously compromising the food security of one-sixth of the world population and damage environmental balance severely. It is in this context that factors affecting agriculture with focus on land use has to be closely studied.

Land is a finite resource and there is conflicting and competing demands on it. For 80 per cent of the world countries, agriculture and land is the primary source of life and livelihood. India holds 2.4 per cent of the world's geographical area (328.73 mha[1]) but supports 17.5 per cent of the world's population (Provisional data of the 2011 Census). India is home to 18 per cent of the cattle population of the world while owning a mere 0.5 per cent of the total grazing area. Of the total 328 mha (total geographical area), land use statistics is available for approximately 305 mha (93%) of the total land. 228 million ha (69%) of its geographical area falls within dry land that encompasses arid, semi-arid, dry and sub-humid land as per Thornthewaite classification. India is blessed with a wide range of soil pattern each particular to the locale. The alluvial soil (78 mha) that covers the great Indo-Gangetic Plains, the valleys of the rivers Narmada and Tapti (Madhya Pradesh), the Cauvery Basin (Tamil Nadu) supports cereals, oil, pulses, potato and sugar cane. The Black Cotton soil (51.8 mha) found in Maharashtra, Gujarat, Madhya Pradesh, Uttar Pradesh, Karnataka, Rajasthan and Andhra Pradesh supports cereals, cotton, citrus fruits, pulses, oil seeds and vegetables. The Red soil of South India and Madhya Pradesh, West Bengal and Bihar supports rice, millets, tobacco and vegetables. The laterite soil (12.6 mha) and desert soil (37 mha) are not found suitable for agriculture.

Water is a resource precious and scarce in India. The variability of precipitation spatially and in quantity can be inferred by the fact that rainfall has been recorded as low as 100 mm in West Rajasthan and 9000mm in Meghalaya in North Eastern India. India receives 4000 cubic kilometre of precipitation in the country in its 35 meteorological sub-divisions. Of this amount, only 50 per cent is put to benefit due to topographical and other constraints. The fact that water is crucial to agriculture in a country that has 68 per cent of its net cultivated area as rain-fed, can hardly be exaggerated. Of the total cultivated area of 142 mha, 97 mha is rainfed. The full irrigation potential of the country has been revised to 139.5 mha out of which 58.5 mha is watered by major and minor irrigation schemes, 15 mha by minor irrigation schemes and 40 mha by groundwater exploitation. India's irrigation potential increased from 22.6 mha (1951) to 90 mha (1995-96) but water usage efficiency is a meagre 30-40 per cent. That is why more than 50 per cent of the total cultivated area is still rainfed. The state of soil and water that mainly determine land and its utility in agriculture is of prime importance to maintain sustainable development. We need to define and examine land use pattern with an emphasis on a viable land use policy taking the above factors into consideration.

Land Use Pattern—The Indian Scenario

Land Use Pattern is determined by physical, economical and institutional framework, ie, the action and interaction of the physical characteristics of land, the economic factors like capital and labour, location of land with respect to factors of infrastructure like transport and institutional framework that determines the inter-relation between all the factors involved. In other words, land use pattern is a complex phenomenon determined by the dynamic equilibrium of factors of agrarian relations, economic development, infrastructure and policy making. It is the synthesis of physical, chemical and biological process on one hand and human process on the other.

The pattern of land use in India can be determined by looking at the post independence scenario. Till 1949-50, land area was divided into a five-fold classification. This was inadequate to meet the agricultural demands as there was lack of uniformity in definition and scope of classification. Hence it was difficult to compare and utilise the classification to improve the existing land pattern. To break up the existing tracts of land into smaller constituencies for better utility and monitoring, The Technical Committee on Co-ordination of Agricultural Statistics (Ministry of Food and Agriculture) recommended a nine-fold use of land in the country. There was the area under agriculture that was the mainstay of farmland. Three-fourth of this area was shared by the states Bihar, Gujarat, Madhya Pradesh, Karnataka and Maharashtra with Maharashtra topping the chart with the highest percent of the net sown area. The area under non-agricultural use comprised the land under water, land used for the construction of buildings, roads, railways and barren agricultural land. The area under forest was 76.52 mha (State Forest Department, 1999). It was classified as Reserve, Protected and Unclassed. Using Remote Sensing Technology, it was ascertained that the actual forest cover was only 63.73 mha. The ownership of forest land was left to the Government of India and community clans wherever applicable. The per capita availability of forest land was 0.08 hectares whereas the optimum area of land required for meeting the basic needs was 0.47 hectares. This immense pressure on forest cover led to the search of potential areas for expansion of forest cover in culturable land tracts. 13.94 mha of the total land form wetland, fallow land and land put to other uses. Forests form an important part of land use. Land allocation for forestry include forest land and land allotted for agro forestry, farm woodlots, wind belts, shelter belts, avenue trees, urban forests, homestead forests and sacred groves. The state of Natural forest in India can be deciphered from table 8.1.

Table 8.1 : State of Natural Forests in India

Area of Natural Forest	51.73 mha
Total growing stock in Natural Forest	2431.30 million cu.m
Total biomass in Natural Forests	4805.7 million tonnes

Source: NFAP, MOEF, Government of India, 1999

Forests in India show the greatest variation and range depending rainfall topography and climactic factors. Forests are both a resource and a habitat and of the 16 detailed forest types given, 38.2 per cent is topical deciduous forests and 30.2 per cent is moist deciduous. The benefits of natural forests include soil protection, fertility, water flora and fauna conservation, microclimate, genetic resource conservation, use of genetic breeding and bio-technology, integrated watershed management and regeneration of eco-systems.

11 mha of the total land comes under permanent pastures and grazing lands. Rajasthan, Uttar Pradesh, Madhya Pradesh, Andhra Pradesh and Orissa cover 75 per cent of the grazing land in India. The forests of India support 40 per cent energy needs of the country out of which 80 per cent needs are in the rural region and 30 per cent fodder needs of cattle remain significant. The livestock statistics of India given in the table is relevant in this context. It is evident that as land remains constant, the increasing livestock population and their needs could be met only with judicious planning and sustainable use of land.

Table 7.2 : Livestock population in India

Year	Total livestock population in (000)	Cattle (in ooo)
1977	369,645	180,140
1982	419,742	192,453
1987	445,286	199,645
1992	470,860	204,584

Source: Agricultural Statistics at a glance, 2001, Directorate of Economics and Statistics, Ministry of Agriculture, Government of India. Note that livestock includes cattle, buffalo, sheep, goat, horse, pig, donkey, mule, camel, yak and 'mithun'.

Area under Common Property Resource (CPR) includes the land that caters to the basic needs and services of the vulnerable sections of the rural poor. This includes village forestry, grazing and watershed drainage to help the farmers in crisis. CPRs should not be confused with wasteland. Whereas CPRs have property rights in the land allocated, wasteland is the ecological characteristics coined to initiate developmental programmes for the recovery of degraded lands irrespective of property rights. Velayutham (2000) has shown that the area under CPR has diminished during the period 1950-1997. Grazing pressure, land degradation resulting from a burgeoning cattle population that increased from a livestock population of 292 million to 462 million during the period resulted in the gross erosion of CPR changing them into wastelands.

Case for Land Use Policy

The way land is used as a means for life and livelihood is not just dependent on the direct users; it is exposed to a wider realm and is decided by all the factors directly and indirectly involved. One of the main problems that is faced today is the depletion of the quality of land and land degradation. Approximately 5-7 million hectares of usable land is lost every year through land degradation. The relative influence of land degradation is 39% in Asia. This translates to half a billion people in the developing world with no irrigation facilities, 400 million living on soil unsuitable for agriculture, 200 million on slope dominated regions and 130 million in fragile forest eco-system. 73 per cent of the earth faces severe and significant problems in agricultural investment while trying to sustain a rising population. A recent pioneering study by three UN agencies including FAO, UNDP and UNEP estimate the severity and cost of land degradation in South Asia to be 2 per cent of the Gross Domestic Product of the region and 7 per cent of the agricultural output. The statistics given below reaffirm the finding.

Table 7.3 : Extent of Land degradation in India (area)

Source of Erosion	Area in mha
Water	103.90
Wind	13.10
Physical Agents	12.23
Chemical Agents	10.30
Other Agents	7.20

Source: National Bureau of Soil Survey and Land Use Planning

The rising trend in land use degradation can be attributed to the following reasons:

1. Deforestation
2. Inadequate land use
3. Unsustainable farming and grazing practices
4. Demographic pressure
5. Lack of adequate technology implementation
6. Markets and legal instruments
7. Climate fluctuation

Demographic Pressure

Demographic pressure is one of the foremost reasons of land degradation as increasing population puts more pressure on arable land, grazing, forestry, wild life, tourism and development. Not surprisingly, population pressure affects 35 per cent of the productive land. The population demands for food, fuel and employment is going to double in the next five decades. This will involve expansion of fragile marginal lands for utility in developing countries as poverty is endemic and institutional capacity for land management is weak. Urbanisation and industrialisation outstrips land capacity. There are serious concerns about land, environmental degradation, decreased productivity and growth rate in the developing world. The population of 1.3 billion living on fragile land is set to double. The vulnerable segment of the population notably the rural poor with moderate assets, land, tradition social capital, human capital and indigenous knowledge are not developed by the institutions. These invisible millions living in disperse settlements in an informal economy are not picked up by the development juggernaut. They lay neglected along with the environmental distress signals.

Land Degradation as a Result of External Features

The net value of land is the sum of two factors- the present value of the revenue stream and the present value of the terminal value of land. There are a number of factors that diminishes the value of land. Intensive farming practices are the foremost among these. Green revolution in India brought in petrochemical technology, pest intensive agricultural method, cross breeding and single species forest plantations which were mindlessly adopted from other parts of the world. Over application of nitrates has led to groundwater contamination, soil degradation and an imbalance in micro nutrients. The extension of area under irrigation has jumped from 19 per cent to 38 per cent in terms of net sown area in four decades. This has led to water logging and salinity. National Remote Sensing Agency and Forest Survey of India has brought out the fact that 60 per cent of the total area under cultivation is degraded. More than one source of irrigation has increased the salinity and alkalinity of soil. Low precipitation coupled with unscientific use of water and drainage facilities take a toll on water resources. Improper cropping patterns and intensive farming practices degrade the quality and value of land.

The consequences of large scale land degradation are two-folded:

(*i*) *The on-site costs*—The technological breakthrough that the Green Revolution offered led us to produce short duration high yielding crops. Intensive land use, increased area under irrigation, prolific use of chemicals to raise the efficiency of production also brought in on-site costs like soil erosion, alkalinity, salinity, micro nutrient deficiency, water logging, depletion and contamination of ground water.

(*ii*) *The off-site costs*—The off-site costs include river and dam siltation, damage to roadways and sewers, siltation of harbours and channels, loss of reservoir storage, disruption of stream ecology, damage to public health and increased frequency of flooding.

Policy Intervention

The rationale for policy intervention should be based on two factors:

(*i*) The significance of off-site costs as a result of land degradation

(*ii*) The costs of on-site degradation even when it is not apparent in the immediate context

This requires a foresight and vision for long term sustainable development through policies, action and awareness brought out through education, training and extension programmes. The objective of the policy intervention should be the following:

(*i*) Restore efficiency to meet the growing consumption needs

(*ii*) Suitable mechanism for scientific management, conservation and development of land resource

(*iii*) Expansion of forest cover to restore ecological balance

(*iv*) Conjunctive use of surface and ground water

(*v*) Preservation of agricultural land

The Integrated Approach

For effective and efficient use of land we need eminently practical plans for land use management. This is included in the integrated approach. To reduce the conflicts and to make trade-offs link social and economic development with environmental protection, sustainable development is the key. The essence of integrated approach is the sectoral planning management. There are a number of issues to consider while adopting approaches and policies. For land use pattern through sectoral approach, we need to plan linkages, formulate economically viable project for each sector and use technology. This would include making Land Use Atlases, system database on land utilisation and management, computerised and updated land records at district, state and national levels. Better legal, political and administrational will is also the key. We need strict laws for land use conversion, survey of land based on climate, water and soil particulars to improve investment and training orientation, publicity and awareness based on local needs. Effective reclamation is needed to check degeneration. This can be done through effective watershed management, reduction of regional imbalances and diversification of land use. Preventive measures on adverse effects from industrial wastes and effluent and development of agro-based industries are also keys to developing an integrated approach.

To monitor the better use of land, Remote sensing satellite technology like Geographical Information System and Global Positioning System can be used. One of the problems frequently encountered while measuring the loss of land value is the difficulty in measurement itself as there are so many variables involved. Empirical or process based models have to be so complex to take into consideration the effects of all the variables. One of the methods is to estimate long term average annual soil loss from arable land using Universal Soil Loss Equation (USLE) or its revised form (RUSLE). There are various mathematical simulation models based on physical process involved in soil detachment, transportation and deposition. Use of Iso-erosion rate map (Singh et.al, 1992) is an example. Soil erodability factor can also be measured. Loss of soil value due to land degradation is needed to understand the environmental costs of agriculture. Production approach that assesses the impact, preventive cost approach that focuses on conservation and defensive expenditure and replacement cost approach that relies on the cost of restoration are the different ways to measure this. There are various econometrics models that can include and evaluate the inputs for alteration and cropping pattern. In India, soil and land survey conducted by Department of Agriculture and co-operation developed land degeneration mapping in the eighth five-year plan through District Information System where soil information system of 30 districts in diverse agro-climactic zones were formulated. Similarly, the Department of Land Resources, Ministry of Rural Development has brought out the Wasteland Atlas of India 2000 after studying different types of degraded wastelands in the country.

Reclamation of waste land is one of the most important aspects of sustainable land use. Agrarian practices can be modified for reclaiming wasteland. For example, application of gypsum consecutively for three years with reduced application in the second and third year will reduce salinity. Integrated watershed management is a preventive method in which soil and water is conserved and cropping pattern is altered to improve land use. Percolation of water into subsoil, reduction of surface water run-off, elimination of soil erosion and increase water availability are the chief aims of such sustainable management practices. For attaining these objectives, check dams along gullies are constructed, bench terracing, contour bunding, land levelling, planting grass along the contours, good vegetal cover on the watershed are deployed. Difference can be brought through Governmental Intervention and policy making. The Soil and Water Conservation Division, Ministry of Agriculture plans to manage 86mha under 30 projects through Integrated Water Management. 30,000 hectares of shifting and semi-stable land dunes have been treated with shelter belts and strip cropping as a conservation measure (TERI Report, 1997). The National Land Use and Wasteland Development Council (1985) was set up with the objective of formulating a National Policy and Perspective Plan for Conservation and Management of Land Strategy. It is time to set right some policies unsuitable for sustainable development. For example, the governmental policy of heavily subsidising electricity for tube well irrigation and chemicals led to poor land quality and eventual abandoning of land. Similarly, the New Economic Policy that encouraged relaxation on land acquired by Non Resident Indians, conversion of agricultural land into non-agricultural land, ceiling of agricultural land holdings eventually led to distorted market value due to speculation. The encouragement given to export oriented agriculture and concessions given to agro-processing industry adversely affected Indian agriculture by increasing the investment costs. Rational Policies to face regional imbalances should be brought in. The commitments of Tropical Forestry Action Plan, World Food Programme, UNCED led Forest Principles and the Government of India's National Conservation Plan should be adhered to. Rational Pricing Policy combined with resource efficiency in agro-processing industry is the need of the hour.

Economic incentives for soil conservation practices, conjunctive use of chemicals with biological inputs, classification of Land use statistics and studying the land use impact on agriculture will help at the macro level. Use of remote sensing technology to study different dimensions of the problem is mandatory. Legislation is in place for conservation of bio-diversity and forests but not to protect soil relations. Such gaps in law should be filled in with appropriate legal protection. New technology and crop management practices should emphasise the integrated systems approach. Meaningful farm research practices will address the concept of linking agriculture with environment. The aim of agriculture should be sustainable crop production with enhanced production envisioned for the long term. Diversification of agriculture should be encouraged. Farming oilseeds and pulses in place of cereals and horticulture wherever applicable demand less water and encourage crop rotation. This permits an understanding of agro climatic conditions, favourable topographic conditions, efficient land use, conservation of soil and maximum use of land resources. Integration of farm forestry with agro forestry will reduce the tremendous pressure on land. Growing a combination of species like agri- silviculture, farm and grove system will make management approach complementary, improve biomass production, regeneration of land resources and increased generation of employment and income.

Thus integrated and sustainable land use comprises prioritisation of critical land sensitivity, understanding land use and forest response, integrated strategy for forest and pest management, diversification of agriculture, crop combination, use of people's indigenous knowledge to attain food and nutritional security, increased productivity and address the environmental concerns. This is the way forward towards an evergreen revolution.

NOTES

mha is Million Hectares

REFERENCES

Mythili, G.M., 'Intensive Agriculture and Its Impact on Land Degradation.'

National Land Use Policy Outline and Action Points, 1998. National Land Use and Conservation Board, Ministry of Agriculture, Government of India, New Delhi.

Pandey, C.M, Singh, J.V. Patel R.A.S, 2008. 'Operational Land Use Policy for Sustainable Agricultural Production': Icon Farm.

Singh, Mridula. 'Land Resources—Need for Land Use Policy'. Land Use Board, Planning Department, Government of Uttar Pradesh.

Singh, Pramod K., 2009. 'Food Security in India: Whether Rational Land Use Policy or Precision Farming is the Answer?', Institute of Rural Management, Anand.

9

A Study on Environmental Management System in Select Companies

— Dr. N. V. Kavitha and Ms. Usha Rani

Introduction

Green Environment is an important issue at both the fronts, one for the economic development and another for the sake of ailment free society. It has been the most remarkable realization of the last century and it is likely to of increasing significance for the present century and beyond for the sake of healthy living of human being and all living things on this very live planet of the universe. The ignorance as well as prolonged disregard with respect, to the nature and on the contrary its cumulative impact at the advent of rapid industrialization that has occurred after the independence of our country, misuse as well as overuse of natural resources due to the rising of standards of living and population explosion has very much resulted in a severe backlash which has ultimately affected the ENVIRONMENT by way of its severe effect resulting in soil degradation, global warming, depletion of stratospheric ozone, environmental pollution, loss of bio-diversity thus resulting in economic disparities in our own country passing through the critical phase of industrialisation and international trade.

This chapter studies the working of E M S in India with special reference to Indian Companies and analysis the benefits derived by such companies. The study reveals that though the number of companies with ISO14001:2004 is increasing, but, not at the pace required for sustainable economic development. This chapter is based on secondary data only, where the data was collected from different company websites. Although rigorous compliance with the standard often resulted in real improvements, these improvements were primarily technical and administrative in nature. However, in most of the cases studied, daily practices remained somewhat decoupled from the prescriptions of the ISO 14001 system, of which employees generally had only a vague understanding. The organizations studied adopted different strategies to reconcile external pressures in favour of adopting this standard and internal constraint associated with a management system whose support varied from one case to the next. However, it is being increasingly realised that a purely regulatory approach to tackle environmental pollution has serious limitations and this needs to be supplemented by a greater awareness and commitment on the part of the industry to manufacture the products in an environmentally acceptable and sound manner under the overall objective of sustainable development. The above objective can only be achieved by adopting a credible Environmental Management System which provides a structured process for periodically reviewing and evaluating the environmental performance that it sets itself, as also for achieving continual improvement.

ISO14001:2004

ISO 14001: 2004 is an environmental management standard. It defines a set of environmental management requirements for environmental management systems. The purpose of this standard is to help all kinds of organizations to protect the environment, to prevent pollution, and to improve their overall environmental performance.

This new ISO 14001 standards was officially published on November 15, 2004. It cancels and replaces the old ISO 14001 1996 standard. ISO 14001 1996 expired on May 15, 2006. Since it was first published in 1996, ISO 14001 has rapidly become the most important environmental standard in the world. Thousands of organizations use it, environmentalists support it, and governments actively encourage its use. ISO 14001 applies to all types of organizations. It doesn't matter what size they are or what they do.

Environmental Management System

An environmental management system is a management structure that allows an organization to assess and control the environmental impact of its activities, products or services. ISO 14001, Environmental management systems—specification with guidance for use, outlines the requirements for an EMS.

According to ISO 14001, there are six key elements of an EMS:

1. An environmental policy
2. Planning

3. Implementation and Operation
4. Checking and Corrective Action
5. Management Review
6. Continual Improvement

The planning stage requires the organization to think and plan for its Environmental Policy. Its policy is the organization's statement of principles and intentions with regard to its environmental performance. This statement is a framework for action because it details the environmental objectives and targets that the organization is committed to achieving within a designated period.

The next step is Implementation and Operation. The organization must have an environmental management system with all staff aware of the organization's commitment to its environmental policy. This will require training to increase awareness and competence on environmental matters. The organization must also document its EMS. The EMS will also have to focus on operational control and emergency preparedness and response.

The EMS should be scrutinized in the Checking and Corrective Action step. It must have a procedure for evaluating compliance with its environmental policy, as well as procedures to ensure that it has the capacity to act as circumstances dictate. It will need records and the capacity to undertake an EMS audit.

The final step is Management Review. Top management is required to review the EMS to ensure its continuing suitability. This step can lead to changes in the environmental policy of the organization as per requirements.

Survey Report: This chapter is based on secondary data only, where the data was collected from different company websites.

Current Position of ISO 14001 Certification in the Country

- Over 66 Industrial Units already Certified to ISO 14001
- Another 71 units currently implementing ISO 14001

From the above Table it is evident that in India, Maharashtra has got major share of 18.25% in getting ISO14001 certified followed by Delhi and Gujarat. Andhra Pradesh only 4 companies only have gone in for ISO 14001:2004 certification.

ISO 14001 - Environment Management System—Significant productivity improvements and financial savings reported by various Companies on ISO 14001 were:

- **Electronics Corporation of India (ECIL) reported—**
    - Increasing the green belt in and around the factory premises.

State-wise list of ISO 14001 Certificates issued

States	No. of ISO 14001 certified companies	% of Companies
Maharashtra	25	18.25
Delhi	17	12.41
Gujarat	13	9.49
STATE	12	8.76
Tamil Nadu	10	7.30
Uttar Pradesh	10	7.30
Karnataka	9	6.57
Madhya Pradesh	8	5.84
Orissa	8	5.84
West Bengal	7	5.11
Andhra Pradesh	4	2.92
Assam	3	2.19
Rajasthan	3	2.19
Bihar	2	1.46
Haryana	2	1.46
Himachal Pradesh	2	1.46
Goa	1	0.73
Pondicherry	1	0.73

Source: http://cpcbenvis.nic.in/newsletter/ems-feb-2010/feb2000iso148.htm

- Tree plantation by VIPs visiting ECIL and development of lawns etc.
- Installation of solar power in place of conventional heating mechanisms in areas like Canteen and Guest House.
- Installation of effluent treatment processes on scientific lines for disposal of used hazardous chemicals and other effluents.

All the above initiatives resulted in ensuring an eco-friendly organizational climate to the external world. The Company also *achieved Certification for Occupational Health & Safety* OHSAS 18001: 2007 from British Standards Institution that serves as a benchmark in respect of concern for health and safety of the concerned stakeholders

- **Indian Aluminium Company (INDAL) reported:**
  - 80% reduction in Water Consumption

- Recovery of Copper, Tin and Lead from Spent Acid, etchants, liquid & solid wastes
- Elimination of the use of toxic chemicals like, formaldehyde, lead and fluorides by substituting with alternate technologies
- Use of poor grade coal by CFBC Boiler
- 50% less requirement for land for ash storage

- **ITC Limited (ILTD Division) reported :**
    - Minimised Water Consumption
    - Minimised Coal Consumption in Boilers
    - Reduced Energy Consumption in Line-II
    - Streamlining of Waste disposal procedures
    - Reduced Ambient Air Temperature near DG Sets
    - Reduced noise emissions
- As far as the hospitality industry is concerned, the list of initiatives taken by the hoteliers to conserve the environment is exhaustive. The Orchid, an Eco-tel hotel in Mumbai is a best example of this. From the basic architecture of the building, to water conservation, to use of rubber wood instead of real wood, to use of energy saving devices, the hotel does it all to qualify as an eco-friendly hotel. The Park in New Delhi, The Ambassador Pallava in Chennai and The Lake Palace in Udaipur may not be as savvy as The Orchid' but they do use energy saving devices to conserve electricity. Moreover all of them reuse biodegradable waste generated in their hotels and also deploy various techniques to conserve water.
- The mother of all was *RETREAT (Resource Efficient TERI Retreat for Environmental Awareness and Training)* located in Gurgaon District. The building is country's first-ever eco-friendly building complex. Home to a state-of-the-art training complex cum conference centre of the Tata Energy Research Institute (TERI), the complex is powered by a photovoltaic-gasifier hybrid renewable energy system, which uses waste biomass and solar radiation as sources of energy. It also boasts of the first solar-roof in India. Air conditioning, equivalent to a conventional 35-tonnes capacity system, is provided by an earth air tunnel, which consumes a fraction of the energy used in a conventional system. The waste-water is treated using plants, which means that the complex emits no waste.
- *Bharat Petroleum Corporation Ltd (BPCL),* for instance, has taken various initiatives to prevent air pollution. It launched an environment-friendly

petrol pump in Delhi. With vapour recovery system, the petrol pump prevents unburned petroleum vapour from entering the atmosphere by converting it into less harmful compounds.

- *Bharat Heavy Electricals Ltd (BHEL)* shares the growing concern on issues related to environment and occupational health and safety. The organisation has launched a host of products like wind electric generators, solar heating systems, solar photovoltaic systems, solar lanterns and battery powered road vehicles in a bid to conserve the environment.

  Likes of *LG electronics* have introduced environment-friendly initiatives such as rainwater-harvesting, solar water heaters for canteen applications and converting effluent, treatment plant (ETP) sludge into bricks.

- *Punjab National Bank* has initiated various environmental drives that include van mahotsav, tree plantation camps, pollution check-up camps, environment awareness camps, maintaining parks, etc. The list is exhaustive. Almost everybody is in the race. And to assist the competitors to take part in the race, there are likes of CoRE, CII's Environmental Management Division (EMD) and Concept Hospitality Ltd, amongst others.

The process used by organizations to integrate the ISO 14001 standard has not yet been the subject of extensive research in environmental management despite the rapid development of this standard, particularly in industrial companies. However, in most of the cases studied, daily practices remained somewhat decoupled from the prescriptions of the ISO 14001 system, of which employees generally had only a vague understanding. The organizations studied adopted different strategies to reconcile external pressures in favour of adopting this standard and internal constraint associated with a management system whose support varied from one case to the next. However, it is being increasingly realised that a purely regulatory approach to tackle environmental pollution has serious limitations and this needs to be supplemented by a greater awareness and commitment on the part of the industry to manufacture the products in an environmentally acceptable and sound manner under the overall objective of sustainable development. The above objective can only be achieved by adopting a credible Environmental Management System which provides a structured process for periodically reviewing and evaluating the environmental performance that it sets itself, as also for achieving continual improvement.

"Climate change is such a huge issue that it requires strong, concerted, consistent and enduring action by governments".

— By Peter Garrett

REFERENCES

Business and the Environment's ISO 14001 Update (1997). Proctor and Gamble.

Forgoing ISO 14001 Registration, Opt for Independent Assessment. Cutter Information Corporation 3: 1-2

MacArthur, J and B. Gordon (1998). ISO 14001 in State Regulatory Offices: A Survey of Activities. Environmental Quality Management 7:14.

Morrison, J., K. Kao Cushing, Z. Day, and J Spier (2002) Managing a Better Environment: Opportunities and Obstacles for ISO 14001 in Public Policy and Commerce.

Thornton, R. (2003). Seeking ISO 14001 Compliance: A Step-by-Step Guideline. DNV Certification. 2003

http://www.dnvcert.com/DNV/Certification1/Resources1/Articles/Environmental/SeekingIS

Environmental Resource Services (2003). ISO 14001, Audits, Assessments, Gap Analysis,

Environmental. 2003. http://www.envsource.com/envsource.htm

"World Trade Needs Worldwide Standards", Henri Schwamm, Honorary Professor, University of Geneva ISO Bulletin September 1997.

ISO 14000 Info Centre, http://www.iso14000.com

Value-based Environment Education and Environment Friendly Living

A Multivariate Analysis

— Dr. N. Sivakumar and Dr. T. Ravikumar

ABSTRACT

This chapter analyses the perceptions of university students in a value-based education system regarding environment friendly living. Using multivariate analysis techniques this chapter analyses the results of a survey conducted among students of Sri Sathya Sai University, a value-based educational institution in India. The study has found that value-based education can promote similarity in perceptions among students and can create a large cluster of likeminded students with environment friendly life styles. The results also show the causal impact of value-based education on environment friendly living. This chapter also analyses the components of environment friendly living in a value-based education system. This chapter finally gives the implications of the study.

Key words: *environment friendly living; value-based education.*

Introduction

"We face an enormous environmental crisis. The worse news is that it is growing bigger at a rate faster than ever. The worst news of all is that if we continue with our present lifestyles, we shall not recover from the debacle for at least 50 to 500 years. The better news is that the final disaster has not overtaken us yet. The best news is that it need never overtake us at all, provided we move smartly and immediately to change our lifestyles. The supremely best news is that if we shift to another track for our lifestyles we shall surely find it more enjoyable, less frenetic and more fulfilling than our present track" (Myers, 2003). The looming environmental crisis thus clearly points out to the importance of leading environment friendly life styles. After analysing the psychological roots of the environment crisis, Russel (1988) states that the root of the crisis is not so much in human behaviour as in the thinking that underlies it and the beliefs and values that underlie the thinking.

Environment friendly living must be learnt properly, especially when young. The university provides a perfect setting to impart the basics of environment friendly living to students. In this chapter the perceptions regarding environmentally friendly living in a values based education system has been analysed using the data from a primary survey conducted among the students of Sri Sathya Sai University, a value-based institution of higher learning in India.

Environment Friendly Living

Environment friendly living refers to life styles which inflict minimal or no harm on the environment (wikipedia, 2009). The serious damages caused to environment have prompted considerable research on environment friendly living. Scholars have analysed various practices and projects of environment friendly behaviour across the world. These include studies on building eco-friendly educational institutions in UK and USA (Bach, 2008, *Shanbhag, 2008), encouraging water bottles usage in Australia (*Leanne, 2007) and promoting environmentally responsible textile designing in India (Ham 2008). Lee (2007) has studied the 'clean plate' project in Korea which aims at reducing food wastage. Geographic analysis also includes studies by Gifford et.al. (2009) which shows spatial optimism bias regarding environmental issues across the globe and a study by the National Geographic Society (2008) which reveals that inhabitants of Brazil and India have the world's most environmentally-sustainable lifestyle and Americans have the least.

Environment friendly behaviour has been understood from a philosophical and religious perspective. Studies have been done from an Islamic perspective (Sadat, 2009), Benedictine perspective (Ouellette et. al. 2005) and in the context of Hinduism (Mazumdar and Mazumdar, 2004; Mazumdar, 2005). Ruback et.al. (2008) have commented that people perceive the religious places differently from an environmental view point because of the different material, social, and symbolic aspects of the locations by analysing the perceptions regarding *Magh Mela* in India. Foster (2000) has tried to philosophise on the issue whether technology is the answer to the current environmental problems and points out that more than technology the solution lies in a society governed not by the search for profit but by peoples' genuine needs and the requirements of socio-ecological sustainability.

Dauncey (2006) and Snelgar (2006) have made efforts to measure environmental friendliness. Amarasekara, (2007) has studied the impact of environment friendly lifestyles in reducing in the ecological footprint. Ways of propagating environment friendly behaviour include creating practices networks (Chiffoleau, 2005), hearing environment pro-messages (Werner et.al, 2008), using green defaults (Pichert and Katsikopoulos, 2008) and usage of soft policies (*Möser and Bamberg*, 2008). While these studies explain varied ways of promoting environmentally living, the impact of cultivation of human values on environment friendly life styles needs to be researched.

Value-based Education and Environment Friendliness

Value-based education is a way of conceptualising education that places the search for meaning and purpose at the heart of the educational process (Hawkes, 2007). Cultivation of human values through value-based education has been emphasised as the most important means to address all the problems of modern society including the environmental crisis (Baba, 1979).

Reser and Bentrupperbäumer (2005), point out that the current practice and reference to the term environmental values in environmental research is in a chaotic and unsustainable state due to lack of clarity and therefore constitutes a particular challenge for environmental psychology. In spite of this, a large volume of research has been devoted to understanding the relationships between value constructs, moral reasoning frameworks and concern for environment (Carrus et.al 2008; Castro et. al, 2009; Shen and Saijo, 2008; Thøgersen, 2006). Studies have found that moral development is positively correlated with ecocentrism (Karpiak and Baril, 2008; Kortenkamp and Moore, 2001). Values of benevolence, altruism and universalism lead to a pro-sustainability orientation towards the environment (Corral-Verdugo et. al 2009; Hansla et.al. 2008). Thøgersen (1999) has emphasised using of intrinsic motivation as a key to encourage environment friendly behaviour.

From an applied perspective, Nordlund and Garvill (2003) have studied the influence of values, problem awareness, and personal norm on willingness to cooperate to reduce personal car use. Ojea and Loureiro (2007) have found that value orientations affect willingness to pay estimates for environmental goods. A positive attitude toward frugality has been found as an effective means of promoting pro-environmental behaviour (Fujii, 2006).

However, studies which attempt to understand environment friendly behaviour in a value-based education system are relatively less. Ravikumar and Sivakumar (2008) have studied how environment friendly living is learnt in a value-based educational environment and show the importance of inculcating values at a young impressionable age. Environment friendly living in a value-based educational system is yet to be understood fully. This chapter is an attempt to fill the important research gap of analysing environment friendly living in a value-based education system.

Aims of the Study

The aims of the present study are to understand environment friendly living in a value-based educational system. The study specifically tries to address the following research issues:

1. To understand whether a value-based education system can lead to similarity of perceptions of students of different years of study regarding environment friendly living (Perception similarity).
2. To analyse whether significantly large clusters of students with varying perceptions of environment friendly living are created in a value-based education system (Perception clustering).
3. To study the causal impact of value-based education in enabling environment friendly life styles among students (Value-based education impact).
4. To explore the components of environment friendly living in a value-based education system.

Hypothesis

Based on the above research issues the following are the hypotheses of the study:

H1 The perceptions of students across different years of study on environment friendly living in a value-based education system are not similar.

H2 A value-based education system creates several significantly large clusters of students with varying perceptions on environment friendly living.

H3 A value-based education system has no causal impact on environment friendly living.

Methodology of the Study

The methodology used for this study is as follows:

Data collection

Primary data was collected from students of Sri Sathya Sai University for this study. More details of Sri Sathya Sai University have been presented in Appendix 1. The details of data collection include:

- *Campus selection*: The data was collected from the students of one of the three campuses of the university namely, Brindavan campus, (situated at Bangalore, India).
- *Class selection*: The students of all the three years of the under graduate programmes offered in the campus were selected for data collection.
- *Data collection tool preparation*: A questionnaire was prepared to study the environment friendly living habits of the students. The questionnaire consisted of 29 statements (coded as Q01 to Q29) to be responded on 5 point Likert scale as follows:

  1 – I strongly disagree with the statement

  2 – I disagree with the statement

  3 – I am neutral i.e. neither agree nor disagree with the statement

  4 - I agree with the statement

  5 - I strongly agree with the statement

  The full questionnaire used in this study has been presented in Appendix 2.
- *Conduct of survey*: The questionnaire was pre-tested and then administered on all the students of the campus. While 298 questionnaires were distributed, 264 completed questionnaires were returned representing a response rate of approximately 90 per cent. The profile of sample studied is given in Appendix 3.

Data Analysis

The data collected was subjected to the following statistical analysis:

- Multivariate analysis of variance (MANOVA)
- Levene's test of equality of error variances
- Cluster analysis
- Regression analysis
- Granger causality test
- Factor analysis

The SPSS (Statistical package for social sciences) and Eviews software were used for this purpose. The descriptive statistics of the scores of statements Q01 to Q29 is given in Table 10.1.

Table 10.1 : Descriptive statistics (N= 264)

Code	Mean	Median	Std. Dev.	Skew-ness	Kurto-sis	Jarque-Bera	Proba-bility	Sum	Sum Sq. Dev.
Q01	4.07	4	0.99	-1.03	3.78	53.06	0.00	1075	255.63
Q02	3.61	4	1.00	-0.35	2.72	6.25	0.04	954	260.59
Q03	4.01	4	0.92	-0.77	3.21	26.84	0.00	1059	224.97
Q04	3.94	4	0.97	-0.97	3.88	49.89	0.00	1039	247.91
Q05	4.44	5	0.87	-1.64	5.60	191.89	0.00	1171	196.91
Q06	4.23	4	0.90	-1.29	4.76	107.42	0.00	1118	213.44
Q07	3.66	4	1.11	-0.50	2.40	14.76	0.00	966	325.32
Q08	3.58	4	0.95	-0.48	3.26	10.97	0.00	946	236.17
Q09	3.99	4	0.94	-0.81	3.48	31.43	0.00	1053	230.97
Q10	3.94	4	0.99	-0.84	3.39	32.54	0.00	1040	259.03
Q11	2.51	2	1.30	0.33	1.92	17.79	0.00	663	443.97
Q12	4.25	4	0.84	-1.06	3.98	60.05	0.00	1121	187.00
Q13	4.61	5	0.75	-2.68	11.71	1150.75	0.00	1218	148.59
Q14	2.25	2	1.23	0.82	2.80	30.26	0.00	593	401.00
Q15	2.55	2	1.34	0.43	1.99	19.49	0.00	672	471.45
Q16	2.38	2	1.13	0.52	2.45	15.27	0.00	628	338.12
Q17	4.04	4	0.95	-1.17	4.48	83.97	0.00	1067	238.54
Q18	1.39	1	0.90	2.69	9.88	838.95	0.00	368	213.03
Q19	3.61	4	1.08	-0.50	2.71	12.05	0.00	953	306.81
Q20	2.30	2	1.12	0.68	2.87	20.52	0.00	606	330.95
Q21	3.82	4	1.09	-0.83	3.30	31.35	0.00	1009	314.63
Q22	3.14	3	1.26	-0.18	1.99	12.57	0.00	828	415.09
Q23	3.64	4	1.21	-0.54	2.33	17.66	0.00	961	384.81
Q24	2.61	2	1.22	0.42	2.26	13.71	0.00	690	392.59
Q25	3.00	3	1.30	0.02	1.95	12.09	0.00	793	445.00
Q26	3.26	3	1.16	-0.17	2.20	8.44	0.01	860	352.48
Q27	1.95	2	1.12	1.11	3.42	55.87	0.00	516	331.45
Q28	3.29	3	1.31	-0.39	2.08	15.90	0.00	869	452.54
Q29	3.47	4	1.08	-0.54	2.75	13.37	0.00	917	307.81

The following sections of the paper discuss each of the issues of the research study.

Perception Similarity

The first issue analysed in the study was the similarity of perceptions of students across various years of study in a value-based education system. This issue dealt with the first hypothesis of the study that the perceptions across various years of study are not similar. For this purpose the data was classified into three groups each pertaining to the year of study. A multivariate analysis of variance (MANOVA) of the perceptions of students of the three groups was then performed. Pallant (2005) and Tabachnick and Fidell (1983) have explained the usage of MANOVA in statistical analysis. Smeeton et. al. (2004) have used the MANOVA technique in analyzing perception similarity. The results of the MANOVA analysis are given in Table 10.2:

Table 10.2 : MANOVA results of perceptions across groups

Test	Value	F	Hypothesis df	Error df	Sig.
Pillai's Trace	0.3072	1.4643	58	468	0.0186
Wilks' Lambda	0.7162	1.4591	58	466	0.0196
Hotelling's Trace	0.3635	1.4540	58	464	0.0206
Roy's Largest Root	0.1998	1.6124	29	234	0.0293

It can be noticed from Table 10.2 that the F values of none of the tests are significant. This shows that the perceptions of students across the various years of study are similar.

Table 10.3 gives the results of Levene's Test of equality of error variances for each of the statements used in the questionnaire.

Table 10.3 : Results of Levene's Test of equality of error variances

Code	F	df1	df2	Sig.
1	2	3	4	5
Q01	0.9367	2	261	0.3932
Q02	1.4675	2	261	0.2324
Q03	0.2160	2	261	0.8059
Q04	1.2360	2	261	0.2922
Q05	0.0930	2	261	0.9112
Q06	0.0143	2	261	0.9858
Q07	0.3842	2	261	0.6814

(Contd...)

1	2	3	4	5
Q08	7.4064	2	261	0.0007
Q09	1.8464	2	261	0.1599
Q10	0.6996	2	261	0.4977
Q11	4.8204	2	261	0.0088
Q12	2.4152	2	261	0.0913
Q13	1.3670	2	261	0.2567
Q14	0.3036	2	261	0.7384
Q15	0.5872	2	261	0.5566
Q16	2.5628	2	261	0.0790
Q17	1.2038	2	261	0.3017
Q18	0.1966	2	261	0.8217
Q19	0.3566	2	261	0.7004
Q20	7.2016	2	261	0.0009
Q21	2.4221	2	261	0.0907
Q22	0.8182	2	261	0.4423
Q23	0.1967	2	261	0.8216
Q24	0.5052	2	261	0.6040
Q25	1.5537	2	261	0.2134
Q26	4.4355	2	261	0.0128
Q27	2.3290	2	261	0.0994
Q28	0.3851	2	261	0.6807
Q29	0.9049	2	261	0.4058

It is interesting to note that the F values are not significant for any statement except Q08 and Q20. This also proves the perception similarity among various groups of respondents.

Thus the first hypothesis (H1) that the perceptions of students across different years of study on environment friendly living in a value-based education system are not similar has been rejected in the study.

Perception Clustering

The next issue studied was whether a value-based education system creates several significantly large clusters with varying perceptions regarding environment friendly living. Following Barr et. al. (1980) and Clatworthy et. al. (2007) who have used cluster analysis in perception clustering, a hierarchical cluster analysis of between groups linkage was performed. The cluster membership of respondents was obtained for a range of 2 to 10 clusters. The frequencies of cluster memberships are given in Table 10.4.

Table 10.4 : Cluster membership frequencies (N= 264)

Cluster Number	Number of clusters created								
	10 clusters	9 clusters	8 clusters	7 clusters	6 clusters	5 clusters	4 clusters	3 clusters	2 clusters
1	250	251	253	253	254	254	255	260	263
2	3	3	3	3	3	5	5	1	1
3	2	2	2	2	2	1	1	3	
4	1	1	1	1	1	1	3		
5	1	1	1	1	1	3			
6	1	1	1	1	3				
7	1	2	2	3					
8	2	1	1						
9	1	2							
10	2								

As most of the respondents belonged to a single largest cluster (cluster number 1), an inclusion-exclusion cluster membership matrix in relation to this cluster was prepared. This showed whether a respondent was a member of the largest cluster or not. The inclusion-exclusion cluster membership for a sample of 12 respondents is given in Table 10.5.

Table 10.5 : Sample Largest Cluster inclusion-exclusion Matrix

Sample Respondent	10 clusters	9 clusters	8 clusters	7 clusters	6 clusters	5 clusters	4 clusters	3 clusters	2 clusters
1	2	3	4	5	6	7	8	9	10
1	+	+	+	+	+	+	+	+	+
11	-	-	-	-	-	-	-	+	+
20	+	+	+	+	+	+	+	+	+
43	-	-	-	-	-	-	-	-	-
50	-	+	+	+	+	+	+	+	+
54	-	-	-	-	+	+	+	+	+
90	-	-	-	-	-	-	+	+	+
107	-	-	-	-	-	-	-	+	+

(Contd...)

1	2	3	4	5	6	7	8	9	10
134	+	+	+	+	+	+	+	+	+
188	+	+	+	+	+	+	+	+	+
232	-	-	+	+	+	+	+	+	+
255	-	-	+	+	+	+	+	+	+

Note: A '+' mark signifies that the respondent belongs to the largest cluster, while a '-' mark signifies that the respondent belongs to a cluster other than the largest cluster.

The percentage of respondents, who belonged to the largest cluster, is given in Table 10.6.

Table 10.6 : % of respondents with largest cluster membership (N = 264)

Number of clusters	Number of members in largest cluster	%
10	250	94.70
9	251	95.08
8	253	95.83
7	253	95.83
6	254	96.21
5	254	96.21
4	255	96.59
3	260	98.48
2	263	99.62

An analysis of Table 10.6 shows that even when the respondents were divided into 10 clusters, the number of members in the largest cluster was a very high 94.70%. This clearly shows that there were not several significantly large clusters with varying perceptions. Infact there was only one very large cluster with uniform perception and a few other exceptional cases.

Thus the second hypothesis (H2) that a values based education system creates several significantly large clusters with varying perceptions on environment friendly living was rejected in the study. Infact the study shows that a value-based education system has the ability to create a very large cluster with uniform perceptions on environment friendly living.

Value-based Education Impact

The third research issue was to analyse the impact of a value-based education system on environment friendly living. For this purpose two indices were created.

Environment Friendliness Learning Index (EFLI)

This index was created by averaging the scores of selected statements in the questionnaire dealing with the learning aspect of environment friendly living for each respondent. The statements included in this index were:

- In the campus, I have learnt to spend money judiciously.
- In the campus, I have learnt to give respect to food.
- I have learnt in the campus to conserve water and electricity.
- The campus education has taught me to give appropriate importance to money in my life.
- Living in the campus has taught me to manage time judiciously.
- The campus life has taught me to live harmoniously with nature.
- In the campus, I have developed admiration for nature.
- One of the important lessons taught by self reliance activities in the campus is time management.
- The daily schedule at the campus is packed with purposeful activity.
- In the campus, I feel I spend a lot of time on extracurricular activities, and
- I do not learn any lessons from self reliance activities.

Environment Friendliness Practice Index (EFPI)

This index was calculated by averaging the scores of the following statements pertaining to implementation of environment friendly practices from the questionnaire for each respondent:

- I feel it is important to preserve the biodiversity on the campus.
- My day on the campus fills me with energy and enthusiasm.
- I am interested in participating in programmes that conserve the natural beauty of the campus.
- When a tube light or fan in a public place or another room other than mine is on, when no one is there at that place, it is my responsibility to switch it off.
- Chanting prayer of offering food to God, before partaking lunch or dinner reminds me to ensure that I eat all the food without wastage.
- I am constantly reminded of the presence of divinity in the surroundings (nature) in the campus.
- In the campus I tend to spend more money compared to when I am away from the campus.

- I feel it is alright to take extra helpings of tasty items during lunch and dinner sessions even though my stomach is full and I have already tasted enough.
- When I buy snacks in the snacks stall at the campus and do not like its taste, it is alright to throw it away.
- I personally feel it is alright to keep the water tap open while brushing or shaving.
- In the campus there are many options where I can spend money excessively.
- I feel that there are many ways by which we may unconsciously fritter away time in the campus, and
- I feel it is alright to allocate some time everyday just to be relaxed doing nothing.

In the case of calculating both indices, the scores of negatively worded statements were reversed to achieve consistency. The EFLI and EFPI were subjected to regression analysis and Granger causality test.

Regression Analysis

The regression model used for analysis was:

$$EFPI = c + x_1 EFLI + e$$

where c and x_1 are regression coefficients and e is the error term. The results of this analysis are given in Table 10.7.

Table 10.7 : Results of regression analysis

	Unstandardized Coefficients		Standardized Coefficients	t	Sig.
	B	Std. Error	Beta		
c	2.8116	0.1421		19.7835	0.00
EFLI	0.2766	0.0361	0.4269	7.6433	0.00

The t-stat of EFLI as shown in Table 10.7 is significant indicating that EFLI significantly impacts EFPI.

Granger Causality Test

The Granger causality test studies causal relationships. In this case, the test was used to analyse whether the EFLI caused the EFPI. Huh (2008) has employed this test in understanding respondent perception linkages in relation to economic development in Asia-Pacific countries. Similarly Yom Din and Slutsky (2008) have used the test to analyse consumer perceptions in Isreal's apple market. The results of this test are shown in table 10.8.

Table 10.8 : Results of Granger causality test (Number of lags = 2)

Null Hypothesis	F-Statistic	Probability
EFLI does not Granger Cause EFPI	29.7515	0.00
EFPI does not Granger Cause EFLI	0.1699	0.8437

Table 10.8 clearly shows that the hypothesis that EFLI does not cause EFPI has to be rejected. This implies that values based education and learning has a causal impact on environment friendly living practices.

The analysis in this section shows the impact of value-based education on environment friendly living. Based on the analysis the third hypothesis namely a value-based education system has no causal impact on environment friendly living needs to be rejected.

Components of Environment Friendly Living

The final research issue dealt with understanding the components of environment friendly living in a values based education system. For this purpose factor analysis was performed to identify the principal factors or components related to environment friendly living. Tsai et.al. (2003) have used factor analysis to study environment friendly marketing. McDonald (1985) and Morrison (2002) have provided a detailed introduction of factor analysis. In the current study, ten factors were identified having eigen values of more than 1, which cumulatively explained 61 per cent of the variance in the data. The factors were rotated using Varimax rotation method with Kaiser Normalization process, which converged in 12 iterations. The rotated component matrix of the factor loadings is given in table 10.9.

Table 10.9 : Rotated component matrix of factor loadings

Code	Component									
1	2	3	4	5	6	7	8	9	10	11
Q01	0.1866	0.1611	0.0667	0.0374	-0.0232	0.6815	-0.0355	0.0338	-0.0152	0.4302
Q02	0.6737	0.0796	-0.2770	0.1183	0.0011	0.0064	-0.2625	0.0283	-0.0574	-0.0689
Q03	0.7634	0.0013	0.0236	-0.1041	-0.0121	0.0823	0.1136	0.1529	-0.0409	0.0198
Q04	0.6073	0.2017	0.0651	-0.1007	-0.0225	0.1265	0.2623	0.1518	-0.1299	0.1537
Q05	0.1864	-0.0394	-0.1067	0.2210	0.1530	0.5000	0.2878	0.1709	0.0314	-0.2533
Q06	0.3308	0.1992	0.0050	-0.4160	0.3030	0.0402	0.1955	-0.0337	-0.1039	0.2313
Q07	0.2796	0.0489	0.1008	-0.1394	0.1112	0.1963	0.0031	0.5634	0.1540	-0.1497
Q08	0.1547	0.1988	0.0269	-0.2786	0.4223	0.0573	0.0174	0.3506	0.1371	-0.1447
Q09	0.1355	-0.0783	0.0730	-0.0204	0.3404	0.2612	0.0486	0.5510	-0.0526	0.1190

(Contd...)

1	2	3	4	5	6	7	8	9	10	11
Q10	0.6481	0.0484	-0.2525	0.0724	0.3064	0.1552	0.0078	-0.0805	0.1103	-0.1132
Q11	-0.0355	-0.0396	0.7440	0.0308	-0.0973	-0.0271	-0.0866	-0.1462	0.2473	-0.0608
Q12	0.3380	0.2396	0.0780	-0.1134	-0.1067	0.0846	0.4111	0.2357	0.1218	-0.4007
Q13	0.0412	0.0770	0.0975	0.0209	0.0755	-0.0312	0.8030	0.1066	0.0232	0.0808
Q14	0.0236	-0.0975	0.1631	-0.0374	0.1227	0.1189	-0.0936	-0.6995	0.1686	-0.1458
Q15	-0.1314	-0.1402	0.8044	0.0549	-0.0493	-0.0934	0.0570	0.0930	-0.0090	0.0075
Q16	-0.0497	-0.0266	0.2489	0.1462	0.0765	-0.5886	-0.0360	-0.0332	0.0989	0.1148
Q17	0.0836	0.2917	-0.0131	0.1327	0.7660	-0.0501	0.0335	-0.0035	-0.1393	0.1428
Q18	-0.0231	0.0581	0.2718	0.1849	-0.1276	-0.2036	-0.5202	0.0682	0.0914	-0.0606
Q19	0.1267	0.7270	-0.0085	-0.1622	0.1274	0.1470	0.1395	-0.0342	-0.0936	-0.1168
Q20	-0.0044	-0.0318	0.2141	0.3253	-0.6037	-0.0122	-0.1674	-0.0855	0.0591	0.0153
Q21	0.4847	0.1036	0.3135	-0.0793	0.1505	0.4879	0.0726	0.1088	-0.0466	-0.0732
Q22	0.0635	0.2068	0.1224	-0.6778	0.1564	-0.0632	-0.0487	0.0249	0.0263	-0.0483
Q23	0.0352	0.7756	-0.0463	0.0119	0.0348	-0.0907	-0.1401	0.1897	0.0054	0.1646
Q24	0.1411	-0.3576	0.2018	0.3650	-0.2358	-0.1949	0.1185	-0.1871	0.0316	0.1314
Q25	-0.1289	-0.0089	0.1837	0.1608	-0.0713	-0.1234	-0.1004	-0.0148	0.7411	0.0522
Q26	0.0239	-0.0675	0.0297	-0.1628	-0.0481	0.0106	0.0744	-0.0372	0.7881	0.0859
Q27	-0.1542	-0.6340	0.1477	0.1510	-0.1824	-0.0819	-0.1506	0.0750	0.0101	0.1805
Q28	0.0175	0.0093	0.1704	0.7213	0.0861	-0.0771	-0.1259	-0.0427	-0.0291	-0.0306
Q29	-0.0024	-0.0864	-0.0473	-0.0188	0.0646	-0.0192	0.1328	0.1072	0.1717	0.7931

Statements in each factor having positive and negative factor loadings of equal to or greater than 0.50 were identified as the aspects making up that factor component. Each factor was appropriately labelled based on its composition. The factor components of environment friendly living identified are shown in table 10.10:

Table 10.10 : Factor components of environment friendly living

No.	Factor name	% of variance explained	Cumu-lative %	Statements included	Mean Score	Factor Loading
1	2	3	4	5	6	7
1	Living environment	8.92	8.92	Q03	4.01	.76
				Q02	3.61	.67
				Q10	3.93	.64
				Q04	3.93	.60

(Contd...)

1	2	3	4	5	6	7
2.	Self reliance	7.16	16.08	Q23	3.64	.77
				Q19	3.60	.72
				Q27	1.95	-.63
3.	Comparative conservation	6.36	22.44	Q15	2.54	.80
				Q11	2.51	.74
4.	Stress free living	6.14	28.58	Q28	3.29	.72
				Q22	3.13	-.67
5.	Time utilisation	5.88	34.46	Q17	4.04	.76
				Q20	2.29	-.60
6.	Nature adoration	5.60	40.06	Q01	4.07	.68
				Q05	4.43	.50
				Q21	3.82	.50
7.	Proactive public responsibility	5.32	45.38	Q13	4.61	.80
				Q18	1.39	-.52
8.	Spiritual foundations	5.29	50.67	Q09	3.98	.55
				Q07	3.65	.56
				Q14	2.24	-.69
9.	Wasteful tendencies control	5.00	55.67	Q26	3.25	.78
				Q25	3.00	.74
10.	Extracurricular activities	4.73	60.40	Q29	3.47	.79

The important components of environment friendly living in a values based education system as pointed out by the study include:

- Creating an environment that encourages the practice of conserving money, food, time and energy.
- Stressing on self-reliance activities that promote environment friendliness.
- Creating a stress free living environment that helps in cultivating environment friendly behaviour.
- Learning to adore and respect nature that encourages environment friendliness.
- Taking proactive public responsibility to promote environment friendly behaviour and thus not restricting it to private life.
- Sustaining environment friendly behaviour through proper spiritual foundations espoused in the system.

- Controlling wasteful tendencies to advance environment friendly behaviour.

Discussion and Implications of the Study

This chapter has studied perceptions regarding environment friendly living in a value-based education system. The various hypotheses made in the study were rejected based on the statistical tests performed. This chapter has also identified the components of environment friendly behaviour in a value-based educational environment. The major inferences from the study are:

- A value-based education system is effective in inculcating a similarity in perceptions regarding environment friendly living. Similar perceptions can in turn lead to common practices.
- Value-based education helps in creating a homogeneous cluster of students who are like minded in relation to environment friendly living. Thus values based education can help in creating the critical mass which can propel the current environment degrading lifestyles to more environment friendly lifestyles.
- Value based education has a positive causal impact on environment friendly living. Thus the importance of value-based education must be stressed in major environmental and educational fora in order to promote environment friendly living for preventing the looming environmental crisis.
- Learning for environment friendly living must begin early in the education system as several components learnt early can provide a strong foundation for future sustainable practices.

Conclusion

This Chapter has analysed the perceptions regarding environmentally friendly living in a values based educational system. The paper has shown the importance of value-based education in creating the proper learning for environmentally friendly behaviour. Such a system will be eminently useful to save the environment and create a secure future for our planet earth.

Dedication: The authors humbly dedicate this chapter to Bhagawan Sri Sathya Sai Baba, the Revered Chancellor of Sri Sathya Sai University, Prasanthinilayam, India.

REFERENCES

Amarasekera, H. (2007). Seventeen Ideas for Environment friendly Living. Available at: www.environmentlanka.com.

Baba, Bhagawan Sri Sathya Sai. (1979). The New Year Pledge. *Sri Sathya Sai Speaks Vol. 14.* Prasanthinilayam, India: Sri Sathya Sai Books & Publications Trust.

Bach, Lisa Kim. (2008). Private School Pursues Earth-friendly Learning Environment. *Las Vegas Review Journal.* Available at: *www.lvrj.com/news/18037109.html.*

Barr B M, Waters N M, Fairbairn K J. (1980). The Application of Cluster Analysis to Entrepreneurial Perception of Regional Economic Environments. *Environment and Planning A, 12,* 869- 879.

Carrus Giuseppe, Paola Passafaro and Mirilia Bonnes. (2008). Emotions, Habits and Rational Choices in Ecological Behaviours: The Case of Recycling and Use of Public Transportation. *Journal of Environmental Psychology, 28,* 51-62.

Castro Paula, Margarida Garrido, Elizabeth Reis and João Menezes. (2009). Ambivalence and Conservation Behaviour: An Exploratory Study on the Recycling of Metal Cans. *Journal of Environmental Psychology, 29,* 24-33.

Chiffoleau, Y. (2005). Learning About Innovation Through Networks: The Development of Environment Friendly Viticulture. *Technovation, 25,* 1193-1204.

Clatworthy Jane, Matthew Hankins, Deanna Buick, John Weinman and Robert Horne. (2007). Cluster Analysis in Illness Perception Research: A Monte Carlo Study to Identify the Most Appropriate Method. *Psychology and Health, 22,* 123-142.

Corral-Verdugo Víctor, Mirilia Bonnes, César Tapia-Fonllem, Blanca Fraijo-Sing, Martha Frías-Armenta, and Giuseppe Carrus. 2009. Correlates of Pro-sustainability Orientation: The Affinity Towards Diversity. *Journal of Environmental Psychology, 29,* 34-43.

Dauncey, Guy. (2006). How Green is Your Campus? *Earth Island Journal, 21,* 2.

Foster, John Bellamy. (2008).Capitalism's Environmental Crisis—Is Technology the Answer? *Monthly Review, 52,* available at: www.monthlyreview.org/1200jbf.htm.

Fujii Satoshi. (2006). Environmental Concern, Attitude Toward Frugality, and Ease of Behaviour as Determinants of Pro-environmental Behaviour Intentions. *Journal of Environmental Psychology, 26,* 262-268.

Gifford Robert, Leila Scannell, Christine Kormos, Lidia Smolova, Anders Biel, Stefan Boncu, Victor Corral, Hartmut Gu¨ nther, Kazunori Hanyu, Donald Hine, Florian G. Kaiser, Kalevi Korpela, Luisa Marie Lima, Angela G. Mertig, Ricardo Garcia Mira, Gabriel Moser, Paola Passafaro, Jose´ Q. Pinheiro, Sunil Saini, Toshihiko Sako, Elena Sautkina, Yannick Savina, Peter Schmuck, Wesley Schultz, Karin Sobeck, Eva-Lotta Sundblad, and David Uzzell. (2009). Temporal Pessimism and Spatial Optimism in Environmental Assessments: An 18-nation Study. *Journal of Environmental Psychology, 29,* 1-12.

Ham Melinda. (2008). Moral Fibre of Life. *The Sydney Morning Herald,* available at: www.smh.com.au/news/environment/moral-fibre-of-life/2008/02/12/1202760301421.html.

Hansla André, Amelie Gamble, Asgeir Juliusson and Tommy Gärling. (2008). The Relationships Between Awareness of Consequences, Environmental Concern, and Value Orientations. *Journal of Environmental Psychology, 28,* 1-9.

Hawkes Neil. (2007). Value-based education. available at: www.values-education.com.

Huh Tae-hoi. (2008). The Impact of Economic Development upon International Conflicts: A Granger Causality Test for Some Pacific-Asian Countries. *Pacific Focus, 11,* 67-90.

Karpiak Christie P. and Galen L. Baril. (2008). Moral Reasoning and Concern for the Environment. *Journal of Environmental Psychology, 28,* 203-208.

Kortenkamp, Katherine V. and Colleen F. Moore. (2001). Ecocentrism and Anthropocentrism: Moral Reasoning about Ecological Commons Dilemmas. *Journal of Environmental Psychology, 21,* 261-272.

Leanne. (2007). Leading an Eco-friendly Existence. *Money,* 106.

Lee Dongho, Seung Woo Kim, Sin Young Jung, Eun Kyoung Lee, Sang Hyun Seo, Young Kook Kim and Kwang Soo Choi. (2007). An Example of a Practical Approach to ESD: Value Education Through "Clean Plate Movement. Available at: www.unescobkk.org/fileadmin/user_upload/apeid/Conference/12thConference/paper/4B3.pdf.

Mazumdar, Sanjoy. (2005). Religious Place Attachment, Squatting, and 'Qualitative' Research: A Commentary. *Journal of Environmental Psychology, 25,* 87-95.

Mazumdar, Shampa and Sanjoy Mazumdar. (2004). Religion and Place Attachment: A Study of Sacred Places. *Journal of Environmental Psychology, 24,* 385-397.

McDonald R.P. (1985). *The Factor Analysis and Related Methods.* NJ, Lawrence Erlbaum Associates.

Morrison, D.F. (2002). *Multivariate Statistical Methods.* Mass., Duxbury Press.

Möser Guido and Sebastian Bamberg. (2008). The Effectiveness of Soft Transport Policy Measures: A Critical Assessment and Meta-analysis of Empirical Evidence. *Journal of Environmental Psychology, 28,* 10-26.

Myers, Norman. (2003). Earth's Top Environmental Problems. Available at: www.populationpress.org/publication/2003-1-myers.html.

National Geographic Society. (2008). Greendex., Available at: www.nationalgeographic.com/greendex/2008_survey.html.

Nordlund Annika M. and Jörgen Garvill. (2003). Effects of Values, Problem Awareness, and Personal Norm on Willingness to Reduce Personal Car Use. *Journal of Environmental Psychology, 23,* 339-347.

Ojea Elena and Maria L. Loureiro. (2007). Altruistic, Egoistic and Biospheric Values in Willingness to Pay (WTP) for Wildlife. *Ecological Economics, 63,* 807-814.

Ouellette Pierre, Rachel Kaplan and Stephen Kaplan. (2005). The Monastery as a Restorative Environment. *Journal of Environmental Psychology, 25,* 175-188.

Pallant, J. (2005). *SPSS Survival Manual: A Step-by-step Guide to Data Analysis using SPSS for Windows (Versions 12-14),* Crows Nest, NSW, Australia: Allen & Unwin.

Pichert Daniel and Konstantinos V. Katsikopoulos. (2008). Green Defaults: Information Presentation and Pro-environmental Behaviour. *Journal of Environmental Psychology, 28,* 63-73.

Ravikumar, T. and N.Sivakumar. (2008). Learning for Environment Friendly Living—A Case Study. *International Conference on Environmental Ethics Education (ICEEE),* Alumni Association of Education, Banaras Hindu University, Varanasi, India, November 16-17, 2008.

Reser, Joseph P. and Joan M. Bentrupperbäumer. (2005). What and Where are Environmental Values? Assessing the Impacts of Current Diversity of Use of 'Environmental' and 'World Heritage' values. *Journal of Environmental Psychology, 25,* 125-146.

Ruback R. Barry, Janak Pandey and Neena Kohli. (2008). Evaluations of a Sacred Place: Role and Religious Belief at the *Magh Mela., Journal of Environmental Psychology, 28,* 174-184.

Russell, Peter. (1988). Psychological Roots of the Environmental Crisis, available at: www.peterrussell.com/Speaker/Talks/Luxembourg.php.

Sadat Nazneen. (2009). Islam and Eco-friendly Lifestyle. *Radiance Viewsweekly*, available at: www.radianceweekly.com/129/2768/ECOLOGICAL-IMBALANCE/2008-10-19/Cover-Story/Story-Detail/Islam-and-Eco-friendly-Lifestyle.html

Shanbhag Jyothi. (2008). Green Technology—Environment Friendly Schools in US for Effective Learning and Teaching. available at: green.tmcnet.com/topics/green/articles/38365-environmental-friendly-schools-us-effective-learning-teaching.htm.

Shen Junyi and Tatsuyoshi Saijo. (2008). Reexamining the Relations Between Socio-demographic Characteristics and Individual Environmental Concern: Evidence from Shanghai data. *Journal of Environmental Psychology, 28,* 42-50.

Smeeton Nicholas J., Paul Ward and Mark A. Williams. (2004). Do Pattern Recognition Skills Transfer Across Sports? A Preliminary Analysis. *Journal of Sports Sciences, 22,* 205-213.

Snelgar, Rosemary S. (2006). Egoistic, Altruistic, and Biospheric Environmental Concerns: Measurement and Structure. *Journal of Environmental Psychology, 26,* 87-99.

Tabachnick, B. G., and Fidell, L. S. (1983). *Using Multivariate Statistics*. New York: Harper & Row.

Thøgersen John. (2006). Norms for Environmentally Responsible Behaviour: An Extended Taxonomy. *Journal of Environmental Psychology, 26,* 247-261.

Thøgersen, John. (1999). The Ethical Consumer. Moral Norms and Packaging Choice. *Journal of Consumer Policy, 22,* 439-460.

Tsai, P.-J., Nagasawa, S., Hirofumi, W., Haeru, S. and Masayoshi. (2003). A Study on the Marketability of Environment friendly refrigerators in China and Japan—1- Analysis of the present market. *3rd International Symposium on Environmentally Conscious Design and Inverse Manufacturing,* 210-213.

Werner Carol M., Carol Sansone and Barbara B. Brown, (2008).Guided Group Discussion and Attitude Change: The Roles of Normative and Informational Influence. *Journal of Environmental Psychology, 28,* 27-41

wikipedia.org. (2009). Eco-friendly/living. Website Accessed on 12th July, 2009.

Yom Din, Gregory and Slutsky, Alexander. (2008). The Direction of Causality in Israel's Apple Market: From Retail to Wholesale, or the Reverse? available at: http://ssrn.com/abstract=115674

APPENDIX 1

A BRIEF NOTE ON SRI SATHYA SAI UNIVERSITY

The Sri Sathya Sai University (formerly known as Sri Sathya Sai Institute of Higher Learning) was founded on November 22, 1981, by *Bhagavan Sri Sathya Sai Baba.* An autonomous body, it has been recognized by the Ministry of Education, Government of India, and the University Grants Commission (UGC), as a Deemed University. The University has been admitted as a regular member of the Association of Indian Universities.

The University which grew out of the Colleges founded earlier by Bhagavan Sri Sathya Sai Baba at Anantapur (Andhra Pradesh), Brindavan (near Bangalore, Karnataka) and Prasanthi Nilayam (Andhra Pradesh.), India, aims at imparting integral education, development of character being considered the primary objective of education.

In practical terms, the programmes offered by the University seek to combine the best of both our ancient traditions, and modern advancements. While the foundations are the eternal human values, the superstructure relates to today's Society. The University subscribes wholly to the concept and practice of national integration and has adopted an open admission policy, based on merit, encouraging the enrollment of boys and girls from all over the country. In order to effectively mould the student's personality, hostel living has been made compulsory and patterned in the ancient Indian Gurukula style.

The National Assessment and Accreditation Council (NAAC) has granted accreditation at the A++ level to the University for five years, from 2002-03. This places the University in the top bracket of the Indian Universities. The NAAC noted that "the Peer Team feels that this University stands out as a crest-jewel among the University education system worthy of emulation by the institutions of higher learning in the country and elsewhere, so that these benefits would be reaped fast and on the widest possible scale"

Salient Features of the University

The University has several distinctive features. The more important among them are:

- *Free Education:* The University does not charge any type of fees—tuition fees, laboratory fees, library fees, examination fees, caution deposit and the like.
- *An open admission policy* enabling students from all over the country to seek admission to various courses, irrespective of income, class, creed, religion or region, making it truly national in character.

- *Merit based selection* through a very comprehensive testing and interviewing procedure giving adequate weightage to intellectual attainments and intuitive insight.
- *A very favourable teacher-pupil ratio* for closer rapport between students and faculty.
- *Residential character* of the University with students and faculty staying on the Campuses.
- *Development of Scientific Research* at the doctoral level relevant to the local and national needs; introduction of educational technology through the installation of a modern space theatre in rural surroundings providing an opportunity for the students and the faculty to develop various kinds of simulation exercises and also formulate programmes of a creative and constructive character.
- *Integrated courses* of five years duration in order to promote talent.
- *Maximum number of working days* through fuller utilization of national holidays and important festivals for educational purposes and extension work.

The success of the University in upholding these high ideals may be judged from the fact that everything operates with clockwork precision. In particular, there is never any student unrest. Examinations are always held on schedule as announced, and the Annual Convocation of the University invariably takes place on November 22. Sai students are scattered throughout the Globe, and wherever they are, they remain committed to the values they had imbibed while studying.

The Residential Hostel life is an integral part of the University's academic programme. Hostel stay is compulsory for all students admitted to the University's programme. The hostel life revolves basically around 3 D's – *Discipline, Duty and Devotion*. Where these three are concerned much is expected from students. A very high standard of discipline is demanded, which, it should be appreciated, is entirely in the interest of students. Infringement of discipline would be viewed seriously by the Hostel authorities; students must therefore ensure that there is absolutely no lapse on their part on this count.

The Hostel routine has been structured, bearing in mind Bhagavan Baba's directive that all aspects of the Student's personality (i.e., body, mind and soul), should receive due and careful attention. The day begins with early rising and prayer (5 a.m.) and ends with prayer and retirement to bed (10 p.m.). During this period, time slots are reserved for various activities—spiritual, cultural, physical, academic and social. Ample scope is provided for students to give full expression to their latent talents in sports, speaking, singing, painting, dancing, etc. Students are also encouraged to participate in community-oriented activities, both in the Hostel as well as the college. Altogether, Hostel life not only complements and supplements class-room instruction, but is delicately interwoven with the latter so as to achieve a holistic moulding of the student's personality and the development of character as well. Harmonious living and the spirit of co-operation as well as selflessness are particularly encouraged.

The philosophy of education of the University is based on the appreciation of the need to provide full scope for the development of mind and heart. Discipline, duty and adherence to basic human values as the best qualities of students in the University, are deeply appreciated.

Further details about the University are available at the University website www.sssu.edu.in

APPENDIX 2

QUESTIONNAIRE USED IN THE STUDY

For each of the following statements give a score between 1 and 5.

1. I strongly disagree with the statement
2. I disagree with the statement
3. I am neutral i.e. neither agree nor disagree with the statement
4. I agree with the statement
5. I strongly agree with the statement

Code	Statement	Your score
1	2	3
Q01	In the campus, I have developed admiration for nature	
Q02	In the campus, I have learnt to spend money judiciously.	
Q03	In the campus, I have learnt to give respect to food.	
Q04	I have learnt in the campus to conserve water and electricity.	
Q05	I feel it is important to preserve the biodiversity on the campus.	
Q06	The daily schedule at the campus is packed with purposeful activity.	
Q07	Chanting prayer of offering food to God, before partaking lunch or dinner reminds me to ensure that I eat all the food without wastage.	
Q08	My day on the campus fills me with energy and enthusiasm.	
Q09	I am constantly reminded of the presence of divinity in the surroundings (nature) in the campus.	

(Contd...)

1	2	3
Q10	The campus education has taught me to give appropriate importance to money in my life.	
Q11	In the campus I tend to spend more money compared to when I am away from the campus.	
Q12	I am interested in participating in programmes that conserve the natural beauty of the campus.	
Q13	When a tube light or fan in a public place or another room other than mine is on, when no one is there at that place, it is my responsibility to switch it off.	
Q14	When I buy snacks in the snacks stall at the campus and do not like its taste, it is alright to throw it away.	
Q15	I spend more money in the general stores and snacks stall in the campus compared to when I am at home.	
Q16	I feel it is alright to take extra helpings of tasty items during lunch and dinner sessions even though my stomach is full and I have already tasted enough.	
Q17	Living in the campus has taught me to manage time judiciously.	
Q18	I personally feel it is alright to keep the tap open while brushing or shaving.	
Q19	Self reliance activities teach me to utilise my energies purposefully.	
Q20	Life in the campus drains my energy.	
Q21	The campus life has taught me to live harmoniously with nature.	
Q22	I feel very relaxed in the campus even though completely engaged in activity compared to staying at home.	
Q23	One of the important lessons taught by self reliance activities in the campus is time management.	
Q24	Self reliance sessions are very exhausting.	
Q25	In the campus there are many options where I can spend money excessively.	
Q26	I feel that there are many ways by which we may unconsciously fritter away time in the campus.	
Q27	I do not learn any lessons from self reliance activities.	
Q28	I feel it is alright to allocate some time everyday just to be relaxed doing nothing.	
Q29	In the campus, I feel I spend a lot of time on extracurricular activities.	

APPENDIX 3

PROFILE OF THE SAMPLE

Detail	Year of Study			Total
	I Year	II Year	III Year	
Number of respondents	100	92	72	264
% of total	38%	35%	27%	100%
Humanities Stream (%)	51%	55%	52%	53%
Science Stream (%)	49%	45%	48%	47%
Average age (yrs)	19	20	21	19.89

11

Forest Policy and Sustainable Forest Management in India

A Brief Review

— Dr. A. Abdul Raheem

ABSTRACT

Forestry represents the second-largest land use in India after agriculture, covering about 641,130 square kilometers, or 22 per cent of the total land base. This sector contributes a little more than one per cent to Gross Domestic Product (GDP). Forests also provide a wide range of environmental and ecological benefits. About 275 million poor rural inhabitants in India depend on forests for at least part of their subsistence and cash livelihoods, which they earn from fuel wood, fodder, poles, and a wide range of non-timber forest products, such as fruits, flowers, and medicinal plants. Seventy per cent of India's rural population depends on fuel wood to meet domestic energy needs. Half of India's 89 million tribal people, the most disadvantaged section of society, live in forest fringe areas, and a significant percentage of India's 471 million livestock are sustained by forest grazing or fodder collected from forests. The National Forest Policy covers the renewable natural resources of India i.e. Forests, Watersheds, Rangelands, Wildlife, Biodiversity and their habitats. The policy seeks to launch a process for eliminating the fundamental causes of the depletion of renewable natural resources through the active participation of all the concerned agencies and stakeholders, to realize the sustainable development of the resources. It is an umbrella policy providing guidelines to the Federal Government, Provincial Governments and territories for the management of their renewable natural resources. In consonance with it thc Provincial and District Governments may devise their own policies in accordance with their circumstances. In India, the criteria and indicators approach for sustainable forest management is being implemented on a pilot basis since 2000. The initiative, known as the 'Bhopal-India' process, has over the years endeavoured to formulate a working framework for the achievement of the goals of sustainability specific to the national forestry conditions. Forests provide a wide range of ecological, economic and socio-cultural benefits for the communities, enhancing their quality of life. However, the dynamics of forest management in a developing country is unique, as the multiple uses of forests are clearly felt in a multi-stakeholder environment. The application and monitoring of criteria and indicators by the communities together with effective institutionalization and capacity-building can provide us tools to review the progress towards our goals of sustainability. This chapter discusses the Forest policy and sustainable forest management in India.

Introduction

Forestry represents the second-largest land use in India after agriculture, covering about 641,130 square kilometres, or 22 per cent of the total land base. This sector contributes a little more than one percent to Gross Domestic Product (GDP). Forests also provide a wide range of environmental and ecological benefits. About 275 million poor rural inhabitants in India depend on forests for at least part of their subsistence and cash livelihoods, which they earn from fuel wood, fodder, poles, and a range of non-timber forest products, such as fruits, flowers, and medicinal plants. Seventy per cent of India's rural population depends on fuel wood to meet domestic energy needs. Half of India's 89 million tribal people, the most disadvantaged section of society, live in forest fringe areas, and a significant percentage of India's 471 million livestock are sustained by forest grazing or fodder collected from forests. Recent years have seen a number of changes in the management of forests. There is a major shift towards a more decentralized and people oriented forestry. Responding to scarcities, villagers have started organizing themselves to reverse degradation and restore productivity. The result has been a renewal of degraded ecosystems. The destruction of natural forests for timber, cropland, fuel wood, pasture, urbanization have had an impact on many poor rural families who are dependent on forest resources for fuel, fodder, food, medicine, housing, etc. The deterioration of forests has accelerated soil erosion, sedimentation of rivers, increased flooding, and overtaxed the land's capacity to regenerate and sustain. It is now being recognized that local communities need to be involved in establishing sustainable forest management systems. Governments are opening a number of opportunities for sustainable forest management and biodiversity conservation by decentralizing authority and responsibility for resource management in different parts of the world. In the Asia-Pacific, attention is being made on community-based forest management programmes. In

Philippines local government units are authorized in the devolution of management responsibilities on some forestry activities. China undergoes land and forest allocation programs. Laos, Vietnam and Nepal rejuvenate transfer of use rights to forest user groups. India practices Joint Forest Management programmes. And New Zealand priorities privatization of forest plantations, similar processes are underway in other parts of the world. The various initiatives have led to greater access and control of forest resources by local people, in turn resulting in improvement in forest protection and management and reducing pressure on resources. Substantial areas of degraded forests have been rehabilitated and new forests are planted. Local people have started supporting forest conservation hereby; they have been able to reap financial returns through benefit-sharing schemes. This chapter emphasizes the Forest policy and sustainable forest management in India.

Present Status of Forest Resources

Forests provide a wide range of goods and various ecological services to us. They are a rich source of biodiversity. A large number of poor people living in and around the forest areas depend heavily on these forests for their livelihood. We need to maintain a good forest cover both in terms of size and quality, and use it in a sustainable manner. Table 11.1, indicates that India has a recorded forest area of 76.52 million hectares that is 23.28 per cent of its total geographical area. The ownership of this forest area rests largely with the Government. It is estimated that 92.47 per cent of the recorded forest area is owned by the Forest Departments, 3.18 per cent by other Government Departments, 2.45 per cent by corporate bodies, and 1.91 per cent by others. The total forest area has been classified into three categories, namely, Reserved Forests (54.44 per cent), Protected Forests (29.18 per cent), and Unclassed Forests (16.38 per cent). There are 87 National Parks and 485 Wildlife Sanctuaries created for *in situ* conservation of biodiversity. These National Parks and Wildlife Sanctuaries covering 4.75 per cent (15.60 m ha) of the total geographical area are referred together as Protected Areas. The network of Protected Areas also include 23 Tiger Reserves spread over 3.30 million hectares overlapping with National Parks and Wildlife Sanctuaries. There are 11 Biosphere Reserves with an area of 4.76 million hectares part of which goes even beyond Protected Areas.

The post independence experience has shown that both extent and quality of forest cover have deteriorated in India. It has been estimated that the actual forest cover of the country is only 19.39 per cent of its total geographical area as against the recorded forest area as 23.28 per cent of the total geographical area. In terms of the quality of the forest cover, only 59 per cent of the actual forest cover of the country is in the form of dense forests.

Table 11.1 : State-wise Geographic Area, Recorded Forest Area and Actual Forest Cover in India

Sl.No.	State/UT	Recorded Forest			Forest cover	
		Geographical area (Sq. Km.)	Area (Sq.Km.)	Per cent	Area (Sq. Km.)	Per cent
1.	Andhra Pradesh	275068	63814	23.2	43290	15.7
2.	Arnachal Pradesh	83743	51540	61.54	68602	81.9
3.	Assam	78438	30708	39.15	23824	30.4
4.	Bihar	173877	29226	16.81	26524	15.3
5.	Delhi	1483	42	2.83	26	1.7
6.	Goa	3702	1424	38.46	1252	33.8
7.	Gujarat	196024	19393	9.89	12578	6.4
8.	Haryana	44212	1673	3.78	604	1.4
9.	Himachal Pradesh	55673	35407	63.6	12521	22.5
10.	Jammu & Kashmir	222235	20182	9.08	20440	9.2
11.	Karnataka	191791	38724	20.19	32403	16.9
12.	Kerala	38863	11221	28.87	10334	26.6
13.	Madhya Pradesh	443446	154497	34.84	131195	29.6
14.	Maharashtra	307690	63842	20.75	46143	15.0
15.	Manipur	22327	15154	67.87	17418	78.0
16.	Meghalaya	22429	9496	42.34	15657	69.8
17.	Mizoram	21081	15935	75.59	18775	89.1
18.	Nagaland	16579	8629	52.04	14221	85.8
19.	Orissa	155707	57184	36.73	46941	30.1
20.	Punjab	50362	2901	5.76	1387	2.8
21.	Rajasthan	342239	31700	9.26	13353	3.9

Source: GOH.

The rest of the forest cover consists of open forests and mangroves. Over the years, a large area of forest land has been formally converted to non-forest use. The size of such converted land is reported as 5760.90 sq km up to 31st October, 2002 (see Table 11.2). Further, a total of 13569.44 sq km forest land is reported as encroached.

Table 11.2 : State-wise Forest Land Diverted for Non-Forestry Purposes in India

S.No.	States/UTs	No. of proposals approved	Forest land diverted (ha)
1.	Andhra Pradesh	184	22626
2.	Arunachal Pradesh	64	2491
3.	Assam	119	1653
4.	Bihar	102	5979
5.	Chhatisgarh	176	15929
6.	Goa	50	389
7.	Gujarat	583	52657
8.	Haryana	312	1582
9.	Himachal Pradesh	356	4905
10.	Jammu & Kashmir	8	1286
11.	Karnataka	296	32408
12.	Kerala	134	30993
13.	Madhya Pradesh	518	228019
14.	Maharashtra	1185	75650
15.	Manipur	9	247
16.	Meghalaya	61	356
17.	Mizoram	42	8528
18.	Orissa	265	27055
19.	Punjab	437	2532
20.	Rajasthan	268	12707
21.	Sikkim	48	623
22.	Tamil Nadu	225	4138
23.	Tripura	91	2315
24.	Uttar Pradesh	180	6484
25.	Uttaranchal	2087	22930
26.	West Bengal	77	9217
27.	Andaman & Nicobar Islands	51	2223
28.	Dadra & Nagar Haveli	87	168
	India	**8015**	**576090**

Source: http://www.Indiastat.com

Forests and Economic Development

India is a large developing country known for its diverse forest ecosystems and is also a mega-biodiversity country. Forest ecosystems in India are critical for biodiversity, watershed protection, and livelihoods of indigenous and rural communities. The National Communication of the Government of India to the UNFCCC has reported that the forest sector is a marginal source of CO_2 emissions. India has formulated and implemented a number of policies and programmes aimed at forest and biodiversity conservation, afforestation and reforestation. Further, India has a goal to bring one-third of the geographic area under forest and tree cover by 2012. Forests are renewable resources and have contributed substantially to the economic development of the country by providing goods and services to the mankind. It also plays a vital role in enhancing the quality of environments and biodiversity. At present 26.6 per cent of the geographical area of the world is covered by forests and per capita forest cover in the world is about 0.64 ha. Of the continents, forests cover in Africa, Asia and Europe are respectively 17.7, 6.4 and 41.3 per cent. In comparison to Asia, the forest cover in India is about 15.7 per cent to her geographical area and per capita forest cover is only 0.06 ha. Both are very low compared to its neighbouring countries. Forest cover in the neighbouring countries like Nepal, China, Sri Lanka etc., are more than that of India. Many developing countries have also per capita forest cover more than India. Forest cover in Indian States and Union Territories is not uniform due to various physical, climates, edaphic and economical factors. The North Eastern-States of India have much higher forest cover than other states and stipulated forest cover set by National Forest Commission of India. The forest cover of India is 63.73 M ha contributing 19.30 per cent of the total geographical area. Out of which 37.74 M ha (92.11%) is dense forests, 25.50 M ha (7.76%) are open forests and 0.49 M ha (0.15%) mangrove forest. In North Eastern States, 58.17 per cent of the total forest cover is dense forest and rest (41.83%) is open forests. There is a substantial decrease in area of open forests in most of the states of this region. Total decrease was about 8630 ha during 1991-99, in these states, whereas, there is a significant increase in forest cover in case of dense forests. Total increase is 6652 ha, which is about 7.5 per cent during the same period. Majority of states show increase in dense forest cover due to efficient forest management. It is revealed that percentage share of forest cover of this region to the total of India has almost remained same during the period. There is a substantial decrease (from 65.2 to 64.2 per cent) in percentages of forest cover in the region. Nearly 2456 sq km of forest area has been decreased in the region during the period. The percentage of forests in each state except Tripura and Sikkim is more than 67 per cent of its total geographical area. Highest percentage of forest is found in Mizoram and that of the lowest is found in Sikkim. Per capita forest cover in Arunachal Pradesh is 0.06 ha which is equal to that of India. Other states of the region have much less per capita forest cover than India as a whole. Arunachal Pradesh is the second largest forest covered state after erstwhile Madhya Pradesh. In 1972-75, total area of forest in the region was 1,30,317 sq. km. In 1980-82 the forest cover was about 1,29,134 sq. km. The forest cover in 1999 was 1,63,317 sq km. It can be realized that during that period the area under forests has decreased continuously except during the period 1989-91. Decline of forest cover in the region is due to various factors like intensive agriculture, shifting cultivation, encroachment of forests land for various developmental activities, illegal felling, increasing rearing of livestock and human interference. Total loss of the forest area in the region is about 1.73 M ha due to shifting cultivation, which is the main factor for rapid decline of forest area. During 1981-87 it was 0.06 M ha and during 1987-99 it was about 1.73 M ha. The maximum loss of forest cover is due to shifting cultivation in Nagaland (0.39 M ha), Mizoram (0.38 M ha) and Manipur (0.36 M ha.). Shifting cultivation is still practiced in these states by the tribal people. Loss of forest cover in Tripura and Sikkim is less because shifting cultivation is less common in these states. Livestock population and density of population per sq km is also high in the North East. There are twelve National Parks comprising 4443.24 ha in the North East India. It shares about 32% of total protected forest area of the region. There are 38 wild life sanctuaries comprising 9540.21 ha in the region. Out of the total protected area, these wild life sanctuaries share 68% of the total. There are 426 Joint Forest Protected and Regulation Committees comprising 31 thousand hectares of the total. Tree plantation in the region has been created under economic plantation of industrial areas, social forestry and soil conservation schemes. Soil conservation scheme is also known as protection of catchments area. J.F.M. is to cover the degraded areas. The net profit shall be shared among the Government beneficiaries and the Village Forest development funds in the proportion of 50%, 30% and 20%. Plantation of different trees in the degraded forest areas has been increasing in different states of the region. Area under plantation is very high in Assam, Mizoram, Sikkim and Tripura under different forest development schemes. Variations in different periods in states are due to social and economical factors. Forest plantation is mostly done in areas affected by shifting cultivation. The common practice of creating plantation is to identify a macro project area of minimum 30 ha. Important schemes of afforestation are tree cultivation and J.F.M., area oriented fuel and fodder project. Important species are planted in the degraded and deforested areas. For efficient management, the area under forest degradation and deforestation has been decreased in the states of North

East India recently. Remote sensing is a vital tool for forest management and development in the area. Its use is increasing year by year for such purpose.

Role of Forest Resources in National Economy

Income from forest resources is aggregated under the head of 'Forestry and Logging' under income from agriculture. Forestry & Logging includes income from the following sources (GOI 1989).

(*a*) Industrial wood—timber, round wood, match and pulpwood:. Recorded and Unrecorded

(*b*) Farmyard wood (outside regular forests): Firewood, Recorded and Unrecorded

(*c*) Minor Forest Products—bamboo, fodder, lac, sandalwood, honey, resin, gum, tendu leaves, etc.

There are large variations in unrecorded production/collection of different products reported by different sources based on different assumptions. For example, the unrecorded production of firewood has been assumed in certain years as ten times of the recorded one. In case of industrial wood, the unrecorded production has been assumed as 10 per cent of the recorded one in certain years. Gross Domestic Product (GDP) and Net Domestic Product (NDP) from Forestry and Logging are calculated as follows.

GDP = Value of output – Repairs, maintenance and other operational costs

NDP = GDP – Consumption of fixed capital

The depreciation in natural capital is, however, not taken into account while calculating NDP. As shown in Table 11.3, the share of income from Forestry and Logging has been declining over the years.

Table 11.3: Percentage Share of Income from 'Forestry & Logging' in GDP

Sl.No.	Year	Percentage of GDP	
		At Current Prices	At Constant Prices (1993-94 Prices)
1.	1970-71	2.08	4.42
2.	1980-81	2.63	2.97
3.	1990-91	1.77	1.70
4.	1999-00	1.11	1.09

Source: CMIE (2001).

Evolution of Forest Policies and Acts

The history of formulation of forest policy in India in recent past may be traced back to the creation of the Imperial Forest Department in 1864 under the colonial rule. The main objective for setting up this department was to ensure sustained availability of large number of sleepers required for railways. The establishment of this department marked a beginning of the shift in the management of forests in India from communities to the State.

Forest Act, 1865: The first Forest Act was enacted in 1865 mainly to facilitate the acquisition of forest areas that could supply timber to the railways without abridging the existing rights of the people. The forest in this Act was defined as "land covered with trees, brushwood and jungle".

Forest Act, 1878: The next Forest Act was enacted in 1878 after realising that many of the provisions made in the previous Act were not adequate for an effective control by the State. The definition of the forest itself inhibited rising of plantations by the State on barren lands. The Forest Act of 1878, therefore, reversed almost all provisions of the Forest Act of 1865 except the provision of 'arrest without warrant'. Some of the important provisions of the new Act were as follows:

(*a*) any land whatsoever could be designated as forest;

(*b*) treatment of customary rights of Indian villager as based on privilege and not on right;

(*c*) a bar to accrual of any further rights of people on Reserved Forests;

(*d*) conversion of Protected Forests into Reserved Forests as and when required;

(*e*) Constitution of a third category of forests as Village Forests. This Act provided a great deal of flexibility to the forest settlement officers that resulted in large variations between different regions in terms of rights of forest dwellers.

Forest Policy, 1894: A resolution on forest policy was made for the first time in 1894. The salient features of the policy were as follows (GOI 1976):

(*a*) The sole object with which State forests are administered is public benefit. In general, the constitution and preservation of a forest involve the regulation of rights and the restriction of privileges of the user in the forest by the neighboring population;

(*b*) Forests situated on hill slopes should be maintained as protection forests to preserve the climatic and physical conditions of the country and to protect the cultivated plains that lie below them from the devastating action of hill torrents;

(*c*) Forests which are the reservoirs of valuable timbers should be managed on commercial lines as a source of revenue to the States;

(*d*) Wherever an effective demand for culturable land exists and can only be supplied from forest area, the land should ordinarily be relinquished without hesitation, subject to the following conditions:

- Honeycombing of a valuable forest by patches of cultivation should not be allowed;
- Cultivation must be permanent and must not be allowed to an extent as to encroach upon minimum area of forest that is needed to meet the reasonable forest requirements, present and prospective;

(*e*) Forest that yield only inferior timber, fuel wood or fodder, or are used for grazing, should be managed mainly in the interest of local population, care being taken to see that the user is not exercised so as to annihilate its subject and the people are protected against their own improvidence.

Forest Act, 1927: The Indian Forest Act 1927 largely involved redrafting of some clauses of the Forest Act 1878. One major change is stated to be its reference to individuals and not individuals or communities while referring to rights on forests.

National Forest Policy

National Forest Policy, 1952: A resolution on the first post-independence Forest Policy was issued in 1952. While this policy retained the basic thrust of the earlier policy, it emphasized a balance across economic, ecological and social benefits from the forests. It thus proposed to classify the forests on a functional basis into: (*i*) protection forests; (*ii*) national forests; (*iii*) village forests; and (*iv*) tree lands. While the functions of protection forests and village forests were the same as laid down in the earlier policy, the national forests were meant for meeting the requirements of defence, communications and industry with a progressively increasing sustainable yield, and the tree lands were proposed for improving physical and climatic conditions and for promoting general well being of people. The provision of centralised management was continued even in this policy.

National Forest Policy, 1988: It was only about 25 years later that the Forest Policy 1988 underscored community participation in protection and development of forests. The objectives of the Forest Policy 1988 have been stated as follows: (*i*) maintenance of environmental stability through preservation and restoration of ecological balance; (*ii*) conservation of natural heritage; (*iii*) check on soil erosion and denudation in catchment areas of rivers, lakes and reservoirs; (*iv*) check on extension of sand dunes in desert areas of Rajasthan and along coastal tracts; (*v*) sustainable increase in forest tree cover through massive afforestation and social forestry programmes; (*vi*) steps to meet requirement of fuel wood, fodder, minor forest produce and timber of rural and tribal populations; (*vii*) increase in productivity of forest to meet the national needs; (*viii*) encouragement to efficient utilisation of forest produce and optimum substitution of wood; and (*ix*) steps to create massive people's movement with involvement of women to achieve the objectives and minimise pressure on existing forest.

Basic Objective of National Forest Policy

The basic objectives that should govern the National Forest Policy are the following:

(*a*) Maintenance of environmental stability through preservation and, where necessary, restoration of the ecological balance that has been adversely disturbed by serious depletion of the forests of the country.

(*b*) Conserving the natural heritage of the country by preserving the remaining natural forests with the vast variety of flora and fauna, which represent the remarkable biological diversity and genetic resources of the country.

(*c*) Checking soil erosion and denudation in the catchment areas of rivers, lakes, reservoirs in the "interest of soil and water conservation, for mitigating floods and droughts and for the retardation of siltation of reservoirs.

(*d*) Checking the extension of sand dunes in the desert areas of Rajasthan and along the coastal tracts.

(*e*) Increasing substantially the forest/tree cover in the country through massive afforestation and social forestry programmes, especially on all denuded, degraded and unproductive lands.

(*f*) Meeting the requirements of fuel-wood, fodder, minor forest produce and small timber of the rural and tribal populations.

(*g*) Increasing the productivity of forests to meet essential national needs.

(*h*) Encouraging efficient utilisation of forest pro-duce and maximising substitution of wood.

(*i*) Creating a massive people's movement with the involvement of women, for achieving these objectives and to minimise pressure on existing forests.

The principal aim of Forest Policy must be to ensure environmental stability and maintenance of ecological balance including atmospheric equilibrium which are vital for sustenance of all life forms, human, animal and plant. The derivation of direct economic benefit must be subordinated to this principal aim.

Strategy of Forest Management

Existing forests and forest lands should be fully protected. Forest and vegetal cover should be increased rapidly on hill slopes, in catchment areas of rivers, lakes and reservoirs and ocean shores and, on semi arid, and desert tracts. Diversion of good and productive agricultural lands to forestry should be discouraged in view of the need for increased food production. For the conservation of total biological diversity, the network of national parks, sanctuaries, biosphere reserves and other protected areas should be strengthened and extended adequately. Provision of sufficient fodder, fuel and pasture, especially in areas adjoining forest, is necessary in order to prevent depletion of forests beyond the sustainable limit. Since fuel wood continues to be the predominant source of energy in rural areas, the programme of afforestation should be intensified with special emphasis on augmenting fuel wood production to meet the requirement of the rural people. Minor forest produce provides sustenance to tribal population and to other communities residing in and around the forests. Such produce should be protected and nourished with due regard to generation of employment and income.

Area under Forests: The national goal should be to have a minimum of one third of the total land area of the country under forest or tree cover. The aim should be to maintain two third of the area under such cover in order to prevent erosion and land degradation and to ensure the stability of the fragile eco system.

Afforestation, Social Forestry and Farm Forestry: A massive need based and time bound programme of afforestation and tree planting, with particular emphasis on fuel wood and fodder development, on all degraded and denuded lands in the country, whether forest or non forest land, is a national imperative. It is necessary to encourage the planting of trees along side of roads, railway lines, rivers and streams and canals, an d on other unutilised lands under State/corporate, institutional or private ownership. Green belts should be raised in urban/industrial areas as well as in arid tracts. Such a programme will help to check erosion and desertification as well as improve the microclimate. Village and community lands, including those on foreshores and environs of tanks, not required for other productive uses, should be taken up for the development of tree crops and fodder resources. Technical assistance and other inputs necessary for initiating such programmes should be provided by the Government. The revenues generated through such programmes should belong to the panchayats where the lands are vested in them; in all other cases, such revenues should be shared with the local communities in order to provide an incentive to them. The vesting, in individuals, particularly from the weaker sections (such as landless labour, small and marginal farmers, scheduled castes, tribal's, and women) of certain ownership rights over trees, could be considered, subject to appropriate regulations; beneficiaries would be entitled to usufruct and would in turn be responsible for their security and maintenance. Land laws should be so modified, wherever necessary so as to facilitate and motivate individuals and institutions to undertake tree farming and grow fodder plants, grasses and legumes on their own land. Degraded lands should be made available for this purpose either on lease or on the basis of a tree patta scheme. Such leasing of the land should be subject to the land grant rules and land ceiling laws. Steps necessary to encourage them to do so must be taken. Appropriate regulations should govern the felling of trees on private holding.

Management of State Forests: Schemes and projects which interfere with forests that clothe steep slopes, catchments of rivers, lakes, and reservoirs, geologically unstable terrain and such other ecologically sensitive areas should be severely restricted. Tropical rain/moist forests, particularly in areas like Arunachal Pradesh, Kerala, Andaman & Nicobar Islands, should be totally safeguarded. No forest should be permitted to be worked without the Government having approved the management plan, which should be in a prescribed format and in keeping with the National Forest Policy. The Central Government should issue necessary guidelines to the State Governments in this regard and monitor compliance. In order to meet the growing needs for essential goods and services which the forests provide, it is necessary to enhance forest cover and productivity of the forests through the application of scientific and technical inputs. Production forestry programmes, while aiming at enhancing the forest cover in the country, and meeting national needs, should also be oriented to narrowing, by the turn of the century, the increasing gap between demand and supply of fuel wood. No such programme, however, should entail clear felling of adequately stocked natural forests. Nor should exotic species be introduced, through public or private sources, unless long-term scientific trials undertaken by specialists in ecology, forestry and agriculture have established that they are suitable and have no adverse impact on native vegetation and environment.

Rights and Concessions**:** The rights and concessions, including grazing, should always remain related to the carrying capacity of forests. The capacity itself should be optimised by increased investment, silvicultural research and development of the area. Stall feeding of cattle should be encouraged'. The requirements of the community, which cannot be met by the rights and concessions so determined, should be met by development of social forestry outside the reserved forests. The holders of customary rights and concessions in forest areas should be motivated to identify themselves with the protection and development of forests from which they derive benefits. The rights and concessions from forests should primarily be for the bonafide use of the communities living within and around forest areas, specially the tribal's. The life of tribal's and other poor living within and near forests revolves around forests. The rights and concessions enjoyed by them should be fully protected. Their domestic requirements of fuel wood, fodder, minor forest produce and construction timber should be the first charge on forest produce. These and substitute materials should be made available through conveniently located depots at reasonable prices. Similar consideration should be given to scheduled castes and other poor living near forests. However, the area, which such consideration should cover, would be determined by the carrying capacity of the forests. The long-term solution for meeting the existing gap lies in increasing the productivity of forests, but to relieve the existing pressure on forests for the demands of railway sleepers, construction industry (particularly in the public sector), furniture and paneling, mine pit props, paper and paper board etc. substitution of wood needs to be taken recourse to. Similarly, on the front of domestic energy, fuel wood needs to be substituted as far as practicable with alternate sources like bio gas, LPG and solar energy, fuel-efficient 'Chulhas' as a measure of conservation of fuel wood need to be popularised in rural areas.

Diversion of Forest Lands for Non forest purposes: Forest land or land with tree cover should not be treated merely as a resource readily available to be utilised for various projects and programmes, but as a national asset which requires to be properly safeguarded for providing sustained benefits to the entire community. Diversion of forest land for any non forest purpose should be subject to the most careful examinations by specialists from the standpoint of social and environmental costs and benefits. Construction of dams and reservoirs, mining and industrial development and expansion of agriculture should be consistent with the needs for conservation of trees and forests. Beneficiaries who are allowed mining and quarrying in forest land and in land covered by trees should' be required to repair and revegetate the area in accordance with established forestry practices. No mining lease should be granted to any party, private or public, without a proper mine management plan appraised from the environmental angle and enforced by adequate machinery.

Wildlife Conservation: Forest Management should take special care of the needs of wildlife conservation, and forest management plans should include prescriptions for this purpose. It is essential to provide for "corridors" linking the protected areas in order to maintain genetic continuity between artificially separated sub sections of migrant wildlife.

Tribal People and Forests: Having regard to the symbiotic relationship between the tribal people and forests, a primary task of all agencies responsible for forest management, including the forest development corporations should be to associate the tribal people closely in the protection, regeneration and development of forests as well as to provide gainful employment to people living in and around the forest. While safeguarding the customary rights and interests of such people, forestry programmes should pay special attention to the following:

- One of the major causes for degradation of forest is illegal cutting and removal by contractors and their labour. In order to put, an end to this practice, contractors should be replaced by institutions such as tribal cooperatives, labour cooperatives, government corporations, etc. as early as possible;
- Protection, regeneration and optimum collection of minor forest produce along with institutional arrangements for the marketing of such produce;
- Development of forest villages on par with revenue villages;
- Family oriented schemes for improving the status of the tribal beneficiaries; and

Shifting Cultivation: Shifting cultivation is affecting the environment .and productivity of land adversely, alternative avenues of income, suitably harmonised with the right land use practices, should be devised to discourage shifting cultivation. Efforts should be made to contain such cultivation within the area already affected, by propagating improved agricultural practices. Area already damaged by such cultivation should be rehabilitated through social forestry and energy plantations.

Damage to Forests from Encroachments, Fires and Grazing: Encroachment on forest lands has been on the increase. This trend has to be arrested and effective action taken to prevent its continuance. There, should be no regularisation of existing encroachments. The incidence of forest fires in the country is high. Standing trees and fodder are destroyed on a large scale and natural regeneration annihilated by such fires. Special precautions should be taken during the fire season. Improved and modern management practices should be adopted to deal with forest fires. Grazing in forest areas should be regulated with the involvement of the community Special conservation areas, young plantations and regeneration areas should be fully protected. Grazing and browsing in forest areas need to be controlled. Adequate grazing fees should be levied to discourage people in forest areas from maintaining large herds of non essential livestock.

Forest-based Industries: The main considerations governing the establishment of forest based industries and supply of raw material to them should be as follows:

(*a*) As far as possible, a forest-based industry should raise the raw material needed for meeting its own requirements, preferably by establishment of a direct relationship between the factory and the individuals who can grow the raw material by supporting the individuals with inputs including credit, constant technical advice and finally harvesting and transport services.

(*b*) No forest based enterprise, except that at the village or cottage level, should be permitted in the future unless it has been first cleared after a careful scrutiny with regard to assured availability of raw material. In any case, the fuel, fodder and timber requirements of the local population should not be sacrificed for this purpose.

(*c*) Forest-based industries must not only provide employment to local people on priority but also involve them fully in raising trees and raw-material.

(*d*) Natural forests serve as a gene pool resource and help to maintain ecological balance. Such forests will not, therefore, be made available to industries for ' undertaking plantation and for any other activities.

(*e*) Farmers, particularly small and marginal farmers, would be encouraged to grow, on marginal/degraded lands available with them, wood species required for industries. These may also be grown along with fuel and fodder species on community lands not required for pasture purposes, and by Forest department/ corporations on degraded forests, not earmarked for natural regeneration.

(*f*) The practice of supply of forest products to industry at concessional, prices should cease. Industry should be encouraged to use alternative raw materials. Import of wood and wood products should be liberalised.

(*g*) The above considerations will, however, be subject to the current policy relating to land ceiling and land laws.

Forest Extension: Forest conservation programme cannot succeed without the support and cooperation of the people. It is essential, therefore, to inculcate in the people, a direct interest in forests, their development and conservation, and to make them conscious of the value of trees, wildlife and nature in general. This can be achieved through the involvement of educational institutions, right from the primary stage. Farmers and interested people should be provided opportunities through institutions like Krishi Vigyan Kendras, Trainers' Training Centres to learn agri silvicultural and silvicultural techniques to ensure optimum use of their land and water resources.

Forestry Education: Forestry should be recogr1ised both as a scientific discipline as well as a profession. Agriculture universities and institutions, dedicated to the development of forestry education should formulate curricula and courses for imparting academic education and promoting postgraduate research and professional excellence, keeping in view the manpower needs of the country. Academic and professional qualifications in forestry should be kept in view for recruitment to the Indian Forest Service and the State Forest Service.

Forestry Research: Priority areas of research and development needing special attention are:

- Increasing the productivity of wood and other forest produce per unit of area per unit time by the application of modern scientific and technological methods.
- Re-vegetation of barren/marginal/waste/mined lands and watershed areas.
- Effective conservation and management of existing forest resources (mainly natural forest eco systems).
- Research related to social forestry for rural/ tribal development.
- Development of substitutes to replace wood and wood products.
- Research related to wildlife and management of national parks and sanctuaries.

Personnel Management: Government policies in personnel management for professional foresters and forest scientists should aim at enhancing their professional competence and status and attracting and retaining qualified and motivated personnel, keeping in view particularly the Arduous nature of duties they have to perform, often in remote and inhospitable places.

Forest Survey and Data Base: Inadequacy of data regarding forest resources is a matter of concern because this creates a false sense of complacency. Priority needs to be accorded to complete the survey of forest resources in the country on scientific lines and to updating information. For this purpose, periodical collection, collation and publication of reliable data on relevant aspects of forest management needs to be improved with recourse to modern technology and equipment.

Legal Support and Infrastructure Development: Appropriate legislation should be undertaken, supported by adequate infrastructure, at the Centre and State levels in order to implement the Policy effectively.

Financial Support for Forestry: The objectives of this revised Policy cannot be achieved without the investment of financial and other resources on a substantial scale. Such investment is indeed fully justified considering the contribution of forests in maintaining essential ecological processes and life support systems and in preserving genetic diversity. Forests should not be looked upon as a source of revenue. Forests are a renewable natural resource.

Sustainable Forest Management

Sustainable forest management encompasses all the three components of sustainability, viz. ecological, economic and socio-cultural well-being. It has been defined by the International Tropical Timber Organization (ITTO) as 'the process of managing permanent forest land to achieve one or more clearly specified objectives of forest management with regard to the production of a continuous flow of desirable forest products and services without undue reduction of its inherent values and future productivity and without undue undesirable effects on the physical and social environment'. Rather, it is always set in the context of decisions about what type of system is to be sustained and over what spatio-temporal scale. Given the abstract nature of sustainability, the criteria and indicators approach provides a framework to define the parameters and goals of socio-cultural, economic and ecological aspects relating to sustainability and assess progress towards them.

Forest Management in India

The forestry sector in India is among the first in the world to be managed on the lines of modern scientific management. Establishment of forest management from the middle of the eighteenth century incidentally coincided with the industrial revolution in the West. The forests emerged as important resources during the pre-independence period, as the demand for raw materials increased, and a need was felt to expand the railway network. Forestry was thus production-oriented at that time. However, the basic change in perception was brought by the National Forest Policy of 1952, from production forestry to focus on meeting objectives of maintaining ecological balance on the one hand and meeting the needs of stakeholders in the best possible way on the other. The 1988 National Forest Policy focussed on the maintenance of environmental stability, conservation of natural heritage by preserving the natural forests and meeting the basic needs of people, and also maintaining the relationship between the tribal and other dependent people, thus encompassing ecological, economic and social aspects of forest management. There is however an urgent needs to monitor and ensure proper implementation of these policy implications. The quantifiable approach like criteria and indicators to monitor and implement these objectives of sustainability is imperative.

Sustainable Forest Management

The pressure on existing forest resources is immense in India. Having only 2.5% of the world's geographic area and 1.85% of the world's forest area, we have 17% of the world's population and 18% of livestock population. In this context, it is imperative to preserve the forests and manage them sustainably, so as to ensure secure livelihood of the forest-dependent communities as well as conserving our biological diversity.

Approach for Sustainable Forest Management

In the forestry sector, there is a paradigm shift from a focus on sustained timber yield to sustainable forest management, encompassing in it environmental, economic and social dimensions. The principle of sustained yield is considered as the focus of forest management ever since the forests were managed on modern scientific basis. It is an accepted norm in forest management and forms the core of modern, organized forestry. Scientific knowledge is needed all over the world to effectively address these issues globally and regionally, and to provide the technical basis for policy decisions. There have been many international initiatives with potential application to define and assess sustainable forest management, such as criteria and indicators, life cycle assessment, cost–benefit analysis, knowledge-based systems and environmental impact assessment. The criteria and indicator method has been widely accepted and immense work has been done towards its refinement and practical application. Over the years, it has developed as a potent tool for assessment, monitoring and reporting of sustainability of forest resources. Currently, about 160 countries are participating in nine regional and international processes of sustainable forest management following the criteria and indicator approach, mostly within the framework of an international initiative, which are specific to various forestry conditions.

The criteria and indicators approach presents a tool for assessing the magnitude and direction of change in given forestry situations, and this provides critical information to the forest managers and other actors for forest-related decision-making. It is an important framework to assist countries collect, store and disseminate reliable science based forest information needed to monitor and assess forest conditions. Criteria define and characterize the essential elements, as well as a set of conditions or processes, by which sustainable forest management may be assessed. The criteria and indicators provide a robust framework not only to define sustainability in the context of individual countries, but also provide a mechanism for understanding, monitoring and analysing national and global trends. These are instruments through which progress towards sustainable forest management may be evaluated and reported. Castaneda defines criteria as the range of forest values to be addressed and the essential elements or principles of forest management against which the sustainability of forests may be assessed. Each criterion relates to a key element of sustainability and may be described by one or more indicators. While indicators are parameters that measure specific quantitative and qualitative attributes and help monitor trends in the sustainability of forest management over time.

International Initiatives: The criteria and indicators approach for sustainable forest management was initiated by the ITTO. At present, there appears to be growing international consensus on the key elements of sustainable forest management. There are nine on-going international and/ or regional criteria and indicators initiatives currently, involving approximately 160 countries with some member-countries participating in more than one process. Seven common thematic areas of sustainable forest management have emerged based on the criteria of the nine ongoing regional and international sustainable forest management initiatives. These were acknowledged by the international forest community at the fourth session of the United Nations Forum on Forests (2004) and the 16th session of the Committee on Forestry (2003). These seven thematic areas include: (*i*) Extent of forest resources; (*ii*) Biological diversity; (*iii*) Forest health and vitality; (*iv*) Productive functions of forest resources; (*v*) Protective functions of forest resources; (*vi*) Socio-economic functions; and (*vii*) Legal, policy and institutional framework.

***The Indian Initiative*:** The criteria and indicators approach developed with development of a specific set of criteria and indicators for specific forestry conditions through international processes among the participating countries. It was realized to develop sustainable forest management in India, to accomplish establishment of a benchmark for sustainability according to the prevailing policy framework. In 1999, a workshop on 'Development of National Level Criteria and Indicators for the Sustainable Management of Dry Forests in Asia' was held at the Indian Institute of Forest Management (IIFM), Bhopal, with support from the Food and Agriculture Organization of the United Nations and the United Nations Environment Programme in collaboration with the ITTO, the United States Department of Agriculture Forest Service, and the IIFM, now referred to as the 'Dry Forest in Asia Process', ten Asian countries jointly developed a regionally applicable set of national-level criteria and indicators relevant for dry forests in the region. The Asia regional initiative was endorsed by the 'National Task Force on Sustainable Forest Management', appointed by the Ministry of Environment and Forests, Government of India. Thus, the Indian initiative of criteria and indicators approach for sustainable forest management was spearheaded by the IIFM in collaboration with ITTO and the Ministry of Environment and Forests, Government of India. A series of national technical workshops and consultation meetings were held to sensitize communities, forest managers, NGOs and researchers about the need for developing a national and state/ forest management unit (FMU) level set of criteria and indicators. A total of 8 criteria and 51 indicators specific to Indian forestry conditions were evolved after a consultative process involving a gamut of stakeholders. The criteria and indicators of the Bhopal-India process have evolved after a lot of deliberations and field-testing over the years.

Present Operational Framework

The applicability of a set of criteria and indicators at the national or FMU level, the set of indicators is unique for a particular management unit. The forest presents a dynamic situation in the field as the forest resources are under the interplay of many situations. In this context, development of a site-specific set of indicators and standardizing their threshold values according the site-specific requirements, are of critical importance. The indicators of the Bhopal-India process were revisited through a workshop in March 2005, when a refined set of 8 criteria and 43 indicators have been evolved. The criteria and indicators approach has over the years endeavored to provide a working framework for the achievement of a site-specific set of sustainability indicators of forests. The criteria of the Bhopal-India process encompass all aspects of sustainability, i.e. ecological, economical and socio-cultural. Hence the criteria will remain the same whether it is for the national or FMU level. Applicability of indicators of sustainable forest management within the broad framework of the criteria varies with the specific forestry conditions. A method for developing FMU-level indicators has been standardized involving stakeholders, viz. foresters, local communities, researchers and academicians, and tested for development of indicators applicable to FMU level. This process involves sensitization of stakeholders to help in building an understanding of sustainable forest management followed by participatory development of indicators, creating and strengthening institutional framework and identification of working groups from among themselves for its operationalization.

Trends and Progress Towards Sustainability

Over the years, there has been a paradigm shift towards community participation in forestry management. However, a system for continuous monitoring of trends and progress towards sustainability is not in place. Some aspects of forest management are being monitored on a regular basis, but in the light of the management objectives, a robust, all-uncommon passing system needs to be developed. Involving the communities in the application and monitoring of the management systems through criteria and indicators can enhance the sustainability of people oriented management initiatives. The system of criteria and indicators can help monitor the direction of change, whether towards or away from sustainable forest management. The forest policy lays emphasis on raising productivity of forests by research and technical inputs, and for management under prescriptions of the working plans. Although the present Indian Forest Policy addresses the ecological (environmental), economic, socio-cultural and legal policy and institutional issues, there appears to be no such inbuilt mechanism to monitor and provide feedback on its implementation. The criteria and indicators approach for sustainable forest management therefore becomes an essential tool to bride this gap. There have also been many efforts for institutionalization of the criteria and indicators approach. The forests in India are managed according to a scientifically sound, written management plan known as the 'Working Plan', and every division has a working plan which is revised after every ten years. Incorporating the monitoring and evaluation frameworks for sustainable forest management in working plans itself is imperative for institutionalization. The National Working Plan Code 2004 mentions incorporation of criteria and indicators in working plans for monitoring and evaluation of sustainable forest management. Some working plans have already incorporated the aspects of criteria and indicators of sustainable forest management, like the Working Plans of Haldwani and Tarai East Forest Divisions of Western Circle of Uttarakhand (2006–07 to 2016–17). Many other State Forest Departments are also working towards incorporation of criteria and indicators in their working plan. The implementation of sustainable forest management in a diverse country like India is a challenging task. To be more effective, criteria and indicators should be incorporated into national forestry legislations and regulation; not only as voluntary application. Being analogous with sustainable development, sustainable forest management also has important implications in the global economic scenario. Besides contributing to environmental, social and economic well-being of the communities, it also facilitates market-oriented tools like certification and eco-labelling. This requires active participation and coordination among the stakeholders for proper implementation. A wider application of criteria and indicators shall require a long maturity process. The Ministry of Environment and Forests, Government of India has already created a Sustainable Forest Management (SFM) Cell in the Ministry in 2006. It is expected to act as a national-level focal point towards SFM in the country. Discussions are also in an advanced stage to create SFM Cells in each state. These SFM Cells are expected to act as a nodal point for all matters related to sustainable forest management in the country and to encourage development of national programmes aimed at sustainable utilization and conservation of forests.

Conclusion

Forest policy in India has progressed well in the areas of employment generation; creation of manmade forest, encouragement of agro-forestry. However, it has not fared very well in the other stipulated objectives. Some threats to forest protection considered in the study are forest fire, poaching, trespass, illegal logging, and grazing which negatively affect sustainable management of forest estates. Thus, there is an urgent need for proper implementation of forest policy as a strong safeguard for providing best option for halting forest decline as well making the required contribution to the well being of the society. One of the biggest challenges towards the outlook of forests in the recent times has been concerns about 'sustainability' of our resources. It has emerged as one of the main concerns of recent policy advocacy. The National Forest Commission in its report released in 2006, has recommended creating an enabling environment to facilitate assessment, monitoring and reporting on national-level criteria and indicators for sustainable forest management. This phenomenon of comprehensive management of forests addressing its ecological, economic and socio-cultural functions developed throughout the world, resulting in improved understanding of the forest managers and awareness among the people. The sustainability of people-oriented management initiatives like joint forest management can be enhanced by involving the communities in applying and monitoring the sustainability by criteria and indicators approach. For application and monitoring of criteria and indicators by the communities, it is imperative that we take care of the institutionalization and capacity-building needs of the communities. The criteria and indicators give an opportunity to monitor and assess the state of sustainable forest management. The approach provides a powerful yet user-friendly tool to forest managers. However, as with other monitoring and assessment frameworks, it ultimately rests with the forest managers to implement and analyse the framework to make sustainable forestry decisions. The criteria and indicators approach besides measuring sustainability of forests at a national level, envisages to monitoring it effectively. Close international cooperation in forest science and related disciplines is required to enable forests to satisfy the manifold human needs in a sustainable way. Though the evolution of regional initiatives for criteria and indicators has been possible because of such cooperation in the first place, we may need to strengthen them for ensuring our goals of sustainability. In conclusion, the government forest policies are good because they protect the forest resources from being destroyed by local people and they also encourage local people to participate in forest resources management. The policies not only encourage people to manage and protect forest resources but also encourage people to increase forest cover by growing more trees along with the agricultural crops. As a result of these policies we can reduce natural disasters. Initially forestry would detain rural poverty and it can augment income finally. On the other hand, the policies have not benefitted equally among all the sections of stake holders. Only some are benefited while shifted their priority from farmland operation to forestry. This endevour will definitely promote livelihood. Sudden spurts in action no doubt is a challenge. The bewildered social status has to be changed. Any indigenous perception will have a threat so also is our make shift forestry. Time alone can best judge the efforts and efficiencies. Future projections are subject to the emphasis and suitable policy framework by the government.

REFERENCES

Agrawal, A. and Sivaramakrishnan, K. (eds) (2001) *Social Nature: Resources, Representations, and Rule in India,* New Delhi, Oxford University Press

Berkes, F. (ed) (1989), *Common Property Resources: Ecology and Community-based Sustainable Development,* London, Belhaven.

Blaikie, P. M. and Brookfield, H. (eds) (1987), *Land Degradation and Society,* London, Methuen.

Brandis, D. (1994), *Forestry in India,* Dehradun, India, Natraj Publishers.

Castañeda, F., Palmberg-Lerche, C. and Castaneda, P. V.,(2001), *Criteria and Indicators for Sustainable Forest Management: A Compendium,* Working Paper FM/5, FAO, Rome, Italy.

De-Montalembart, M.R (1996). *Cross Section Linkages and the Influences of External Policies and Forest Development,* Unasylva: International Journal of Forestry and Forest Industries, 182.

FAO, Report of the FAO/UNEP/ITTO/IIFM/USFS, (1999), *Workshop on Regional Initiative for the Development and Implementation of National Level Criteria and Indicators for the Sustainable Management of Dry Forests in Asia. Bhopal, India,* 30 November–3 December, FAO – Regional Office for Asia and the Pacific, Bangkok.

FAO/CCAD/CCAB-AP (1997), *Criteria and Indicators for Sustainable Forest Management in Central America,* Experts' Meeting, Lepaterique Process of Central America, Tegucigalpa, Honduras.

Gadgil, M. and Guha, R. (1995) *Ecology and Equity: Use and Abuse of Nature in Contemporary India,* London, Routledge.

Ghate, R. (1992), *Forest Policy and Tribal Development,* New Delhi, India: Concept Publishing Company.

GoI (1952), *National Forest Policy for India,* Ministry of Environment and Forests, Government of India.

GoI (1988), *National Forest Policy,* Ministry of Environment and Forests, Government of India.

Handmer, J., Norton, T. and Dovers, S. (eds) (2001) *Ecology, Uncertainty and Policy: Managing Ecosystems for Sustainability*, Harlow, Prentice-Hall.

IIFM (2000), *Bhopal-India process for Sustainable Management of Indian Forests*. Indian Institute of Forest Management, Bhopal, June .

ITTO, (1992), *Criteria for the Measurement of Sustainable Forest Management*, ITTO Policy Development Series No. 3, International Tropical Timber Organization, Japan.

Kotwal, P. C. and Chandurkar, D (2003), *Towards Sustainable Forest Management in India*. Indian Forest, 129.

Obaseki JK (1973). *Some Ingredients of Forest Regeneration and development*, Report of forest operation, Ministry of Agriculture Natural Resource.

Poffenberger, M., M.B. McGean and A. Khare.(1996). *Communities Sustaining India's Forests in the Twenty First century*. Village Voices, Forest Choices: Joint Forest Management in India, New Delhi: Oxford University Press.

Prasad, R., (1999), *National Forest Policy Imperatives: Criteria and Indicators of Sustainable Forest Management in India*. In Proceedings of the National Technical Workshop on Evolving Criteria and Indicators for Sustainable Forest Management in India (eds Prasad, R. et al.), IIFM, Bhopal.

Rametsteiner, E. and Simula, M. (2003), *Forest Certification—An Instrument to Promote Sustainable Forest Management*? J. Environ. Manage., 2003, 67.

Ministry of Environment and Forests,(2007), *India's Initial National Communication to UNFCCC (NATCOM)*, New Delhi, 2004; available at http://www.natcomindia.org/natcomreport.htm http://envfor.nic.in/nfap/.

Forest Survey of India,(2003), State of Forest Report 2003, Ministry of Environment and Forests, Dehra Dun.

Ravindranath, N. H., Sudha, P. and Sandhya, R., (2001), *Forestry for Sustainable Biomass Production and Carbon Sequestration in India*. Miti. Adap. Strat. Global Change.

Ballabh, V.; K. Balooni and S. Dave (2002). *Why Local Resource Management Institutions Decline: A Comparative Analysis of Van (Forest) Panchayats and Forest Protection Committees in India*, World Development, 30(2).

Centre for Monitoring Indian Economy (2001). *National Income Statistics*. Economic Intelligence Service, December.

Dhanagare, D.N. (2000). *Joint Forest Management in UP: People, Panchayats and Women*, Economic and Political Weekly, September 9.

Government of Haryana (undated). State-wise Geographic Area, Recorded Forest Area and Actual Forest Cover in India (1998-1999). Department of Forests. (http://www.Indiastat.com)

Government of India (1989). *National Accounts Statistics: Sources and Methods*. Central Statistical Organisation, Dept. of Statistics, Ministry of Planning, New Delhi.

Government of India (2001). *Statistical Abstract of India 2001*. Ministry of Statistics and Programme Implementation. (http://www.Indiastat.com)

Government of India (2002). *Tenth Five Year Plan (2002-2007), Volume I: Dimensions and Strategies*. Planning Commission, New Delhi.

Government of India (2003). *Forest Resources in India: An Overview* (http://envfor.nic.in/fsi/sfr99/chp2/t21b.html).

Guha, Ramchandra (1983a). *Forestry in British and Post-British India: A Historical Analysis (Part I & II)*, Economic and Political Weekly, 18(43), October 22.

Guha, Ramchandra (1983b). *Forestry in British and Post-British India: A Historical Analysis (Part III & IV)*, Economic and Political Weekly, 18(45 & 46), November 5-12.

Government of India (1976). Report *of the National Commission on Agriculture 1976, Part IX: Forestry*. Ministry of Agriculture and Irrigation, New Delhi.

Indian Council of Forestry Research and Education (2000). *Forestry Statistics of India 2000*. (http://www.Indiastat.com)

Ministry of Environment and Forests (2003). *Annual Report 2002-03*. (http://envfor.nic.in/report/0203/ar-main.htm).

National Dairy Development Board (1985). *Meeting Rural Fuelwood and Forage Needs through Tree Growers' Cooperative Societies—A Pilot Project Proposal*. Anand.

National Dairy Development Board (1985). *Meeting Rural Fuelwood and Forage Needs through Tree Growers' Cooperative Societies—A Pilot Project Proposal*. Anand.

Saxena, N.C. (1995). *Forests, People and Profit: New Equations for Sustainability*. Natraj Publishers, Dehradun.

Saxena, Rakesh (1996). *The Vatra Tree Growers' Co-operative Society* in Katar Singh and V. Ballabh (ed.), *Co-operative Management of Natural Resources*. Sage Publications, New Delhi.

Saxena, Rakesh (2000). *Joint Forest Management in Gujarat: Policy and Managerial Issues*, Working Paper 149, August, Institute of Rural Management, Anand.

Singh, Satyajit (1999). *Collective Dilemmas and Collective Pursuits: Community Management of Van Panchayats (Forest Councils) in the UP Hills*, Wastelands News, May-July, 29-45.

12

Assimilate Environmental Issues in the Organizational Governance to Harmonize Stakeholders' Interests

— Md. Tapan Mahmud and Mohammad Tariq Hasan

ABSTRACT

A business runs by, of and for the stakeholders. To continue the successful run of reaping profit for a longer time horizon, business organization must balance out the interests of all its stakeholders. A governance process based on these stakeholders' interests might be the only key to the said balancing. Since, the resources are limited and consequences are overlapping, it is very hard on the business' part to balance their interests. So, there must be a common issue, to which all the stakeholders feel positive. Environmental concern is one of them. This chapter tries to examine the impact of embedding environmental concern in a stakeholder based governance process, and see whether the harmonization pans out or not. In the process, the role of environmental accounting at the original governance process is also highlighted.

Keywords: *Stakeholders' Interests, Governance, Environmental Issues, Environmental Accounting.*

Introduction

Environmental discussions are at the top of burning questions for the last decade. Each and every action we take someway has a direct or indirect impact on the environment. Business activities had the largest amount of toll on the balance of natural environment. Recently, proposal has been raised to accumulate an environmental fund to help the LDCs. Since the LDCs are not among the industrialist countries, the developed (industrialist) countries were asked rationally to take the blame.

Business organizations are not the sole ranger, it is influenced and it influences all other entities that falls in its encompassment. Environment is one of those along with other stakeholders. Stakeholders' interests are to some extent mutually exclusive. Companies are ongoing concerns that look forward for unknown time horizon. To survive for such a long tenure, it is imperative from the organizations' point of view to harmonize the interests of all the stakeholders concerned.

Governance is the way, by which the skippers of the organizations keep pace with the ongoing dynamism of business world. If the stakeholders are pleased, the successful run of the organization can be made sure. So, most of the organizations' governance process is now based on stakeholders' interests; yet pleasing all the stakeholders at a time is a colossal Ask. This chapter states on the point of embedding environmental issues in the governance process, and tries to find out a balanced outcome, which is the interest harmonization of all the stakeholders in question.

Stakeholders and Their Diverse Interest

The people who are influenced by the decisions and aftermath of those decisions of a business'; and the people who can influence those decisions and apparent consequences, may be termed as stakeholders. There are chunks of homogeneously interested people roaming around a particular business organization just for a basic reason, which is to optimize his / her self-interest. The company should take into consideration the needs, interests and influences of peoples and groups who either impact on or may be impacted by its policies and operations (Frederick et al., 1992). However, the interests of the stakeholders and the interest of the business organization hinges on the same string.

There are lots of stakeholders; such as shareholders (only owning stakeholder), employees, activists, customers, suppliers, government, creditor, lenders, media etc. It is very hard on the organizations' part to maintain the interests of all the said parties at the same degree. If one's interest is prioritized others' interests naturally become dwarfed; because, after all the scarcity principle applies to all sources and it is also a zero-sum game. Therefore, the managers, more often than not goes for the 'Balancing' approach of interests maintaining.

As time went by, the stakeholder concept has taken on greater importance due to public interest, greater coverage by the media, concerns about corporative governance and its adoption as a policy within the scope of the 'Third Way' (Hutton, 1999; Greenwood, 2008).The traditional view of the organization was just to please the shareholders with favourable financial feedback. Conversely, the modern view refutes this approach switching to please all the stakeholders. Ironically though, this transmission did not happen automatically; the managers were bound to follow this dynamism. Diminishing trend of information asymmetry, openness of the market, increasing opportunity to raise vocal, diversity of ownership, and the emergence of 'ethical investors'[1] worked as a stimuli behind that move (Brooks, 2004). So, the harmonization of the interests of all the stakeholders becomes an inevitable option for the managers. The manager also realized the inter dependence of business and the environment. Because, almost all the factors of production are retrieved from the environment, and the products produced helps to improve the living standard of society.

Since, the harmonization is the only option to maintain the interest of all the stakeholders, integrating environmental issues and care in the organizational governance might help in strengthening the inter-dependence of business-environment; and please all the stakeholders thereby.

Governance Process Based on Stakeholders' Interests Embedding Environmental Issues

Governance process sets the tone for the whole organization. A close look at the figure 12.1 may provide a preliminary idea about it. Here the process is designed in such a way, by which stakeholders' interests might be assured. Getting the environmental issues integrated at the vital areas stars the discussion here.

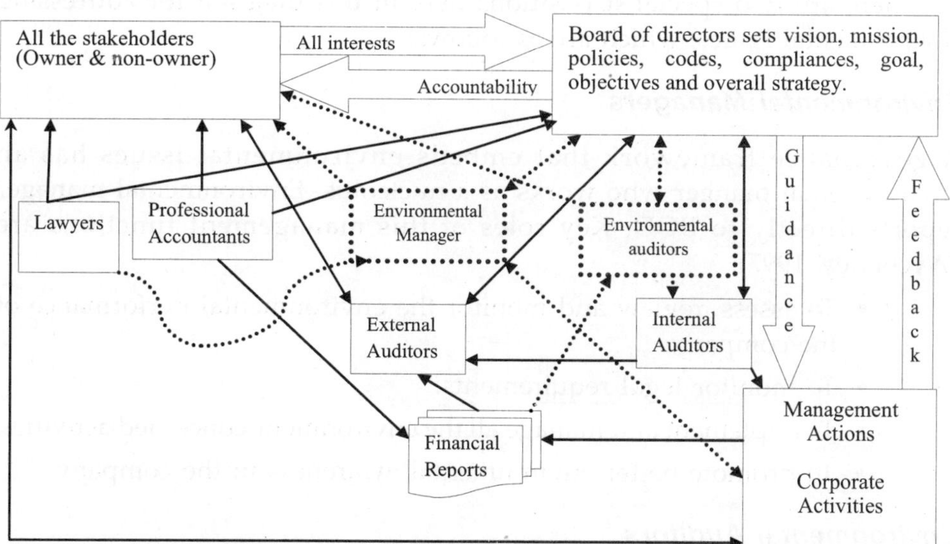

Fig. 12.1 : A corporate governance framework based on the stakeholders' interests, embedding environmental concerns

Freeman (1984) argued that business organizations should be concerned about the interests of other stakeholders when taking strategic decisions. In setting the vision, mission, policies, codes, compliances, goal, objectives and overall strategy the Board should consider and embed the environmental issues. While stating a vision Board should use those words that highlight the environmental concern, while stating mission BOD should include environmental terms in explaining the 'Who we are', and 'What we do' parts. Managers do regular corporate activities and provide financial statements. In the process, they get guidance from the BOD and provide regular feedback to them. Environmental issues should be highlighted and reconciled in the said process of 'guidance-feedback'. Special financial and accounting issues are addressed by the privately hired professional accountants of the company. They report to the BOD about the wrongdoings. Here the professional accountants should design an infrastructure for accounting the environmental issues. Internal auditors goes around the overall corporate activities and report to the BOD. Here internal auditors should confirm that the environmental issues placed in the policies, code of conduct, objectives and compliances are maintained. Due to the SOX proposals, the company's lawyers will be expected to make the BOD aware of problems if management does not respond appropriately, when told of improprieties. Along with this, the lawyers should enlist the environmental issues and consider them among improprieties, when left undone.

There are two specialist positions here in this diagram for addressing environmental issues; which are as follows:

Environmental Managers

A governance framework that embeds environmental issues has an environmental manger who works as a nucleolus. Environmental manager reports directly to BOD. Key roles of this management functions are (Wycherley, 1997):

- To assess, review and monitor the environmental performance of the company;
- To monitor legal requirements;
- To implement and manage all the environment-concerned activities;
- To promote better environmental awareness in the company.

Environmental Auditors

Environmental auditing is a determinative function (Medley, 1997). Credibility is a crucial aspect of environmental auditing. Initially audit was done to determine compliance with regulation. It has since advanced to determine compliance with management's environmental controls. The audit is based on the reliable environmental representation in the accounting record and performance. Auditor has specific roles in verifying the environmental accounts along with the figures arising from objective and subjective assessment of positive and/or negative externalities arising from corporate activities.

Turning the Facts into the Figures

People believe more in facts and figures rather than projection, so the enumeration of environmental issues is a vital concern. Here comes the inclusion of environmental accounting in the original accounting and governance framework. Environmental managers view environmental accounting as providing the financial data with the technical-functional improvements required by the specific role of the environmental managers.

A survey conducted among the environmental managers (Wycherley, 1997) reveals that environmental accounting's basic utility stems from the ability of providing measures of key environmental data.

Environmental accounting is an inclusive field of accounting. It provides reports for both internal use, generating environmental information to help make management decisions on pricing, controlling overhead and capital budgeting; and external use, disclosing environmental information of interest to the public and to the financial community. Internal use is better termed as environmental management accounting. (Bartolomeo et al., 2000).

To reap the benefits of Environmental Accounting following accounting wings might be in great use:

Environmental Cost Accounting (ECA)

The utility of assessing costs to products and process is defined by cost accounting (Lally, 1998). However, in environmental cost accounting cost are accounted for by their specific source.

ECA finds out all activities related to an environmental issue and by specifying homogeneous cost pool determines the cost related to those activities. Environmental actions include environmental infrastructure design, pollution, prevention and environmental management. ECA helps to find out the true cost of a product by eliminating arbitrary allocation of environmental overhead. ECA in producing environmental cost might take the assistance of the following two costing frameworks (Grinnell and Hunt, 2000). One is the 'ABC' framework; which looks for the 'cost drivers' at the organizational level by dividing the activities in unit, batch, product sustaining and facility. Another is a 'Cost-of-quality' framework, which branch out environmental costs in prevention, appraisal, internal and external failure.

There are some other sub-accounting disciplines that also may help in finding out the cost related to a particular environmental attachment; which are as follows:

- *Full Cost Accounting (FCA):* Full cost accounting describes how goods and services should be priced to reflect the true costs (including environmental and other social cost). Depending on the type of accounting system involved it can thus relate to national, financial, or managerial/cost accounting. With full cost accounting, natural resources would be redefined as assets on company ledgers; and environmental cost would be built into a product cost.
- *Total Cost Accounting (TCA):* This costing approach try to capture all the direct and indirect (externalities) cost related to a particular product/service, process and project. This costing approach incorporate wider time horizon, time value of money, vague hidden cost etc. This approach can include uncertain or less quantifiable costs such as the potential long term impact on the biosphere.
- *Life Cycle Cost Analysis (LCCA):* This sort of analyzing approach provides a framework for finding the total cost of design/development, production, use and disposal of the product with an intention of reducing the total cost, over the total life span of a particular product. It adds in costs emerging from effluent control, effluent treatment, effluent disposal, Eco-Taxes, rehabilitation, energy; and subtracts cost savings from recycling and reuse.

Environmental Management Accounting (EMA)

EMA borrows most of the information from ECA. It is defined as the generation, use and analysis of financial and related non-financial information, to support management within a company or business (Bartolomeo et al., 2000). EMA integrates in a great extent the governance and environmental issues and thus assist to deploy environmental policies.

EMA analyzes environmentally related financial cost and benefits that contribute to the increasing level of capital expenditure and operating expenses; for pollution control equipment and environmental taxes. It also incorporates possible environmental initiatives, for example, incentive-based regulation in its analysis and reporting (Fryxell and Vryza, 1999).

The environmental reports are integrated in nature. The data sources are based in design, engineering and operations records, rather than broad areas such as energy, costs and waste minimization. The broad data are transformed as input to the accounting system. This sort of reporting abolishes the need for allocating environmental costs directly to products and process. Also, the nature of environmental costs determines the capital investment assessment method. Discounted cash flow method is preferred to Payback period, because the benefits from environmental capital investments are realized in a longer time horizon rather than a short one (Grinnell and Hunt, 2000).

Harmonization of the Stakeholders' Interests

It is impossible to maintain all the stakeholders' interests at the same level, which was stated earlier; someone has to be offended to defend someone's interest. Insertion of environmental concern might help to shorten the distance between the offended & defended and harmonize the interests in a great manner thereby.

Though, organizations have shifted from a point of view of serving only the shareholders' interest, profitability is still one of the major concerns. Shareholders are also shifted from the short time dividend seeking motive to longer time horizon. Firms who are concerned about the context, in which they are operating in, are historically reaping more benefit in the long run than the firms who are not doing so (Peters and Waterman, 1982). Environmental concerns not only incur costs, but also save a lot of money. Nynex saved $2.5 million by printing customer invoices at both side of the page; whereas Qatar State saved $600000 on its corrugated packaging by changing the shape of its motor oil bottles from round to rectangular (Wasik, 1996).

Various governments of the world also take initiatives to favor those organizations that are environmentally concerned. According to the degree of environmental consciousness, Indonesian government categorized their companies in three categories, namely; 'Green', 'Black' and 'Red'. The 'Green' companies would get tax relief and easier access to bank credit for their highest degree of consciousness, the 'Black' companies would be penalized by court and the 'Red' companies would be deprived of bank credit (Embassy of Indonesia, 2010)[2]. In July 2007, China government launched a policy named 'Green Credit'. According to that policy the government instructed banks not to give loans to high energy consuming and polluting industries. The firms who already had loan, but violated environmental conditions, found their loan called in. In the eastern Jiangsu province alone, more than one billion Yuan, (US $ 137 million) in loans have called in from companies who failed to pass environmental assessment or to implement China's environmental protection regulation (Green Credit Policy, 2008)[3].

Expectation and pressure from the consumer and activists has always been on the card, lately. In June 2009, 'Greenpeace'[4], released a report showing that companies like Gucci, Wal-Mart, Nike, and Timberland have such a procurement policy which is linked to the deforestation of Amazon. Immediately after the release of this report, the fallout in the sales revenue of these organizations was evident; which was originally impacted by a mass corporate boycott from customers. In December 2009, Unilever cancelled a $32.6 million contract with Sinar Mas[5], because the palm oil Sinar Mas supplies was farmed at a deforested arena (Butler, 2010). On the same note, employees that work in a marked organization, feels embarrassed in the society. The declining position of the company and the negative media coverage turns the shoulder of the employees down. In the long run, the company fails to provide the prior benefits that they were used to provide to the employees and the turnover slope booms up. So much investment that was put behind the workforce drains out to other companies.

Banks as the main creditors and financer of the companies have panned out certain restrictions and pre-requisites on loans regarding the environmental issue. Bank America Corporation gave loans to a forest product company of $7 million, but stipulated that the loans can't be repaid by deforestation. The corporation also refused to lend in a project in the Middle East, because of the excessive emission from the proposed plant (Moving Money Responsibly)[6].

Now, we have a complete picture about the identicalness of movement from the stakeholders' point of view; when it comes to the environmental issues. Recent pragmatic phenomena plots this identicalness as we notice the reaction from the shareholders, banks/creditors, activists, media, consumer, employees and from government about environmental concerns. Though, value chain activity is the real engine that formulates the ultimate value, organizational governance is the steering that directs and hold it together. Therefore, if the environmental issues can be assimilated in the organizational governance process, the diverse interests of the stakeholders would be harmonized for sure.

Conclusion

A harmonization based on a common ground, which was environmental issues, was shown; using the stakeholder based governance process. An anti-consideration is; whenever we boycott a seller or supplier, we are hurting some stakeholders, yet in the long run we would find a net beneficial outcome by continuing this sort of approach. Interestingly, there are also some consumers who are not ready to pay for the extra amount which is arousing for additional environmental care. This sort of short term and contradictory orientation should be addressed positively. On top of it, a multidisciplinary approach should be adapted with the help of environmental science, environmental accounting, environmental law and regulation, finance and risk management, management policies and control system to avail the said harmonization.

REFERENCES

Bartolomeo, M., Bennett, M., Bouma, J.J., Heydkamp, P., James, P. and Wolters, T. (2000), "Environmental Management Accounting in Europe: Current Practice and Future Potential", *The European Accounting Review,* Vol. 9 No.1, pp. 31–52.

Brooks, L. J. (2004), *Business & Professional Ethics for Directors, Executives and Accountants,* Thomson South-Western, USA.

Butler, R. (2010), "In the Fight to Save Forests Activists Target Corporations", http://e360.yale.edu/mobile/feature.msp?id=2267, January 14, 2011.

Frederick, W., Post, J. and St Davis, K. (1992), *Business and Society: Corporate Strategy, Public Policy, Ethics,* 7th ed., McGraw-Hill, New York, NY.

Freeman, R. (1984), *Strategic Management: A Stakeholder's Approach,* Pitman, Boston, MA.

Fryxell, G.E., Vryza, M. (1999), "Managing Environmental Issues Across Multiple Functions: An Empirical Study of Corporate Environmental Departments and Functional Co-ordination", *Journal of Environmental Management,* Vol. 55, pp. 39–56.

Greenwood, M. (2008), "Classifying Employees as Stakeholders", Working Paper 4/08, Working Paper Series, Department of Management, Business and Economics, Monash University, Melbourne, April 14, p. x.

Grinnell, D.J., Hunt, H.G. (2000), "Development of an integrated course in accounting: focus on environmental issues", *Issues in Accounting Education,* Vol. 15 No. 1, pp. 19–42.

Hutton, J. (1999), *The Stakeholders Society,* Blackwell, London.

Lally, A.P. (1998), "ISO 14000 and Environmental Cost Accounting: the Gateway to the Global Market", *Law and Policy in International Business,* Vol. 29 No. 4, pp. 501–538.

Medley, P. (1997), "Environmental accounting - What does it mean to professional accountants?", *Accounting, Auditing and Accountability Journal,* Vol. 10 No. 4, pp. 594-600.

Peters, T. J., Waterman, R. H. (1982), *In Search of Excellence,* Harper& Row, New York.

Wasik, J. F. (1996), "The New Economics of Ecology: Why The Green Bottom-line Works for Business",http://www.envirolink.org/external.html?www=http%3A//www.envirolink.org/articles/jan97-1.html&itemid=sbn861521142183, January 17, 2011.

Wycherley, I. (1997), "Environmental Manager and Accounting", *Journal of Applied Management Studies,* Vol. 6 No. 2, pp. 169-184.

FOOTNOTES

1. Ethical investors are those investors that not only look for the profit but also the ethical validation of the way by which the profit was reaped. Environmental concerns are one of the most important ethical issues.

2. Link: http://www.embassyofindonesia.org/news/2010/12/news097.htm, January 15, 2011.
3. Link: http://www.china.org.cn/english/environment/242659.htm, January 16, 2011.
4. Greenpeace is a non-governmental environmental organization with offices in over 40 countries Greenpeace states its goal is to "ensure the ability of the Earth to nurture life in all its diversity".
5. Sinar Mas group is Indonesia's largest palm oil exporting company. It was accused of aggressive deforestation.
6. Link: http://www.envirolink.org/external.html?www=http%3A//www.envirolink.org/articles/feb97-3.html&itemid=sbn61528142813, January 14, 2011.

13

Forest Policies in India

A Historical Analysis

— Mr. Bipul Kumar Rabha

ABSTRACT

This chapter analyzes the historical perspective of different forest policies that have been implemented in India to conserve forest resources. We find that the acts, which did not take into concern local people's requirement of forest resources, were over and over again amended. Based on the importance of forest resources both in British and Post-British period forests are divided into different categories and are regulated by different rules.

Keywords: *Forest Polices, Forest Rights, Tribals, Traditional Rights, Protection, Conservation, India.*

Introduction

In an era plagued by climate change and global warming societies can no longer afford to ignore the importance of forests. Initially forests have been analyzed by economists and policy makers as a source of economically valuable resources. However, in the later analysis several other types of values have been attributed to the forests. Forests contribute towards ecological existential value and livelihood subsistence for people. Forests resources also possess intrinsic value such as ethical and spiritual value (Sagoff, 2004). Since forests are extremely valuable in several ways degradation of forests and deforestation arc such processes that acquire immense significance and this call for a serious analysis of these problems and, therefore, it has been thought to implement acts to conserve forest.

There was no any forest policy in India before the British came. The colonial rulers were very conscious about destruction of valuable forest resources of the country and introduced different acts to conserve the forest. The forest conservation policies have been trying to reconcile the conflicting objectives of exploiting forests for economic development, ecological balance and livelihoods and rights of people dependent on forests. This chapter analyzes historical perspective of different forest policies implemented in India to conserve the forest.

Policies to Conserve Forest in India

The Forest Act of 1865

India was a country with large forest area before British came. The wastelands and forests were not exploited by the rulers of pre-British era in India (Guha, 1983). The British had already destroyed their forests area when they came to India. Therefore, their eyes were on India's dense forestlands and resources, which would be the source of revenue and exports. Introduction of railways intensified the exploitation of Indian forests. Many forest areas were destroyed because of laying railway tracks. This led to massive exploitation of forests. Concerned about the massive deforestation, the Governor General Lord Dalhousie issued a memorandum for systematic conservation of forests. Based on that memorandum Dietrich Brandis, Superintendent of Forest, and German Botanist was appointed as the first Inspector General of Forests by the Government of India. Based on the suggestions given by Brandis the Imperial Forest Department was formed in 1864 with the assistance of German foresters and in the next year formulated the first forest act in Indian history—*The Forest Act of 1865*. This act was formulated to regulate exploitation of forests and for its management and preservation. The first attempt was initiated to regulate the collection of forest produce by the forest dwellers (Guha, ibid & Kulkarni, 1987).

This act soon became controversial since it had no provision for the use of forests resources by tribals and other forest dependent village communities. It gave total monopoly powers over forests to the central government. Therefore, in future, it was resolved that forest policies should recognize rights of local villagers over some of the forest resources (Haeuber, 1993).

The Forest Act of 1878

In 1878, Indian forests policy was designed addressing the shortcomings of *The Forest Act of 1865*. The forests in India were classified into three main categories (Haeuber, ibid)—(*a*) *Reserved Forests;* (*b*) *Protected Forests;* and (*c*) *Village Forests*. The Government of India owned the forests, which were classified as reserved forests. These types of forests were intended to provide ecological stability and to sub-serve the developmental objectives of the government. The main objective of this type of classification of forests was to protect them from use by the local people. The protected forests were defined as those forests, which would become reserve forests in future once they had been demarcated and covered by working plans. These forests consisted of valuable tree species and therefore restrictions were imposed on activities such as grazing. The village forests were the forests that were reserved for the subsistence requirement of tribals and other forest dependent village communities which full governing powers had been given to the village authorities.

The forests areas, which were controlled, by the local rulers and Rajas realized that the British had aimed to exploit the forests resources in India through the settlement process. Secondly, the officials (colonial officials) noted that the act had led to serious discontentment amongst the agricultural classes, particularly where there were no buffer Zamindar classes (Haeuber, ibid). The ultimate aim of the colonial government during that period was to monopolize all ownership rights over the forests (Tucker, 1987). J A Voelcker, an agricultural expert, submitted a report in 1893 cautioning the colonial government that the tenancy system of the government had considerably broken up village communities and for most part these communities were reduced only to heterogeneous groups living together rather than communities (quoted by Haeuber, 1993).

The Forest Policy Resolution of 1894

Based on the caution alarm sounded by the Voelcker report the colonial government issued the *'The Forest Policy Resolution of 1894'* with greater emphasis on the local demands for forestlands including clearing lands for agricultural extension. To fulfill these objectives the forests classification was modified into four categories: (*a*) *Protective Forests*-reserved to maintain environmental stability; (*b*) *National Forests*-reserve for providing sustained supply of commercial timber; (*c*) *Minor Forests*-forests for use of village people e.g. fuel wood, fodder etc.; and (*d*) *Pasture Lands* (Haeuber, ibid).

The above classifications were for the forests, which were under the management of the state. Again, the classification did not include the wastelands in the definition of forest. Although this forest resolution claimed to be considerate about the local demand for forest resources, it remained primarily a mechanism for restricting popular access to forest resources. The use of forest resources was primarily aimed at sub-serving the imperial economic interests.

The Indian Forest Act of 1927

The Government of India under the British Raj again reformulated the Indian forest policy in *The Indian Forest Act of 1927*. The purpose of this forest policy was to codify all the functions of the forest officials. The basis of the regional division of forest was the act of 1894. In addition, this forest policy made provisions for the private management of forest in certain cases. This act also proscribed the punishments meted out to those accused of forest offences (Kulkarni, 1987). Tribals and other village communities that enjoyed traditional rights suddenly found themselves being seen as criminals by the administrative for using the forests for their subsistence.

There was a great change in Indian forest policy in 1935 as a consequence to the *Government of India Act of 1935*; adopted in the British parliament. This act created a dual system of governance and forests were included in the provincial list i.e., forest administration came under the authority and control of provincial governments.

Those who were part of nationalist movement were of the opinion that the existing colonial forest policies neglected village and minor forests. However, the policies continued to emphasize restrictions on user rights and continued to manage the forests by using the colonial classification of forests into reserved and protected forests which was meant to sub-serve imperialist interest. Robert Wallace, professor of agricultural economy, University of Edinburgh, criticized the colonial forest policies stating that the policy causes massive exploitation of valuable trees which was not in favor of cultivators but sub-served the interests of contractors employed for supplying forest resources to meet the extraneous demands mainly of the British (Kulkarni, ibid). The Inspector General Howard stated in this regard emphasizing that preservation of physical and climatic conditions should be given priority and a minimum amount of forest should be maintained to ensure the country's well being (Haeuber, 1993).

The National Forest Policy of 1952

After independence Indian leadership revised the forest policies, which reflected the new developmental aspirations. It stated that forest policy should be based on paramount consideration of national needs. The leaders thought that forest policies would be instrumental in determining the inter-state relations apart from playing a crucial role in industrial and agricultural development. This was the basis for reviewing the forest policies by the *Central Board of Forestry (1950)*. Based on recommendations of this board *'The National Forest Policy of 1952'* was formulated. The act stated that the state governments in the country would formulate and enact legislations for conserving and managing their forest resources. The policies also recognised the specific local priorities—for instance importance of plantation of trees on rivers banks to restrict soil erosion. Keeping such objectives in view, *Central Board of Forestry* recommended that one third of country's land area should be covered with forests and proportion of forestlands should be 60 per cent and 20 per cent in the mountains and plains respectively. It means that forest cover should help stabilized the natural environment of the country. The classifications of forests were same as in *'The Forest Policy of 1894'*, except changing the terms of the last two categories. In this act the terms were *Village Forest* and *Tree Lands* instead of *Minor Forest*, and *Pasture Land* respectively (Haeuber, ibid).

This policy was criticized on different grounds. First, according to Kulkarni (1987), the concept of national need was interpreted in a very narrow sense. While the destruction of forests for construction of roads, building of irrigation and hydroelectricity projects were named as national interest, the cultivation lands without any tree cover were treated as encroachment. Second, according to *Scheduled Areas and Scheduled Tribes Commission (1960)*, traditional rights of tribals were not recognised. The status remained the same as in the colonial *'The Forest Policy of 1894'*; only difference was that the marginalization of *Nistar Rights* (1) includes the category of the *'rights and privileges'* in 1894 in 1952 was replaced *'rights and concessions'* (Kulkarni, ibid). Third, the forest policy failed to achieve its objectives e.g. it aimed at achieving reforestation of one third of total geographical area of the forestland where forest cover was lost. But in reality due to unrestricted and unregulated diversions of forests for various non-forestry uses the forest cover got further reduced (Darlong, 2002).

In 1963, the sub-committee of the Central Board of Forestry stressed remedial, preventive and punitive measures to enhance forest conservation. As for example-the traditional burning of forests during certain seasons and cultivation in forest areas were to be prohibited and such activities would be regulated more strictly. Forest officials were given additional powers to punish the offenders of forestlands and resources. The forest department increased the list of minor forests including *'gum'* and *'wild animals and skins, tusks and horns'* and damage to these forest products would be dealt with through more stringent provisions.

In 1976, *National Commission on Agriculture (NCA)* felt that Indian forests provided a great potentiality for forest based industrial development. This, it was argued, would reduce unemployment problem of the country, basically in case of rural unemployment. It also felt that unrestricted use of forests by rural people would rapidly destruct the forest resources. The commission ultimately aimed to abolish the *Nistar Rights*. The main purpose of the NCA was that the traditional rights should be eliminated as soon as possible and rights be given instead to forest based industries, which could contribute towards the economic development of the country. The redefinition of property rights over forest resources were transferred from villagers to the industrial sector in case of minor forests, which would be brought under the planned management of modern industries. Following the centralization of management of forest, it was felt that it would increase the foreign exchange earnings through export of forest based industrial products while simultaneously discouraging domestic consumption. Based on the above objectives the NCA reclassified the forest into three categories: (*a*) *Protection Forests*—occupying areas vulnerable to erosion such as hill slopes, watershed and river banks; (*b*) *Production Forest*—comprised of valuable or potentially valuable timber bearing stands manage to meet the demands of existing and future industries. *Production Forests* were again divided into three categories. (*i*) *Mixed Quality Forests*—consisting of timber stands of low economic value which could be clear felled and converted into stands of valuable economic species yielding higher production and greater economic returns; (*ii*) *Valuable Forests*—comprised of valuable timber stands providing high revenues, but which could yield higher revenue per hectare if converted and replanted with economically valuable species; and (*iii*) *Inaccessible Forests*—situate in remote areas that were unexploited largely due to insufficient infrastructure, these forests would be reached through a programme of forest road extension. (*c*) *Social Forest*—covering wastelands, Panchayat lands, village commons and lands on the sides of roads, canal banks and railway lines as well as minor forest consisting of marginal and depleted forest areas. These forests would meet the small timber, fuel wood, grazing, fodder and recreation needs of the population (Haeuber, 1993).

No doubt that the classification of production forests was completely detrimental to ecological and sustainable development objectives. This process leads to monoculture in terms of the tree species, which is ecologically undesirable. Further, between clear felling and planting, there is time lag, which puts stress on the flora and fauna of those forest areas. Although this process is aimed at realizing economic development of the country, it ignores the ecological costs on account of possible extinction of certain wild life species, which have symbiotic relation with certain low valued tree varieties along with extinction of certain tree varieties. Social forestry was introduced with the objective of recognizing a role for the traditional rights of local people. But the skeptics raised questions as to how can most degraded forest area be socially useful? It is a policy anomaly that the problem of deforestation caused by clear felling of existing forest for economic development was to be solved by plantation drives implemented through social forestry programme. It could not therefore achieve its objectives. As for example—a study by Muthayya & Loganathan (1992), in Karnataka found that people were interested in planting trees in their own lands rather than on common lands. Dhanagare (2000) says that there was no cooperation from the revenue department staff, which had an important role to play in the plantation drives of common lands involving local village communities. Chhatre & Saberwal (2006) points to the conflicting objectives, lack of organic link between local people's objectives and its functionaries which implies that the incentive structures build into conserving forests were not properly evolved.

The *Central Board of Forestry* subcommittee (1963) and the NCA (1976) also recommended for more juridical powers to the forest officials if the objectives of forests conservation are to be achieved. The forest officials were to be given extraordinary powers to arrest and hold those accused of forest related crimes without warrant, magisterial powers were to be vested with the forests officers to initiate action against offences on the spot (Haeuber, 1993). The recommendations of the NCA were in violations of the traditional rights of local people over forests. The commission recommended adopting a revised forest policy, which would be implemented effectively. These recommendations were opposed to those made by the *Scheduled Areas and Scheduled Tribes Commission*. It should be noted here that according to the *Government of India Act, 1935*; forest was a subject in the state list. But this was transferred to the concurrent lists after the 42nd amendment made to the constitution of India in 1976. However, *'The Forest Conservation Act of 1980'*, made the prior approval of central government a necessity to use forest resources for any purpose.

The Indian Forest Act of 1981 and The National Forest Policy of 1988

The recommendations of the NCA were put to public scrutiny in the early 1980s and after which *'The Indian Forest Act of 1981'*; was issued. The forest act increased the state control on forest resources by increasing the categories of forests and forest produce that were brought under its control. The act became controversial due to forced action by Government of India. On August 7, 1982; the *Central Board of Forestry* convened a meeting of the state Forest Ministers and recommended new forestry legislation. In 1987 a final draft of the proposed act was circulated for public scrutiny. The act maintained that the forest policy must be to ensure environmental stability and ecological balance. Based on that draft a new *'The Revised National Forest Policy of 1988'* was formulated by the Government of India.

This act encourages involvement of people in the development and protection of forests. All the states government with the exception of Uttar Pradesh, Assam, Manipur and Nagaland, India adopted the Joint Forest

Management (JFM) system for forest conservation based on the instructions given by the Government of India (Poffenberger & Sinha, 1996). But eventually, all the states have adopted the JFM program. The purpose of setting up the JFM system can be classified into three categories (Pattnaik & Dutta, 1997)—(i) *Environmental*-to protect the existing forest and water resources and prevent their depletion and to encourage the regeneration of degraded forest lands; (*ii*) *Economic*—to efficiently manage of forest and water resources with the aim of providing income and subsistence to those that are directly dependent on forests; and (*iii*) *Socio-political*—involvement of the local communities in decision making on forest use. The act was again amended in the years 1992 and 2003. The two amendments did not change the main issues of the original act. Only changes made were with respect to solve rules governing the responsibilities of the functionaries within the government for the sake of convenience in the forest management.

The India's Forest Rights Act of 2006

The newly issued *'The India's Forest Rights Act of 2006'* grants the *"rights to hold and live in the forest land under the individual or common occupation for habitation or for self-cultivation for livelihood by a member or members of the forest dwelling ST or other traditional forest dwellers"* (Ramnath, 2008). It suggests gradual giving up of shifting cultivation and other forest dependent ways of life that could deplete forest resources. The government has recognized the *Schedule Tribes (STs)* and other forest dwellers as the primary actors in carrying out programmes relating to improving the sustainability of forest environment. Combining tribal rights and environmental agenda can only attain sustainability of forests. The new controversy triggered off by this act is whether clubbing together of Tribals and other Non-Tribals forest dwellers is justified (AITPN, 2006; Bhuiler, 2008). There is a question here whether government in doing so has done well by mixing the tribals and other forest dwellers, because tribals are indigenous to forests and have traditional rights over the forests. Their life in forests cuts across several generations. Their community life, labour and the memories of their history cannot be separated out from the forest life unlike other Non-Tribal populations. Tribals therefore have greater existential, emotional, psychological and cultural attachment with forest all of which are significant in their own valuation framework than other forest castes or Non-Tribal forest dwellers. On the other hand, forest and forest related livelihood activities are the last resort when other options of livelihood are not available. The denial of choice here is suggestive of superimposition of a concept of development that is alien to the tribal understanding of 'development'.

Conclusion

Different forest policies have been implemented in India to conserve the forest resources. We have found that the acts, which did not take into concern local people's requirement of forest resources, were over and over again amended. Based on the importance of forest resources both in British and Post-British period forests are divided into different categories and are regulated by different rules.

Acknowledgements

I would like to thank Dr G Vijay, Assistant Professor of Department of Economics, University of Hyderabad for his valuable comments on this paper.

NOTES

Nistar Rights: The traditional rights of people living in forest areas together products such as fuel wood, fodder, foods and medicines necessary for survival needs (World Bank, 2006).

Resolution No. 3-1/86-FP, dated, December, 1988 (Darlong, 2002: 25).

The instruction was circulated on June 1, 1990.

Act, chapter 2, 3 (a) (Ramnath, 2008).

REFERENCES

AITPN (Asian Indigenous and Tribal Peoples Network) (2006): "India's Forest Rights Acts of 2006: Illusion or Solution", The Occasional Briefing Papers of AITPN, December, Viewed on 24 December 2010 (http://www.aitpn.org/Issues/II-09-06-Forest.pdf).

Bhullar, Lovleen (2008): "The Indian Forest Rights Act 2006: A Critical Appraisal", *Law, Environment and Development Journal*, Vol. 4/L, pp. 20-34.

Chhatre Ashwini and Saberwal Vasant (2006): *Democratizing Nature: Politics, Conservation and Development in India* (New York, New Delhi: Oxford University Press).

Darlong, V T (2002): "Forest Policies and Legislations Vis-à-vis: Forest Resources Management in North East India", in B Datta Ray & K Alam (ed), *Forest Resources in North East India,* (New Delhi: Omsons Publications).

Dhanagare, D N (2000): "Joint Forest Management in UP, People, Panchayat and Women", *Economic and Political Weekly,* September 9, pp. 3315-3324.

Guha, Ramachandra (1983): "Forestry in British and Post British India: A Historical Analysis", *Economic and Political Weekly,* October 29, pp. 1882-1893 and November 5-12, pp. 1940-1945.

Haeuber, Richard (1993): "Indian Forestry Policy in Two Eras: Continuity or Change?" *Environmental History of Review,* Vol. 17. No. 1, pp. 49-76.

Kulkarni, Sharad (1987): "Forest Legislation and Tribals: Comments on Forest Policy Resolution", *Economic and Political Weekly,* December 12, pp. 2143-2148.

Muhayya, B C and M Loganathan (1992): "Community Participation in Social Forestry (A Dialogical Assessment)", *Journal of Rural Development*, Vol. 11(6), NIRD, Hyderabad, Andhra Pradesh, India.

Pattnaik, Binay K & S Dutta, (1997): "JFM in Southwest Bengal: A Study in Participatory Development", *Economic and Political Weekly*, December 13, pp. 3225-3232.

Poffenberger, M & S Sinha (1996), "Communities and States: Re-establishing the Balance in Indian Forest Policies", in Mark Poffenberger and Betsy Geam (ed), *Village Voices, Forest Choices: Joint Forest Management in India* (Delhi: Oxford University Press).

Ramnath, Madhu (2008): "Surviving the Forest Rights Acts: Between Scylla and Charybdis", *Economic and Political Weekly*, March 1, 43(9), pp. 37-42.

Sagoff, Mark (2004): *Price, Principle, and the Environment* (Cambridge University Press).

Tucker, Richard P (1987): "Dimensions of Deforestation in the Himalaya: The Historical Setting", *Mountain Research and Development*, Vol. 7, No. 3, pp. 328-331.

World Bank (2006): *India-Unlocking Opportunities for Forest Dependent People*, Agriculture and Rural Development Sector Unit, South Asia Region (Oxford University Press).

14

Environmental Ethics in Corporate World
Some Issues

— Dr. Santosh Singh Bais

ABSTRACT

Rapid industrialization, inspite of its positive effects on economic development of the world, has very seriously threatened the world's natural environmental balance. There is a growing pressure from environmentalists, government, society, customers, employees and competitors on business firms to be environment friendly. Theses days, protection of environment has become a key issue all over the world. Though swift industrialization is an essential pre-requisite for overall economic growth, yet it is damaging the environment drastically, water pollution, air pollution, solid and toxic waste pollution and other environmental contamination are common in many production processes.

The inspiration for environmental ethics was the first Earth Day in 1970, when environmentalists started urging philosophers who were involved with environment groups to do something about environmental ethics. Environmental ethics is a subject without definition and without consensus. And yet, every person on this planet makes everyday decisions that relate to environmental ethics. Questions as simple as 'what should I eat?' or 'How should I move from place to place?' all raise environmental and ethical issues. Environmental ethics is very recent as an academic discipline and there is much to studied an acted upon. The need for an environmental ethics is, however, critical. Recognizing that environmental ethic alone is not enough; we must all live the environmental ethical way. This chapter draws the attention of environmental ethics among the corporate customers.

Key Words: Ethics, Pollution, Natural, Industrialization, Development

Introduction

In the last two decade there has been increasing concern about the threat to the environment caused by economic growth and its more undesirable side effects. This concern was expressed much earlier in the developed countries. Rapid industrialization, in spite of its positive effects on economic development of the world, has very seriously threatened the world's natural environmental balance. There is a growing pressure from environmentalists, government, society, customers, employees and competitors on business firms to be environment friendly. These days, protection of environment has become a key issue all over the world. Several factors and forces are responsible for destruction of environment. Of these growing hazardous industrialization is a major culprit. Though swift industrialization is an essential pre-requisite for overall economic growth, yet it is damaging the environment drastically, water pollution, air pollution, solid and toxic waste pollution and other environmental contamination are common in many production processes. Environmental degradation and development are considered as two sides of the same coin. The environmental degradation, in fact, started with the propagation of human race. This process of environmental degradation was accelerated with the development of socio-economic activities i.e. agriculture, industrialization, drugs and pharmaceuticals, transport, civil construction including roads and buildings etc. with growing population, the requirements of foodgrains and other consumer items increased greatly, leading to further degradation of environment.

In other words rapid industrialization has created environmental disturbances of three types namely:

1. Depletion of non-renewable natural resources;
2. Deforestation; and
3. Degradation and destruction

Thousands of years ago great Indian sages in 'Prithvi Sukla' had stated the importance of keeping the earth free from pollution and any disturbance caused to its equilibrium. The message of environment protection is thus not new. Environment as a term is very widely used and means different things to different people. It is used in management literature to refer to the external environment in which the organization functions. Ecologically, environment refers to the sum of all the external conditions and influences affecting the life and development of organism (Webster-1961). Two main aspects of the environment are biotic and abiotic (living and non-living).

Environment refers to all the surrounding things, conditions, and influences affecting the growth or development of living things (World Bank

Dictionary-1989). Environment as an area of study is thus a conglomerate of all basic and applied sciences, engineering, socio-economic aspects, management, and law.

Environment, as the United Nations Committee describes, is the sum total of identified and in identifiable natural resources, existing in finite quantities on earth and, of the quality of the environment of the milieu, which constitutes an important element of the quality of renewable resources.

In the generic sense, it is the aggregate of surrounding things, conditions, or influences. In specific sense, it is a thin layer of life supporting systems called biosphere, divided into physical and biological environment.

Evolution is a concept in which along with the welfare and happiness of the present generation, the rights of the future generation should be secured. Environment is the pivot on which the world's economic condition stands. It is God-given Home where living creature gets shelter. We all depend on it for our survival. Unfortunately, in spite of this universal truth, man is misguided by thinking that cultural values lie in the artificial shining of the material advancement. In fact, it is a life value which carries its own seeds of destruction.

Environment management is the optimal utilization of the finite resources between different possible uses. Environmental criteria and economic considerations demand that such an allocation be efficient, simultaneously, the available resources should be protected from degradation, and scarce and diminishing resources should be conserved. Environmental degradation affects the quality of the environment and threatens the livelihood of many people.

Three decades ago the international community gathered in Stockholm for the United Nations conference on human environment to sound an alarm about the perilous state of Earth and its resources. That landmark event is widely credited with environmental issues being placed on the international agenda, leading, in turn, to the establishment of environment ministries at the national level, and increased awareness of the impact that even local decisions can have, on the global environment. Every activity generates unavoidable environmental impact of some kind or the other, but the ability of people and societies to adopt themselves to and cope with the change is varied. Environment degradation results to poor health and reduced quality of life.

(*a*) Poor environmental quality is directly responsible for some 25 per cent of preventable diseases.

(*b*) Air pollution is a major contributor to a number of diseases.

(*c*) Globally 7 per cent of all deaths and diseases are due to water, and lack of sanitation and hygiene.

There are two basic reasons for our concern with environmental pollution, firstly Home, health and welfare and secondly sustenance and survival of mankind. While addressing the world conservation strategy on March 6, 1980, the Indian Prime Minster, Smt. Indira Gandhi, spoke that in India the interest in conservation is not a sentimental one, but the rediscovery of the truth well known to our ancient sages.

Environment Management

In the 21st century, organizations are rapidly changing their structures, systems, work processes and activities. This changing environment calls for enterprising managers to manage and respond to the changes in an appropriate manner. It is therefore, necessary for them to develop a clear focus and direction to facilitate proper decision making process. The features of 21st century are:

(1) An era of information revolution.

(2) The traditional supply chains are fast disappearing, paving way to new virtual supply chains.

(3) The relationship among organizations, their customers, suppliers and government is also undergoing a drastic change.

(4) Organizations are becoming extended enterprises.

(5) There is an increasing concern about the environmental performance and reporting practices.

It is no longer possible to ignore the needs of the society and quite appropriately, management education must address new areas of interest. In light of this, issues concerning protection, conservation and management of physical environment are to be addressed with a view to imparting knowledge, increasing awareness, and developing the required skills to solve the environmental problems.

Conflict between the enterprise and the community or government may result from incompatible values and goals or scarcity of resources. Successful environment management internalizes environmental concern through measures taken at the decision making stage. Environment management is not 'Management of the environment' it is the management of activities within tolerable constraints imposed by the government with full consideration of ecological factors. Environment management also includes the preparation of plans and legal evaluation of administrative and technical solutions to various environmental problems in terms of both preventive and remedial measures, taking into account the multidisciplinary approaches to development.

Environment management covers functions designed to facilitate comprehensive planning that takes into account the side effects of man's activities and thereby protects and improves the human environment for the present and future generations (United Nations—1972). Thus the study of environment management covers the conscious and planned efforts and activities undertaken by the government departments and agencies to minimize damages to the environment and measures undertaken to regulate the ongoing activities in different areas. The impact of environment management decisions are:

A. The enterprise and the community are part of one system.
B. Good environment management decisions reached are balanced solutions for the enterprise as well as the community.
C. Sound environment management, which is cost effective since it achieves higher productivity that increases work force motivation.
D. Environment management a series of compromises using limited resources to achieve multiple goals.

Sustainable Development—A Remedy

The issue of environment and sustainable development is certainly on the top of global agenda. While environment and related problems have been discussed by expert over a decade, the concept of sustainable development was popularized by the Brundtland Commission Report in 1987 and later by the Rio declaration in 1992 in the present era of rapid urbanization, over population and unabated industrial growth all around the world, a constant need a shift focus from development to sustainable development has repeatedly been felt.

Sustainable development stands for sustainability and it represents an approach to development which is concerned with such fundamental human concerns like poverty, environment, equality, democracy development and peace. The term sustainable development was coined by Barbara ward, the founder of the international institute for environment and development.

The concept of sustainable development broadly means that the development initiatives be initiated in such a way that the future generation can enjoy the benefits of nature without any comprise.

Sustainable development is also often defined as development that improves health care, education and social well being, which is necessary for economic development. Human resource development report, 1991 of the United Nations Development Programme says "Men, women and children must be the centre of attention with development woven around people not people around development".

In 1992, the United Nations Conference on environment development in Rio-de Janeiro, the earth summit called for sustainable development, "to ensure socially responsible economic development while protecting the resources base and the environment for the benefit of future generation.

In the words of Robber Repetto "Sustainable development is development strategy that managers all natural resources and human resources as well as financial and physical assets for increasing long term wealth and well-being.

Definitions of sustainable development are increasingly stressing that development must be participatory and must involve local people in decisions that affect their lives. It also requires transformation of the technological base of industrial civilization, requiring new technology which is cleaner, more efficient, requiring fewer natural resources. Sustainable development is thus that process of economic development which aims at maintaining the quality of life of both present and future generations without harming natural resources and environment. In short it is the process of development which can be sustained over a long period of time without causing fall in the quality of life of future generations.

The important elements in the attempt to achieve sustainability have been on regulation, consumer awareness, company's solution of end of pipe problems, and company's green product development. The government of each country has developed guiding principles of sustainability from the Stockholm conference. The United Nations have given impetus to these Stockholm principles by providing the agenda 21 through the Earth Summit at Rio in 1992.

Implications of Sustainable Development

- The development work undertaken by a state must be related not only to the present but also to the future. That is, the decision makers should keep it in their view that today's development does not become a disaster for tomorrow.
- Development work should be total or comprehensive. That is, while undertaking development in one direction; other directions must also to be taken into account.
- The development work of a state should keep in view its effect on other countries. Thus no state has the right to make its development at the cost of the interest of other countries.

The concept of sustainable development good and sound economic growth, that can be maintained with minimum environmental impact. The factors that can promote sustainable development are the following:

- Population stabilization and health care

- Integrated land use planning and watershed management
- Re-vegetating marginal land and greening the uncultivated area
- Air pollution control in industrial pockets
- Water pollution control in rivers
- Use of non-polluting renewable energy
- Waste recycling and reuse
- Conservation of Biological diversity
- Human settlement without congestion
- Environmental education and awareness

Environmental Ethics and Corporate World

"A decision is right when it tends to preserve the integrity, stability and beauty of the biotic community. It is wrong when it tend to be otherwise" this is how Aldo Leopold, a naturalist, defined environment ethic. The birth of environmental ethic as a force is partly a result of our concern for our own long term survival as well as our realization that humans are but one form of life and that we should share the earth with our fellow human beings. One of the first to recognize the degradation of the environment and to voice the concern for nature was Henry David Thoreau, the well known American writer and naturalist.

Environmental ethics deals with the following topics genetic engineering, cloning, resource allocation, animals and vegetarianism, air and water pollution, radiation, ozone crisis and global warming, population and environment, econ-feminism, indigenous peoples, and spiritually and the environment.

Environment ethics is a subject without definition and without consensus. And yet, every person on this planet makes everyday decisions that relate to environmental ethics. Questions as simple as "what should I eat?" or "How should I move from place to place?" all raise environmental and ethical issues. Environmental ethics is very recent as an academic discipline and there is much to be studied and acted upon. The need for an environmental ethic is however, critical. Classical ethics has always been concerned with relations between humans, and only recently has it been accepted that we have some obligations towards the non-human world. This ethic is very selective and does not extend to such lower animals as bugs or bacteria, not to mention plants. We recognize our duty to preserve wilderness areas for aesthetic enjoyment and scientific study and to conserve resources for future generations, but we do not treat a tree with same respect as we do to a human.

We believe that we should care about non-human life and the natural environment, not for our selfish personal ends but because it seems to be the right thing to do. But there seems to be no ethical theory that explains this attitude. Perhaps the solution to these problems lies in expanding the moral community. If we can include animals and the environment generally in our moral community, perhaps we can lean how to treat them ethically. Environmental ethics that does not bother to find reasons for preserving 'non-living' Nature should review its position.

In a reverse way, in the case of problems of pollution, it is not a question of taking something out but putting something in—sewage, chemical, radioactive and heat wastes into water, noxious and dangerous fumes into the air, and distracting and unpleasant advertising sings into the line of sight.

Environmental Law

The Stockholm conference was the beginning of the awakening of national consciousness on environmental issues in India. The Bhopal Gas Tragedy gave the real impetus to this issue. Though Air Act and the Water Act were already in existence, the Environment protection act enacted only in 1986 as a response to the gas tragedy, which created a nation wide uproar.

The relationship between economic development and environmental degradation was first placed on the international agenda in 1972, at the UN conference on the Human Environment, held in Stockholm. By 1983, when the UN set up the World Commission on Environment and Development, environmental degradation, which had been seen as a side effect of industrial wealth with only a limited impact, was understood to be a matter of survival for developing nations.

The Rio convention Governments—108 represented by heads of state or governments—adopted three major agreements aimed at changing the traditional approach to development. They were:

1. Agenda 21—a comprehensive programme of action for global action in all areas of sustainable development.
2. The Rio Declaration on environment and development—a series of principles defining the rights and responsibilities of states.
3. The statement of Forest principles—a set of principles to emphasize the sustainable management of forests worldwide.

In addition, two legally binding conventions aimed at preventing global climate change and the eradication of diversity of biological species were opened for signature at the summit, giving high profile to these efforts:

- The United Nations frame work convention on climate change.
- The convention of Biological diversity.

The rise in the awareness of environmental degradation due to the impact of modern industrial development in the 1970s brought a major change in the perceptions at the national and regional levels. The new 'environmental establishments' include many significant non-governmental organizations formed to voice public concern. India responded to environmental problems, which dates back to April 1972, when the Prime Minster, Smt. Indira Gandhi, established a National Committee on Environmental Planning and Coordination (NCEPC).

Environmental protection and improvement were explicitly incorporated into the constitution by the constitution (42nd Amendment) Act of 1976. Article 51A (g) in a new chapter entitled 'Fundamental Duties' imposes a similar responsibility on every citizen 'To protect and improve the natural environment'. Article 253 states notwithstanding anything in the foregoing provisions of this chapter, parliament has power to make any law.

As environment regulation grew more stringent and its enforcement became more vigorous, industrial challenge to agency action is likely to increase. Although there are over 200 central statues that have some bearing on environmental protection. In India, the environmental debate was set in motion in the parliament on August 11, 1980 under the title of 'Rape of Earth', led by the Minister of Environment, Shri Dig Vijay Singh. An integrated department called 'Department of Environment, forest and Wildlife' in the Ministry of Environment and Forest came into being with effect from September 25, 1985. Minimal National Standards for pollution discharges from specific industries have been formulated and control measures implemented in a phased manner. About % of the large and medium industries in the country have so far installed pollution control devises.

Environment Protection Act, 1986

Under the act, the Central Government has been vested with powers of entering and inspecting any place through any person or agency authorized by it. After a review of the existing legislation on Environment, the Environment Protection Act, 1986 has been legislated to plug the gaps and to provide a single focus for environmental issues. The Central enactments—Water (Prevention and Control Pollution) Act, 1974 and the Air (Prevention and Control of Pollution) Act, 1981—have been reviewed extensively and suitably amended to make the provisions more effective. The government agencies have generally adopted three major functions. These are:

1. Policy formulation
2. Policy implementation
3. Policy Enforcement

Although it embodies the colonial polices of the pre-independence era, the Forest Act of 1927 remains in force. This act consolidates, with minor changes, the provisions of the Indian Forest Act of 1878 and it's amending Acts. The Wildlife (Protection) Act, 1972, clearly states that the main objective is to protect the wild animals and birds, particularly rare species.

After the Bhopal Gas Tragedy and supreme courts' judgment in the ShriRam Gas Leak Case, the 1987 amendment to the Factories act introduced special provisions on hazardous industrial activities. The 1987 amendment empowers the states to appoint site appraisal committees to advice on the initial location of factories using hazardous processes.

The Atomic Energy Act of 1962 and the Radiation Protection Rules of 1971 govern the regulation of nuclear energy and radioactive substances in India. Under the act, the Central Government is required to prevent radiation hazards, guarantee public safety and the safety of workers handling radioactive substances, and ensure the disposal of radioactive wastes.

The Insecticides Act 1968 was decided to implement the recommendations of the Kerala and Madras Food-poisoning cases inquiry commission, which inquired into several deaths from insecticides-contaminated food in April and May 1958. The act established a Central Insecticides Board to advise the Centre and the state on technical aspects of the act.

In 1972, Parliament enacted the Wildlife Act pursuant to the enabling resolutions of 11 states under article 252(1) of the constitution. The act provides for state wildlife advisory boards, regulations for hunting wild animals and bird, establishment of sanctuàries and national parks, regulations for trade in animal products and trophies, and judicially imposed penalties for violating the act.

The Water Act of 1974 was the culmination of over a decade of discussion and deliberation between the Centre and the states. The history and the preamble of the water act suggest that only state governments can enact water pollution legislation.

Alarmed at India's rapid deforestation and the resulting environmental degradation, the Central Government enacted the Forest (Conservation) Act in 1980. As amended in 1988, the act requires the approval of the Central Government before a state 'deserves' a reserved forest, uses forest land for non-forest purposes.

In the wake of the Bhopal Gas Tragedy, the Government of India enacted the Environment (Protection) Act of 1986 under Article 253 of the Constitution. The purpose of the act is to implement the decisions of the United Nations Conference on the Human Environment of 1972.

Industrial Response for Environment

Environmental issues and concerns are common to all sectors and all activities. If the deterioration continues, the whole system of life will be thrown out of gear. United Nations Environment (UNECP) programme was designed to be "the environmental conscience of the United Nations". The major focus for UNECP has been the study of ways to encourage sustainable development-increasing standards of living without destroying the environment. A growing number of international agreements have been reached in an effort to improve the world's environmental status. Standards are prominent means for direct regulation of environmental quality in most of the developed world. They are:

1. Ambient Environmental quality standard
2. Effluent or emission standard
3. Technology-based standard
4. Performance standard
5. Product standard
6. Process standard
7. Permits and licence

Industrial units are required to obtain from the concerned state pollution control board consent to operate the unit. Such consent is subject to the unit complying with the prescribed standards.

Environment Policy in Coca-Cola

The Coca-Cola India is in the business of beverages that refresh people. It will carry out its operations in ways that Protect, Preserve and Enhance the Environment. Its activities are guided by Coca-Cola eKOsystem, which provides a framework to transform this principle in actions. Towards this objective, it shall endeavour to:

- Establish, maintain and operate facilities to comply with all applicable Environmental Safety and Health laws, Statutes and Consents.
- Formulating sound environmental objectives and targets and integrate a continuous process review in all essential elements of corporate management.
- Conservation of natural resources specifically in water, energy and fuel by continually improving its usage and reducing wastage.
- Working as catalyst to enhance collection of post consumer PET bottles through awareness programmes and synergizing relevant agencies for getting better pricing to the consumer.

- Seek co-operation with Public, Private and Governmental Organizations in identifying solutions to relevant environmental issues.
- Advertising initiatives are to be critically evaluated while advertising in eco-senstive areas; not put advertisement on Historical Monuments, Religious, Political Buildings and Structures and other specially protected and sensitive areas.
- Using cooling equipment with environment friendly technologies.
- Managing fleet operations in a manner to minimize environmental impacts by ensuring good maintenance, improving and tracking fuel efficiency and effectively managing wastes.
- Ensuring procurement policies that consider the environmental impact of packaging materials and all direct and indirect process aids used within the operation.
- Ensuring all operations implement eKO Management System and requirements under ISO 14001 before December 2004.

Environment Policy in Hero Honda

Hero Honda is committed to demonstrate excellence in its environmental performance on a continual basis, as an intrinsic element of its corporate philosophy. To achieve this it commits itself to:

- Integrate environmental attributes and cleaner production in all our business processes and practices with specific consideration to substitution of hazardous chemicals, where viable and strengthen the greening of supply chain;
- Continue product innovations to improve environmental compatibility;
- Comply with all applicable environmental legislation and also controlling our environmental discharges through the principles of 'alara' (as low as reasonably achievable);
- Institutionalize resource conservation, in particular, in the areas of oil, water, electrical energy, paints and chemicals;
- Enhance environmental awareness of our employees and dealers/ vendors, while promoting their involvement in ensuring sound environmental management;

It will communicate this policy to all its employees and would make it available to interested parties. In 1989, the Institute of Petroleum Safety, Health and Environment Management (IPSHEM) were established with the objective of promoting standards of safety, health and environment in petroleum sector in India. The Institute is committed to upgrade and develop human resources with a view to minimize the overall risk to human life, damage to property, process and the environment.

1. Environment Monitoring—offshore and onshore.
2. Ambient Air Quality Monitoring
3. Environment Baseline Data Generation
4. Environment Auditing
5. Environment Impact Assessment (EIA)
6. Environment Database
7. Oil Spill Modelling
8. Environment Management Plan (EMP)

Environment Policy in ONGC

The development activities of the ONGC have planned on sound ecological principle and must incorporate appropriate environmental safeguards.

1. Environmental impact assessment, with the details required by the 'Department of Environment' has prepared at the earliest stage of project formulation and necessary financial provisions for various environmental programme and safeguards are indicated in the project estimates.
2. Environmental norms prescribed by the Central and state government, statutorily empowered to do so, in the matter of air and water quality, noise, land use, afforestation etc. has strictly observed in the design, construction and operation of all facilities of the corporation.
3. The widest possible range of information on practical options available for the design of the project has gathered and analyzed for final decision making technology that ensures energy economy, environmental safeguards, recycling of resources and utilization of wastes should be adopted for all projects.
4. Releases of hydrocarbons, chemicals and other materials would be controlled so that it does not disturb the flora and fauna. Releases containing viruses, pathogenic bacteria and parasites, which survive in marine life, would be completely eliminated and precluded from entering marine waters.
5. Productivity of the environment adjacent to the project areas and resource of the coastal waters should not be adversely affected. No action harmful to the potential for marine resources such as

fish, salt, corustacea, etc. should be permitted. Coastal marine areas should not be subjected to unplanned salutation, erosion, changes in flow pattern and coastal contours.

6. Microbiological activity of significance to marine and estuarine life and people dependent on the coastal waters has fully protected.
7. Aesthetic, cultural and social patterns and historical characteristics of the areas covered by or adjacent to the ONGC's prefects should not be unduly disturbed by the project activities. Scenic landscapes, historical heritage and cultural monuments should be preserved and the environment around them should be kept clean and hygienic.
8. As far as possible, a minimum area of 500 metres from the high tide mark in respect of coastal projects located near river banks should be kept clear of all structures so that beach activities or river front development are not adversely affected.
9. Effective mechanisms for monitoring the environment and for collection of the required data of various parameters of the environment for the purposes of surveillance should be set up within each project.
10. Work environment in the operational areas should be conducive to safe and healthy working conditions. Good housekeeping is an integral part of sound environmental management.

Promoting a healthy, safe, productive, and aesthetically satisfying environment is the responsibility of ONGC.

Environment Policy in Tata Steel

Tata Steel reaffirms its commitment to provide safe working place and clean environment to its employees and other stakeholders as an integral part of its business philosophy and values. We will continually enhance our Environmental, Occupational Health and Safety (EHS) performance in our activities, products and services through a structured EHS management framework. Towards this commitment, it will:

1. Establish and achieve EHS objectives and targets;
2. Ensure compliance with applicable EHS legislation and other requirement and go beyond;
3. Conserve natural resources and energy by constantly seeking to reduce consumption and promoting waste avoidance and recycling measures;
4. Eliminate, minimize and/or control adverse environmental impacts and occupational health and safety risks by adopting appropriate

'state-of-the-art' technology and best EHS management practices at all level sand functions.

5. Enhance awareness, skill and competence of our employees and contractors so as to enable them to demonstrate their involvement, responsibility and accountability for sound EHS performance.

Environment Policy in Ranbaxy

Caring for the Environment is a core corporate value and as a part of this commitment. The Company enunciated its EHS policy in 1993. The Company's EHS policy provides for the creation of a safe and healthy workplace and a clean environment for employees and the community. It aims at higher international standards in plant design, equipment selection, maintenance and operations. The policy seeks to manufacture products safely and in an environmentally responsible manner. The implementation of the EHS Policy is ensured by institutionalizing a robust EHS Management system, adequately supported by well defined organizational structure.

As a part of EHS processes at the corporate level, besides laying down guidelines on systems, policy and training, the corporate EHS office monitors compliance, maintains and disseminates information on laws and regulations. EHS performance review meetings are held on regular basis to monitor the progress against agreed EHS improvement plans. Close cooperation between all units and individuals is the key to maintaining high standards of environment protection and safety in all the plants.

The key processes at location level comprise of regular safety surveillance, inspections and audits, Permit to work system for operational/maintenance safety, Fire prevention and protection activities, operation of the ETP/Incinerator, disposal activities related to hazardous wastes, regular monitoring of the environment internally and also through approved laboratories. Monthly reports address EHS initiatives, compliance and various records under the statutory requirement, training of employees including contract employees on EHS awareness, interaction with the residential associations/nearby community etc., celebration of National safety day, fire day, and Environment day etc. for EHS awareness among employees.

The manufacturing facilities for bulk drugs and dosage forms comply with the stringent requirements of Good Manufacturing Practices (GMP) and Good Laboratory Practices (GLP) and are approved by International health and regulatory Agencies like FDA—USA, MCA—UK, WHO etc. These practices and approvals ensure that an effective framework is always in place, not only for manufacture of high quality products, but also for effective use of resources and reduction of wastes as well as high safety and hygiene standards.

Ranbaxy has made significant improvements in process safety of the existing manufacturing facilities by providing extensive instrumented safety protection systems. The intended safety features are incorporated in the basic design of the new projects.

Investments have been made on process improvements as well as effluent treatment plant up-gradation using the latest membrane based technology, multi-effect thermal evaporation system and state-of-the-art Incinerator. These investments have helped to reduce discharges of contaminants into the environment. With the facilities installed at Toansa for recycling of the treated effluent, the site has achieved the status of 'zero discharge site'.

The Company also engages with the concerned authorities and industry in devising responsible laws, regulations and standards and thus making safety, occupational health and environmental information and expertise available to its employees and the community at large. Ranbaxy has made EHS concerns and practices a necessary factor in appraising its employee performance.

Recognition of the safety and environmental performance came through a number of prestigious awards during the last year. National Safety Award by Ministry of Labour and Employment for 'Lowest Average Weighted Frequency Rate', Greentech Environment Excellence—Silver Award in Pharmaceutical sector and National Award for 'Excellence in Energy Management' as an 'Excellent Energy Efficient Unit' for the Toansa Plant, were amongst them.

Environmental Accounting

Environmental Accounting is an attempt to identify and bring to light the resources exhausted and costs imposed on the environment by a business unit without considering these facts, maintaining accounts and interpreting the results there of may give a dubious picture of the business corporation. There is an increasing need for accounting for the environment and the economy in an integrated way because of the crucial functions that the environment plays in economic performance and in the generation of human welfare. Therefore, it is a primary responsibility of every citizen of the planet especially corporate citizen to evolve a system of accounting to record that benefits and costs rendered by environment to a business corporation and costs and the benefits tendered to environment by a business corporation and justifying these costs and benefits are large constituents of environmental accounting. The objectives of environmental accounting.

- Taking the total stock of assets or resources related to environmental issues, and changes therein.

- Estimation of the total expenditure on protection or enhancement of environment,.
- To identify that part of gross domestic product which reflect the costs necessary to compensate for the negative impact of economic growth, i.e. the so called defensive expenditure to protect environment?
- Assessment of Environmental costs and benefits.
- Elaboration and measurement of indicators, relating to environmentally adjusted product and income.

Much of the use of environmental accounts has been in industrialized countries, especially Europe, Australia and Canada. The asset accounts are complied by most countries, but not used very much in assessing sustainability. Sustainability can only be measured if all assets are included. Including natural capital as part of a country's is an important step towards better measure of sustainability. However, most countries do not include all environmental capital, or all the environmental goods and services that natural capital provides.

A responsible behaviour pattern from the part of the industrial unit will involve regular review and audit of the following environmental issues:

- Assessment, control and reduction of environmental impact.
- Resource management, including water.
- Waste avoidance, recycling, reuse, transportation and disposal
- Evaluation, control and reduction of noise.
- Prevention and limitation of environmental accidents.
- Information and training of staff on environmental issues.
- External information on environmental issues.

Responsible environmental management reporting does take place through the company's annual reports. Though the reporting practices are restricted to large companies, it is interesting to see the level of identification that is taking place in the company and the extent of owning the responsibility. Though it may still take a few years for companies to look at themselves strategically on the extent of environmental management practices, the search has begun in Indian companies. Though it is difficult to quantify anything from the statements, it does tell you that the environmental processes are in place in the company, and the company is keen on declaring itself as an eco-friendly company. It is always possible to get detailed reports from the companies. Some of these companies have also gone ahead to certify them for the ISO Environment Management.

Conclusion

Finding for environmental protection is the best way for a nation to avoid the need for costly environmental regulations. The Environmental ethics is new and, like the vital issues, it will undergo transformation as new data are made available and we are able to interpret rationally and live with nature. Education of the public to environmental problems and solutions is of prime importance. Recognizing that environmental ethic alone is not enough, we must all live the environmental ethical way. We must also recognize the power of nature and feel humble in the realization that we are just a very small part in a wonderful and still mysterious system.

REFERENCES

"Environmental Management" by Bala Krishnamoorthy PHI Private Ltd. New-Delhi 2005.

"Business and Society: Ethics and Stakeholder Management" by Carroll, A.B. South-Western: Cincinnati Ohio, 1992.

Downs, A., Ups and Downs with Ecology: The 'Issue Attention cycle' The Public Interest, 1972.

Passmore, J., Man's Responsibility to Nature, 2nd Ed., Duckworth, London, 1980.

Rene, Dubos "A Theology of the Earth,:" A lecture reprinted in Western Man and Environmental Ethics, Barbour, I.G Ed. Reading, Addison – Wesley, Mass., 1973.

"Environmental Accounting Linkages with Management Control Systems" Dr.Heera Sunil Oza. The Management Accountant, June 2005

Self-organizing Complexity, Conscious Purpose and Sustainable Development—Ernest Garcia Environment and Global Modernity.

"Sustainable Development" by Dinesh Arora by Third Concept, April 2004.

"Integrated Approach to Sustainable Development" by B.C Bose –Rajat Pbulication 2001 New-Delhi.

"Environment and Development" edited by M.S Rathore Ravat Publication, 1996, Jaipur and New Delhi.

"Economic Growth and Environment" by Dr. Mrs. S Murthy RBSA Publishers, Jaipur.

"Issues in Environmental Accounting and Reporting" by Dr. A Banerjee, Indian Journal of Accounting, June 1999.

Concerned websites on Environment.

15

Capacity Building for Effective Local Governance

Indian Perspectives

— Mr. Sangappa Hosmani

ABSTRACT

Local governance is being promoted in India because it is believed that it provides a structural arrangement through which local people and communities can participate in the fight against poverty at close range. However, it is acknowledged that various capacities of a multiplicity of stakeholders and actors need to be strengthened to meet the requirements of effective and responsive local governance. As we know that the most vibrant democratic institution at the grassroots level in India is Panchayati Raj Institutions (PRIs) which is figured to be participatory, accountable, responsive, and transparent and citizen friendly local self-government. The 73rd and 74th Constitutional Amendments provided the constitutional provisions for constructing and operating of such bodies at the local level in India. Some of these provisions are inclusive and democratic in nature such as one-third reservation of seats for women and schedule castes and tribes (dalits) and decentralization of power etc. But the nature of functioning of these bodies for last few years exposed ineffectiveness and inefficiency in governance and delivering of services to the local people. The effective local self-governance indeed is still a distant dream and needs enormous interventions to realize its potential. This dream can possibly be realized by the way of comprehensive understanding of capacity building in terms of governance. This chapter discusses a comprehensive meaning of capacity building, issues and challenges related to capacity building for effective local governance in India. It also attempts to view Panchayati Raj Institutions (PRIs) as institutions of local self-governance and not as mere implementers of centrally determined development programmes.

Keywords: Participatory, Transparent, Governance, Responsive Accountable etc.

Introduction

After the independence the Indian state offered a democratic form of governance to its citizen by adopting the Constitution in 1950. The Constitution enshrined a host of rights to the Indian citizenry along with a federal structure of the government. The Constitution since its adoption has undergone several Amendments to incorporate many significant social and political requirements of the contemporary society. The 73rd and the 74th Constitutional Amendments brought in 1993 provided the Constitutional framework for constituting democratically elected governance mechanisms at the local level. The provisions in these Amendments have some far reaching implications with respect to democratic governance and local development. By providing one-third reservation for women and proportionate reservation for other socially excluded and deprived sections (tribals, dalits etc.), the Constitutional framework for local governance mechanisms in India has enormous potential for affirmative action. One of the most important roles for these local governance institutions is to plan for local development and ensure social justice in consistence with the citizens' needs and aspirations.

Objectives of the Study

The objectives of the study are as follows:

(*i*) To view Panchayati Raj Institutions (PRIs) as institutions of local self-governance and not as mere implementers of centrally determined development programmes.;

(*ii*) To give emphasis on bottom-up comprehensive planning based on micro-planning;

(*iii*) To emphasis on active participation in decision making by women and other weaker sections with a view to enhance their role, status and leadership in local self-governance;

(*iv*) To assert PRIs' access to and control over local natural and human resources as well as other development resources being available with state and national governments;

(*v*) To strengthening PRIs' roles, systems of governance, accountability and transparency and inter linkages.

Need of the Study

The experience of functioning of these local bodies in the past 10 years in India makes it clear that effective local self governance is still a distant dream and requires enormous interventions to realize its potential. This is particularly so because such democratic decentralization is coming after nearly 50 years of centralization in the state machinery, public resources and bureaucratic structures. As a result, hierarchies of government departments and agencies have generated vested interests and exercise their responsibility to apply public resources in an unaccountable manner. On the other hand, nearly five decades of state led model of development delivered from the top has created a sense of passive dependence on government agencies, programmes and resources among citizens in rural and urban areas. As a result, there is a need of the study in this area to have an organized system of governance at the local level.

Framework of Capacity Building

There is a lack of consensus on the meaning of capacity. Capacity as a multi-dimensional aspect consists of awareness, knowledge, skill, self-confidence and actions. Capacity in this context can be defined as the totality of inputs needed by an actor to realize its purposes. Applied to local bodies, this will ensure that such institutions are able to function effectively as institutions of local self-governance in the perspective elaborated above.

Capacity of such institutions can be seen in three distinct though inter-related aspects:

(i) *Intellectual Capacity* implies capacity to think, reflect and analyze reality independently and in pursuit of self-defined purposes of local self-governance.

(ii) *Institutional Capacity* includes procedures, systems, structure, staffing, decision-making, transparency and accountability, planning, implementation and monitoring. It also includes mechanisms for building linkages with other institutions and actors.

(iii) *Material Capacity* consists of material resources, physical assets, funds, systems and procedures to mobilize revenues; access and control over physical and natural resources and infrastructure; systems and procedures required for adequate management of funds and such infrastructure.

Viewed in the above sense, capacity building comprises consistent training of individuals (involved in local governance) for organizational strengthening, institutional learning, exposure, horizontal sharing and solidarity. Capacity building is also a long-term process of strengthening a local body based on systematic learning of new knowledge, skills and attitudes. This can be expected only in the system of democratic decentralization that offers opportunities for popular participation, improved accountability, responsiveness and transparency of local bodies, increased effectiveness and efficiency of government service. In other words capacity building approach as described here, comprises of a broad set of interventions which promotes the development of competent, responsive and accountable local self-government, the establishment of mechanisms by which different population group can equally participate in local decision making process and evolution of civil society players and organization.

Local Governance

Governance is a multifaceted compound situation of institutions, systems, structures, processes, procedures, practices, relationships, and leadership behaviour in the exercise of social, political, economic, and managerial/ administrative authority in the running of public or private affairs. Good governance is the exercise of this authority with the participation, interest, and livelihood of the governed as the driving force. Local governance therefore refers to the exercise of authority at local community level.

Capacity Building of Gram Sabha as Civil Society

Effective functioning of local self-governance requires decentralization of policies, strategies, legal frameworks, programmes and activities, the transfer of authority, responsibilities and resources from Central Government to local government structures and the empowerment of grass-root communities which enable them to determine plan, manage and implement their socio-politico-economic development. It also needs active, engaged and organized citizenry. But in reality, the families and communities have been increasingly divided on the basis of caste, religion, ethnicity and gender in our society. The marginalized (women, dalits and tribals) sections of the community are systematically excluded from political participation by rural elites (higher caste) in support with local authority and strong patriarchal system. Therefore the most significant involvement needed is to strengthen Gram Sabha as contemporary civil society formation in each village. Capacity enhancement interventions at this level demand an appreciation of the collective identity of Gram Sabha. A strong Gram Sabha also requires institutional mechanism to function effectively, effective conduct of periodical Gram Sabha meetings for development, planning and implementation of policies and programmes and collective decision-making in common public good. Large scale Pre-Election Voters Awareness Campaigns (PEVAC) can be organized in partnership with other voluntary organizations, State Election Commission and local bureaucracies and Massive educational interventions on various aspects of election including how to cast votes through street plays, street meetings, and distribution of posters, pamphlets etc. to make the common people a well informed electorate..

After the election, series of orientation meetings explaining the roles of Gram Sabha as a collective entity, discussing problems and issues and identifying needs and priorities of the people shall be organized. These orientation meetings also serve the purpose of initiating dialogue between various marginalized groups and elected representatives of PRIs (Gram Panchayat.

However, in most cases citizens particularly the marginalized are not aware about dates and places of such meetings. The very first step of participation—attendance in the decision making meetings have been purposefully obstructed by the vested power lobbies in the villages. In many places campaigns are organized to inform the local citizens before the actual Gram Sabha meetings. Informational and educational materials (like posters, handbills, leaflets, brochures etc.), folk performances (like folk songs, street plays, mimes etc.), video film shows and rallies can be extensively used to inform about Gram Sabha meetings to the local citizens. Recently, Panchayat Resource Centres (PRCs) have been created to access information from the government departments regarding various development schemes and resources and circulate the same to the members of Gram Sabha and Gram Panchayat.There are many informal local community based associations in the villages. Some of them are traditional associations based on caste or kinship, cultural-religious associations, and many new associations like self-help-groups, Mahila Mandals (women's groups), youth groups, village education committee, forest protection committee, watershed committee, etc. formed by government or NGO development programmes. A significant aspect of strengthening local demand system is to build the capacity of these traditional and contemporary local associations. For which, series of orientation meetings with these community based organizations, specially designed training and workshops on variety of issues and themes (like structure and functions of PRIs, Role of Gram Sabha, Participatory Micro Planning, Community-based Monitoring, Roles of Citizen Leadership, Group Formation and Management, Self Development etc.) can be conducted on regular basis. This enables the traditional and contemporary local associations to work collectively with the Gram Panchayat and the Gram Sabha.Pre-Election Voters Awareness Campaign and Panchayati Raj Jagrukta Abhiyan and Joint workshops, seminars, symposiums and research projects with academic institutions can be organized in partnership with local voluntary organizations to work with local self-governance. Finally there is a vast arena of public education for society at large so that different individuals and institutions such as the media, academic institutions, youth groups, human rights organizations and others, need to be sensitized and oriented to the challenges faced by local bodies in building their capacities to accomplish their constitutionally mandated purposes.

Capacity Building of Elected Representatives

The elected representatives of Gram Panchayat (numbering between 7-11 members) represent a village or a cluster of villages. In addition, there is a Sarpanch—elected as Chief of Gram Panchayat directly by all members of Gram Sabha. In some ways, this body is the first and most direct representative body of local self-governance.

However, Gram Panchayat as a vehicle for exercising representative leadership with transparency and accountability to Gram Sabha is a distant ideal.

(*i*) To understand the autonomous and basic democratic nature of Gram Panchayat as a collective decision-making body, the most significant step is to focus on preparing collective identity and developing a common perspective and intellectual appreciation of the Gram Panchayat.

(*ii*) Gram Panchayat as transparent and accountable local body includes mechanisms for conducting meetings, preparing minutes, sharing information with Gram Sabha, securing participation and contribution of Gram Sabha, developing participatory micro plans, procedures and systems, effective implementation and monitoring of these plans, securing and mobilizing resources and maintaining transparent systems of financial management, etc. The capacity building intervention at this level also needs to address the question of enhancing the material base of Gram Panchayat to make them financially autonomous and sustainable entities. Capacity enhancement interventions in this area particularly focus on mobilizing local resources from the village.

(*iii*) The most significant interventions in capacity enhancement at this level is required to focus on building individual leadership of each of the elected representatives. This is particularly relevant for women, dalits and tribals. These newly elected leaders are experiencing political participation in public space for the first time in their life. Thus, enhancing their leadership roles requires capacity enhancement in several ways:

(*a*) To access authentic information about the system of local governance, their roles and responsibilities and financial resources available to them (women, dalits and tribals) in audio-visuals, folk forms, etc.

(*b*) To provide opportunities for homogenous groups of women, dalits and tribal to share their experiences and to participate in joint camps and big Sammelan.

(*c*) To learn new skills like how to conduct a meeting, how to prepare minutes, how to prepare village plans, how to manage funds, etc. which can be promoted through training, practical demonstration and hand-holding. Therefore, capacity enhancement interventions aim at individual strengthening and empowerment of new leaders in local governance.

Capacity Building of Elected Representatives on Vertical and Horizontal Linkages

Given different tiers of local bodies, vertical linkages across them and horizontal linkages between different tiers of local bodies and commensurate tiers of local administration are also needed to be strengthened by involving the primary school teachers, village level workers, Aanganwadi (pre-school) workers, multi-purpose health workers, forest guards, etc. According to constitutional provision, all the above-mentioned government functionaries should be accountable to Gram Panchayat. However, this is not a reality anywhere in India so far. Gram Panchayat needs to learn how to assert their rights and supervision over the concerned government functionaries and relevant government development programmes and resources. Structured learning opportunities shall be created separately for Gram Panchayat, as well as jointly with concerned government officials and their supervisors.

Another area of horizontal networking is building relationships and support mechanisms with other elected representatives in neighbouring villages, blocks and districts. Capacity building here needs assessment studies for elected representatives to enhance their practical understanding about local governance. In addition, structured educational events on-site support for undertaking participatory micro planning and budgeting exercises, administration and financial management of Gram Panchayat, Informational materials like posters, handbills, manuals in local languages and simplified version of the State Act can be prepared and disseminated among the elected representatives.

Capacity Building of Government Officials

Firstly, orientation and attitudinal change for government officials at all levels has been a major challenge in working with responsive and accountable bureaucracy. A primary vehicle for bringing this about is through civil service training institutions at the district, state and national levels. This may imply improving pedagogy and quality of facilitators in such government civil service training institutions.

Secondly, capacity enhancement for government officials has to do with specific skills that they may need to work with Panchayati Raj Institutions. For example, in the system of top-down development interventions, lowest level government officials have no skill in planning and monitoring since all of that has been centralized. They need to learn skills in promoting micro plans (including budgeting) as well as social audit and community monitoring of implementation of these plans.

Thirdly, partnerships and joint initiatives can be tried out with state and district level government training institutions in providing inputs on preparing and delivering training modules for government officials and Panchayat functionaries. Many multi-stakeholder dialogues can be organized on various development issues in partnership with local government authorities.

Capacity Building of Other Actors

Sensitization and attitudinal changes are also a major arena of capacity enhancement for political leadership at all levels. Barring a few individuals, the political culture in most political parties and among active and elected politicians is one of the disregard for the activities and motivations of ordinary people to take responsibility for village level development. Capacity enhancement interventions are most urgently needed to sensitize and re-orient donors. Despite general discussions, concrete shifts in donor policies, resources and programmes towards strengthening institutions of local governance should be carried out. Carefully selected communication strategies, meetings, dialogues and workshops can be been utilized for such capacity enhancement interventions. The political leaderships shall be invited to participate in many multi-stakeholder dialogues at the district and state levels.

Conclusion

The above description explains the challenges facing effective capacity development for effective local self-governance. Volume of this capacity focuses on promoting participation in local public institutions. Obstacles to such participation are cultural, systemic, institutional and human. As a result, inclusion of the marginalized is a primary challenge of capacity enhancement interventions. Local governance can be made more transparent and accountable to local community only if civil society assertions are coherent and persistent. The interface between strong civil society and effective local governance can be secured more organically if capacity building interventions are properly designed and implemented. Changing attitudes and beliefs are at the very heart of democratic functioning. This implies a culture of dialogue, consultation and consensus building. These values and processes need to be nurtured through sustained capacity enhancement interventions.

REFERENCES

James N. Rosenau: Editor (with Ernst-Otto Czempiel), Governance Without Government: Order and Change in World Politics (Cambridge University Press, 1992)

James N. Rosenau: The Dramas of Political Life: An Introduction to the Problems of Governance (Duxbury, MA: Duxbury Press, 1980).

Rai, Manoj et. al., 2001. The State of Panchayats: A Participatory Perspective; PRIA, New Delhi.

Tandon, Rajesh 2002. Voluntary Action, Civil Society and the State; Mosaic Books, New Delhi.

Tandon, Rajesh and Kaustuv Kanti Bandyopadhyay, 2003. Capacity Building of Southern NGOs: Lessons from International Forum on Capacity Building; PRIA, New Delhi

16

Traditional Institutions Supporting Sustainable Management of Natural Resources in Central Arunachal Pradesh, India

— Mr. Rajiv Mili, Mr. L. Jitendro Singh,
Mr. Prasanna. K. Samal and Mr. Mihin Dollo

ABSTRACT

Traditional communities living in the margin of the forest are extensively dependent on natural resources for their livelihood sustenance. Earlier, it was believed that the resource management systems of tribal communities were unsustainable and unscientific. However, recent research findings have proved that traditional ecological practices are efficient and practical management options towards sustainable development. Roles played by the Traditional Village Institutions have been recognized by the governmental agencies through appointing village head 'Gaon Burah' and also by giving emphasis on codification of customary practices into formal laws as well as enactment of Scheduled Tribes and Other Traditional Forest Dwellers (Recognition of Forest Rights) Act, 2006. These informal customary norms and practices have evolved with specific socio-culture, and suited to local ecological setting. A survey was conducted during 2006-2009 in order to investigate the efficient and sustainable natural resources management systems of Adi community, a major and dominant tribe comprising of numerous sub-tribes, inhabiting the central part of the bio-culturally hotspots region of Arunachal Pradesh in Eastern Himalaya. The community has distinct land use system called Patat, which is a unique ecological design to sustain the crop productivity, as well as to meet fodder demands and other ethno-bioresource needs for livelihood sustenance. Across the study villages, 83 numbers of patches (Patat) have been recorded. Of that, 5 are maintained as bamboo groves, 7 patches for grazing land (Lurang) and rest are used for agricultural purpose. The efficient management of Patats through village Institutions helps in maintaining adequate fallow period of nearly 14-34 years that sustains the agro-ecosystem by recuperating soil nutrients. Traditional institutions, Kebang and others such as Asi Among Committee, Dosing Social Welfare Committee (DSWC) etc. are playing pivotal role in managing natural resources. The present study highlights the traditional institutions and their role in sustainable natural resource management among Adi community in central Arunachal Pradesh.

Key words: Adi community, Patat, Lurang, Bamboo groves, Kebang, DSWC, Customary practice.

Introduction

The north eastern region of India is well acknowledged for its high biological and cultural diversities. The region harbours huge potential of forest based natural resources that include numerous endemic wild flora and fauna of conservation interest, varieties of indigenous crops and livestock, which sustain the livelihood of upland ethnic communities as well as provides ecological services to lowland inhabitants. Geo-culturally the region has been occupied mostly by the ethnic communities comprises of 130 major tribes and 300 sub/minor tribe with varied cultural identities. Since time immemorial, these ethnic communities are living in close association with nature that makes them rich in knowledge of utilization, management and conservation of the natural resources. They are not only the custodian but also the bio-ecological managers of natural resources (Hore, 2005; Bisht, *et.al.* 2007; Mili *et. al.,* 2007). The community manages these resources with their age-old traditional ecological knowledge (TEK) which has been acquired from their ancestor with thousands of trial and error practices (Singh, *et.al.* 2007; Gupta 2007). They have unique management practices and strategies, which have been governed by traditional institutions through various traditional laws and customary practices. Owing to the importance of the traditional institutions in management regimes, researches in recent past lean back on the traditional ecological practices as efficient and practical management tools towards sustainable development. Over the years, Traditional Village Institutions have been recognized by the governmental agencies through appointing village head 'Gaon Burah' and also by giving emphasis on codification of customary practices into formal laws as well as enactment of Scheduled Tribes and Other Traditional Forest Dwellers (Recognition of Forest Rights) Act, 2006. These informal customary norms and practices have evolved with specific socio-culture and ecological setting that may help in policy planning and developmental interventions.

Arunachal Pradesh is not only having high ethnic diversity with 26 tribes and 110 sub/minor tribe but also has rich traditional resources conservation practices well managed through diverse Traditional Institutions (TI). TI has been playing a pivotal role over the sustainability of natural resources (Dollo, 2007). The Adis, a major tribe of the state is known for its highly efficient TI (*Kebang*) and rich ecological knowledge relating to sustainable natural resource management and utilization. For example, sustainable utilization of land resources through *patat* system and effective livestock-agriculture management thorough *Lurang* are unique ecological designed developed through informal experimentation by the community. In order to have an understanding of the significance of the Traditional Institutions in the management of resources, a study has been conducted among Adi tribe of Siang belt through documentation of the Traditional Institutions.

The Study Area

The study was conducted in two districts, i.e East Siang and West Siang of Arunachal Pradesh extending between 93.57° to 95.23° E and 27.69° to 29.20° N. Both the districts are bounded in the north by China, east by Upper Siang and Lower Dibang Valley districts, south by Lakhimpur and Dhemaji districts of Assam and west by Upper Subansiri and Lower Subansiri districts of Arunachal Pradesh. The district West Siang covers an area of 8,325 km^2 that has been divided in to 20 circles under 8 Community Developmental Blocks (CDB) in 6 subdivisions (Anon., 2005) having a total population of 1,03,917 where more than three-fourth (79.68%) are living in rural areas. Literacy rate is 49.29% where males are marginally higher (58.83%) compared to females (41.17%). Administratively the district East Siang has been divided in to 12 circles under 4 subdivisions covering a total geographical area of 4,005 km^2. The total population of the district is 87,397 (Anon., 2007) of which 74.86% are living in rural area.

The study site is mountainous terrain forming a part of Eastern Himalaya and comprising of a cross section of foot hill region adjoining ridges. According to agronomic classification five major soil regions that range from alluvial loam to clayey rich organic content have been conceived in this area. It lies in a monsoon region falling within the hot and humid belt of Indian climatic zone. But the region has diverse climatic condition due to varied topographic features. Four seasons have been recorded in the area-Winter season mainly from December to February; Pre monsoon season from March to May; South-Western monsoon mainly confined to June to September and the post monsoon season or the transition period during October and November. The rainfall over the extreme south eastern plains of this area exceeds 400 cm with mean annual rainfall of 250 cm. However, foothill and valley regions experience higher rainfall compared to surrounding mountainous areas.

The temperature of the area varies considerably from place to place, depending upon the elevation and exposure to the sun. December and January are normally the coldest months during which daily mean temperature in the plain in the extreme south is nearly 15°C only. The minimum being 5 to 10°C, and temperature rises rapidly from March onwards and continues to rise till July, after which it remains more or less steady till September. July and August are the warmest months when the daily mean temperature of about 27°C prevails over the plains, while the maximum temperature is in the order of 30°C.

Diverse topographic conditions, varied rainfall and temperature largely influence the natural vegetation of the region, which created different vegetational patterns with huge diversity of flora and fauna. The southern parts of the region are situated in low altitude, and the dominant vegetation types are tropical evergreen and semi-evergreen forests.

The People and Culture

The study site is inhabited by the Adis, normally settled in the central region and constitutes a major tribe in the state of Arunachal Pradesh. They are divided into two broad groups on the basis of some differences in material culture, hair dress and social institutions. These are the Padam-Minyong and the Galo group. The former has been divided in to ten sub/minor groups viz. the Minyongs, Padams, Panggis, Pasis, Ashings, Milangs, Komkars, Shimongs, Karkos and Boris. On the other hand, the Galo group consists of four subgroups viz. the Galos, Pailibos, Ramos and Bokars. Each sub tribe has its own way of migration history in oral form. In recent past the Galos are recognised as a major tribe. They belong to the mongoloid stock and are factual and not philosophical in nature (Nyori, 1993).

The *Dere/Moshup*, community hall is an important traditional social institution of every Adi village. In olden days young boys were given training by their elders on agricultural activities, war techniques and other socio-cultural attributes. Most of the socio-political and religious matters are discussed in *Dere/Moshup*,. Like the boys, the girls had a community hall known as *Rasheng/Risheng* in every village in ancient time. The girls who attain puberty were being trained up by their elders on household activities, weaving, spinning and agricultural activities. In recent past, the importance of community hall (*Rasheng)* is losing value due to influence of modern education and socio-cultural diversification. The Adi community has the system of local-self government system called *Kebang* or the village council. The village council is time-honoured socio-political institution deriving its authority from tradition. The function of the *Kebang* is of three folds i.e judicial, administrative and developmental.

The *Ponung* and *Tapu* are some of the famous dances of the tribe. These dances are simple, rhythmic, colourful and participative. Donyi-Poloism is the main religion of the community. They are clan exogamous and community endogamous (Roy, 1960; Srivastava, 1988; Nyori, 1993). The Solung is the main socio-religious festival of the Adis being observed in village as well as community level on September 1st in every year. Since, agriculture is the mainstay of the community hence, the Solung festival is primarily connected with the agricultural activities of the people (Pathak, 2007). Besides, there are many other important festivals of the community such as Unying, Etor etc.

Methodology

The study was conducted in East Siang and West Siang of Arunachal Pradesh during 2006 to 2008. Preliminary survey was conducted in 27 villages (Table 16.1), while extensive survey has been confined to three circles i.e. Pangin and Boleng circles in East Siang district and Rumgong circle in West Siang district covering four representative villages. All the four villages are inhabited by Adi community. A semi-structured questionnaire was used for generating socio-economic information at the village level. The *Gams* (Village Chief) and elderly persons were interviewed with the help of a translator to trace the origin and historical background of various traditional social institutions and their role in management regimes. Besides, informal discussion and secondary information was gathered from different Line Departments of the state. Secondary literature was consulted from various reports, bulletins and monographs published by central and state Government departments, Universities and other research institutes. To draw out conclusion, extensive field verifications and surveys were conducted across the study villages.

Table 16.1 : Administrative setup and representative villages in the study districts

District (HQ)	Subdivision	Circle	Village	Distance from district h/q
1	2	3	4	5
East Siang (Pasighat)	Boleng	Boleng	Lileng	98 km
			Rengo	100 km
			Dosing	102 km
			Pareng	102 km
		Rebo-Perging	Riew	116 km
		Pangin	Pangin	76 km

(Contd...)

1	2	3	4	5
			Rottung	78 km
			Koreng	50 km
		Riga	Riga	136 km
			Pangkang	140 km
			Parong	117 km
			Sitang	137 km
Upper Siang (Yingkiyong)	Yingkiyong	Yingkiyong	Halleng	7 km
			Shimong	8 km
		Geku	Gabuk	26 km
			Komkar	26 km
			Geku	25 km
West Siang (Along)	Rumgong	Rumgong	Rumgong	66 km
			Jomoh	59 km
			Mopung	61 km
		Kaying	Kaying	45 km
			Kerang	47 km
			Paksin	48 km
		Jomlo Mobuk	Pesing	14 km
			Pangkeng	16 km
			Jomlo Mobuk	17 km
			Roying	19 km

Results and Discussion

Traditional Institutions

The Kebang is a unique socio-cultural and political institution of the Adi community. It is a local self government system that administers day to day affairs of the community. The institution is solely responsible for matters of common interest in the village or community. The Kebang normally looks after the resources of the village, socio-cultural issues that are linked with the village community, political issues like boundary disputes, inter and intra village conflicts resolution etc. The Kebang is governed by a group of elderly people known as Gams, choosen from within the village on the merit of their personal influence and ability to resolve cases in traditional norms (Roy, 1960; Nyori, 1993). Earlier the Gams were known as *Milung* nominated initially based on the activities performed and selected finally when they attain maturity in terms of age and performance. Generally they are selected from each clan. Since the community believes in democracy, every citizen has the equal right to express his or her opinion before the Kebang. No autocracy has known to them and in the absence of a distinct class of nobility, oligracy has remained equally unknown (Roy, 1960). The Kebang is held in community hall locally known as *Dere/Moshup* which is normally located in the centre of the village. The Kebang meetings are conducted under the chairmanship of the senior most gam called Kebang Abu accompanied by the group of gams represented from different clans.

Role of Kebang in Resource Management

Hierarchically, the Kebang has a three tiered structure based on the population size and area occupied (Figure 16.2). The lowermost unit or body is called *Dolung Kebang* (intra village) followed by *Bango Kebang* (inter village or group of councils) and the top most body is the *Bogum Bokang Kebang* (community level). Each category enjoys the right and exercises its duties within its jurisdiction (Figure 16.2). The *Dolung Kebang* regulates the agricultural field selection and distribution, construction of road, community halls and houses in the village etc. The Kebang directs activities according to traditional norms and customary practices of which it is supposed to be repository and it punishes those who violate the rule in any way and looks after welfare and well-being of the village community (Roy, 1960).

The Kebang evolved its own norms and function by allowing the villagers to access natural resources falling within the village jurisdiction, manpower mobilization, efficient sharing of local resources, etc. Kebang's role in equitable distribution of land resource and access to other natural resource as well as conservation efforts not only helped in sustainable management but also help in communal harmony. The villager may use any given plot of forestland on the hill slopes for agricultural purpose only by clearing vegetation. Re-cultivation of the cultivated plot depends entirely on the replenishment of soil fertility through the natural process of regeneration of vegetative cover over a period of time.

Agriculture and Forest Resource Management

Like many other upland communities of north eastern India, the Adis also primarily depend upon agriculture and forest based natural resources for their livelihood. Shifting agriculture locally called *Mopi Arig,* which is the main agricultural practice of the community is being governed by the Kebang. The cultivation practices have well-planned agriculture calendar, which comprises of several steps from plot selection to harvesting and merrymaking activities and in each step the Kebang plays a pivotal role. The Kebang decides and selects the opening of a new agricultural field for current year. After selecting the plot, it has been divided into some smaller blocks and allotted among the families. The villagers clear the selected forest patch together. The remains of logs and branches of trees and other herbaceous flora are allowed to dry for 15 to 20 days and set to fire. The construction of fencing is done before or after the sowing of seeds, which is location specific. Male farmers are involved actively in felling of trees and construction of fencing while females are involved mainly in sowing, weeding, harvesting and carrying. In every step of the cultivation phase, the community performs ritual ceremonies to enhance the agronomic yields by protecting crops from insect-pest and other natural calamities. All these activities are carried out in group, which not only helps in reducing excess labour input but also tremendously helps in maintaining community harmony and integrity.

The Kebang also plays an important role in forest resource management. The forest cover under the village jurisdiction is owned by the individual families or clan, which has been demarcated by putting pointed stone in the peripheral zone. During course of migration the family head had been allotted forest land by the Kebang to nurture their crops and establish settlement under the territory of the Kebang. Gradually those allotted forest lands have now been owned by the individual families or clan who are still under the governance of the Kebang in the case of selling and other resources utilization. It is well acknowledged that the area is full of forest wealth that has the potential to sustain the upland ethnic community. Sustainable utilization of forest wealth is being maintained efficiently by the community under the leadership of the Kebang. For that the Kebang releases strict notice orally, which has to be obeyed by the villagers at any cost. Meanwhile, if anybody found to be violating the Kebang's norms, the violator would be imposed a penalty based on the gravity of the violence. The forest resources such as bamboo, cane, timber, leaves etc. could be extracted sustainably for the household utilization like construction of houses, granaries, bridge and agricultural implements. The income generated from forest resources are used in the construction of community hall, road and bridge, welcome ceremonies of VIP's and guest, community functions like festivals, rituals and other rites.

Other Institutions

Asl Among Committee (AAC) in Rumgong Village

Asi-Among Committee is the governing body to look after the forest resources of the Rumgong village for sustainable utilization and management. Committee permits the villagers for extraction of resources for which a minimum royalty is charged. In exceptional cases, outsiders coming for certain developmental activities may also extract resources from the forest with due permission of the committee and a lump-sum amount is charged based on the size and amount of materials collected. The committee comprises of 10 members at present represented by one individual from each *Kumdang* (lineage). The representative member of the *Kumdang* should be the head of the family staying at the village so that he can contribute and participate in the decision making process of the committee.

Dosing Social Welfare Committee (DSWC) in Rengo Village

Due to increasing pressures on Kebang the villages have founded certain village level social institutions to look after the community resources in village territory and also to support the Kebang. Dosing Social Welfare Committee (DSWC) is one of such kind in Rengo village. The committee was founded in 1984 to look after the natural resources of the villages falling within the Dosing area. A president (*Rutum*) associated with secretary (*Luge Ige bone*), a treasurer (*Murko Rutum*) and all the Gams of the locality constitute the committee with three year tenureship.

Resource extraction and unlawful activities within the jurisdiction of village is strictly regulated by the committee. Royalty is collected for the extraction of resources under the guideline of committee. Penalty is imposed for the violation of committee norms and guidelines particularly in resource extraction and other unlawful activities. The resources can be collected in between *Besing* (December) and *Lobo* (May) month. The common property resources can be accessed sustainably by the villagers only for construction of granaries, houses etc. The committee collects fund from various sources; for example payment for one truck of boulders and sand for Rs.30/, illegal fishing in river i.e Rs. 3000/day, penalty for using thread net Rs.10000/day, use of explosive Rs.20000/Day (on Simang River). On special occasions like well come of visitors, VIPs etc, the villagers are allowed to fishing for 1-2 days from the river Simang. The collected fund is utilized for community functions and ceremonies. Some portions of the collected fund are also used for education of poor students. For example, any student who is qualified for medical or engineering course, he/she may be donated Rs.10000 from the committee. The eligible student may also get loan from the committee without interest for the period of one year. However, he must return the same amount to the committee by the end of the year. A small portion of the fund is used for donating villagers for medical treatment. In such case a villager may get a maximum amount of Rs.10000/ towards medical treatment. Moreover he may also be eligible for getting loan from the society without interest. Villagers may get loan from the society to establish business on compound interest. Outsider may also get loan @20% interest rate from the society. In such case the person must take a guarantor.

Functions of DSWC:

1. The committee looks after the common property resources like bamboo, cane, fire wood, leaves etc. under the village jurisdiction.
2. The committee checks the illegal supply of common property resources from Dosing area.
3. The committee also checks the illegal selling of sand, stones, boulders etc. from Dosing area. However, the resources can be taken with due permission from the committee. For that a minimum payment is made against the person that extracts the resources.

The Patat(s)

The *Patat* is a traditional way of land management, where the land has been divided into numerous patches or blocks for efficient and sustainable utilization in agriculture and other activities maintained by the Adi farmers. As many as 83 such blocks (Table 16.2) have been recorded from four study villages of East Siang and West Siang districts of Arunachal Pradesh of which 60 patches are under operation for cultivation purpose, while rest 23 patches are not used for agricultural purposes. Highest numbers of 27 *patats* have been recorded from Rengo village followed by 25 in Rumgong and lowest of 13 in Pangin village. The management system is quite unique. The cultivation phase varies from place to place based on the availability and fertility of land. In Rumgong village a single patch has been brought under cultivation for one year only with two seasons of cropping, whereas in Rengo and Pangin village the same plot is being used for 2-3 years. The first year of cultivation is locally called as *Rikpa;* second and third year of cultivations are called *Rigang* and *Rigang Abi,* respectively. Opening of new patch for cultivation is decided by the entire village lead by the Gams and community leaders in consultation with the farmers. The meeting for making decision is being conducted in the community hall (DERE) of the village. Once the *Kebang* passes resolution nobody can cultivate a single piece of land individually for agriculture other than the plot allotted by the community for the year. This helps in reducing excess labour input in construction of fencing and maintaining unity among the villagers. Fallow phase has been efficiently managed to recuperate the soil nutrients to meet the demand of crops, which is correlated with *patat.* For example in Rumgong village there are 25 *patats,* out of which only 15 are used for shifting agriculture and the fallow phase is of 14 years. However, fallow phase are depends on the number of cropping years in one *patat.* (Table 16.2). Transition has been recorded. Earlier all the *patats* were used for shifting cultivation, while in the present stage, some of the *patats* have been abandoned which may risk the future sustainability of shifting cultivation (Table 16.2).

Table 16.2: Number of *Patats* maintained, cropping period and jhum cycle of four representative villages

Village	No. of Patats	Currently cultivated Patats	Cropping Year(s)	Jhum cycle
Rumgong	25	15	1	15
Rengo	27	16	2	32#
Pangin	13	12	2-3	24-36#
Koreng	18	18	2-3	24-36#

#based on preliminary investigation.

The Lurang

Since agriculture is the primary occupation often sometime the only source of subsistence for the upland communities, it is of utmost important to protect their crops field from loss or damages caused by the domestic, semi domestic and wild animals. Over the centuries the Adi tribe has managed their animals by keeping them in a fixed place. For that all the villagers collectively construct an enclosure where Mithuns (*Bos frontalis*) are kept together in a location opposite or farthest to the current shifting cultivation field. The enclosure is locally called as *Lurang,* which may be of a *patat* or a number of *patats*. The management of Lurang is strictly governed by the village authority comprising the Kebang and villagers. It has been constructed collectively by the villagers irrespective of the owners of the mithun, shifting cultivators, wet rice cultivators, employers etc. The entire area of the *Lurang* has broadly been divided in to two equal halves (*Merom*) locally called as Higo Merom and Hangga Merom. The villagers also divide themselves in to two parties for managing the same. The Merom system exists in all Adi villages though the terminology may vary from village to village. For example in Riga, the system is called Humbung Merom and Hirang Merom, in Jomo village it is called Kuming Merom and Jajum Merom, in Molom it is called Kuming Merom and Yabang Merom, in Dosing, Rumgong and Yeksi it is called Higo Merom and Hangga Merom.

All male members of the village take part in construction of Lurang except those who are below 10 years old and those old men who attain the age 70. The persons(s) who will not go for this activity will be imposed fine (*Ajeng*) of Rs.100/day (the minimum wages rate of the society). However in certain emergency cases like serious ill health and examination, villagers are exempted from paying fine. Only males are involved in Lurang construction. Females normally do not take part in this activity due to the following reasons.

(1) During Lurang construction the females are engaged in other activities like clearing of debris and seed broadcasting in agricultural field.

(2) Since Lurang construction is a labourious job it is a hazardous work for them.

(3) From the time immemorial in Adi tradition this particular activity has been carried out by the males only, hence it would be against their culture if the females are involved in the practice.

The Lurang is shifted (Table 16.3) according to the shifting of cultivation plot. For example in the year 2008 in Rumgong village the Lurang will be constructed in Kigong Patat, which was situated opposite to the Tirlung Patat the current cultivation patat. In 2006 the Lurang was situated at Hi-ir/ Lampu, which was opposite to the Pomging Patat the cultivation plot of the year. In general it is constructed in the month of April (*Luking polo*) and the mithuns are kept up to October (*Dongkiyong polo*). The mithuns remain free for six month (from October to March). The Lurang may continue up to three consecutive years at the most.

Table 16.3 : *Lurang*—an encloser for mithun in Rumgong village

Sl.No.	Name of the Lurang	Year of construction
1	Kigong	2008
2	Kigong	2007
3	Hi-ir/Lampu	2006
4	Rumgong	2005
5	Kigong	2004
6	Moyang	—
7	Motum	—

—indicates non-availability of record

Bamboo Conservation in Rumgong Village

The entire land use/cover of Rumgong village have been divided in to 25 patches locally called Patats. Of that 5 patats are dominated by bamboo vegetation (Table 16.4). It has been recorded that the harvesting of bamboo shoot is strictly prohibited, except at Diging Patat. Farmers viewed that the extensive harvesting of bamboo shoots may affect the potential of mature bamboo production and may also reduce clump size. It has been observed across the study villages and also reported in literatures that the bamboo is the most useful natural resource for the farmers of the region, which provides basic livelihood sustenance i.e. food to household materials and agricultural fencing. In all the patats, mature bamboos are harvested sustainably particularly for household materials, ritual ceremonies and house construction. This indicates the efficiencies of traditional resources management practices evolved by the Adi community over the period of time.

Table 16.4 : Bamboo dominated *patats* of Rumgong Village

Sl. No.	Name of the Plot	Direction	Distance from village (km)	Potentiality	Accessibility
1	Ngehin	North-East	9	++++	Restricted
2	Moyang	South-West	0.7	++++	Restricted
3	Biyit	West	11	+++	Restricted
4	Diging	South-East	6.5	+++	Open
5	Pomging	North-West	1.2	+	Restricted

Note: + indicate low; ++ average; +++ good and ++++ excellent.

The restrictions imposed on the harvesting of young bamboo shoots from four recorded bamboo dominated patats of the Rumgong village are Ngehin, Moyang, Biyit and Pomging. The reason behind is that these particular patats are quite congenial for harvesting of any bamboo product and farmers viewed that their resources will shrink immediately if not regulated. On the other hand, in case of Diging Patat there is no such restriction since it is topographically inaccessible for collection of bamboo material from this *Patat*.

Asi Among committee is solely responsible for the management of bamboo groves in the village. The community exercises customary norms to manage their bamboo resources. Selling or illegal supply of bamboo is strictly prohibited. No outsider is permitted to extract any product from restricted *patats*. Anybody found to violate the customary practices will be imposed penalty from Rs.500 to 2000. The fund raised from such activity is used for the welfare of the community.

Conclusion

Sustainable resource management and conservation are intricately linked with socio-cultural and ritualistic practices of the Adi community. Revitalization and codification of the customs are options for maintaining the ecological processes in fragile Eastern Himalayan region. Traditional institutions of the community are efficient forums for management of natural resources, which are slowly eroding under interventions. Sustainable traditional management practices of Adis need recognition and revitalization to check the erosion of time-tested ecological knowledge. *Patat* may be an efficient tool for sustainable management in shifting cultivation, which is one of the most debated forms of agriculture. Besides, *Lurang* is another important agriculture related livestock management practice that reduces the risk of crop damage, which can be replicated in other regions as a management tool.

Acknowledgement

The authors are thankful to the Director G.B.Pant Institute of Himalayan Environment and Development (GBPIHED), Almora, India, for providing facilities and necessary guidance; Mr. Taro Mize, ADC (Rumgong, West Siang District), Mr. Tabom Mize (Rumgong Village), Mr. Tapum Tabi (Rengo Village) and Mr. Tadi Panor (Pangin Village) for their co-operation during field and household survey. Thanks are also due to the villagers and farmers of Rengo, Dosing, Pangin, Koreng Village (East Siang) and Rumgong village (West Siang) for their help during field investigation.

REFERENCES

Anon. 2005. West Siang District. District at a Glance (http://westsiang.nic.in/glance.htm)

Anon. 2007. District Profile—East Siang at a Glance (http://eastsiang.nic.in/html/profile-esd.htm)

Anon. 2007 . Solung -Adi festival (http://www.webindia123.com/arunachal/festivals/festivals.htm)

Bisht, I., Mehta, P. and Bhandari, D. 2007. Traditional Crop Diversity and Its Conservation on-Farm for Sustainable Agricultural Production in Kumaun Himalaya of Uttaranchal State: A Case Study. *Genet. Res. and Crop Evol.* 54(2): 345-357.

Dollo, M. 2007. Traditional Farmers Groups Supporting Sustainable Farming. *LEISA* 23: 22-24.

Gupta, A.K. 2007. Indigenous Knowledge and Innovations for Managing Resources, Institutions and Technologies Sustainability: A Case of Agriculture, Medicinal Plants and Biotechnology. *W.P.No.2007-07-09*, Indian Institute of Management, Ahmedabad, India

Hore, D.K. 2005. Rice Diversity Collection, Conservation and Management in North-eastern India. *Genet. Res. Crop Evol.* 52: 1129-1140.

Mili. R. 2007. Bamboo: Prospect for Sustainable Development in North East India. *MORE Expression*. 1:11.

Mili Rajiv, Arya S.C., Dollo, Mihin and Samal Prasanna K. (2007). Managing Agrobiodiversity: Traditional Ecological Practices, Transition and Future Implications. In: *Regional Seminar on Traditional Knowledge Systems and Community Development in North East India.* 18-19th August, 2007. NERIST, Nirjuli, Arunachal Pradesh. p.46.

Nyori, T. 1993. The Adis, People and Their Culture, *Omsons Publication*, Rajouri Buliding, New Delhi, India

Pathak, G. 2007. Solung—A Festival of the Adis of Arunachal Pradesh (http://www.articlesbase.com/art-and-entertainment-articles)

Roy, S. 1960. Aspects of Padam Minyong Culture. Director of Research, Govt. of Arunachal Pradesh, Itanagar

Singh, J.S., Pandey, U. and Tiwari, A.K. 1994. Man and Forests: A Central Himalaya Case Study. *AMBIO* 12(2): 80-87.

Singh, R.K., Mishra, A. and Das, S.K. 2002b. *Ethnotaxonomy and Fertility Management Dimension of Soil: AnAppraisal of Farmer Wisdom*. Technical Bulletin. Indian Council of Agricultural Research, New Delhi, India. pp. 25-27.

Srivastava, L.R.N. 1988. *The Gallongs*. Director of Research, Govt. of Arunachal Pradesh, Itanagar. pp. 128.

17

Changing Trends in Traditional Customs and Rituals

— Mrs. N. V. Kavita, Mrs. Anuradha and
Mrs.Swena Shanti Mathur

ABSTRACT

India with a rich heritage and culture has upheld its traditional outlook in various aspects, across different sections of population. The characteristic tradition of past had held many values towards sustaining the nature with minimum exploitation of natural resources, life sustaining practices, thus, maintaining its originality. Ploughing of paddy fields with bullocks and following traditional water harvesting methods, performing traditional customs and rituals such as Vanmahotsvam, Pushkaram were the most contributing factors towards sustainable development in the recent past. With changing times, there is drastic declination to many such useful practices due to increased stress on the resources, busy work schedules and modernisation of various activities and workings. The value-based knowledge systems has changed and evolved with more emphasis on short term goals thus creating a magnitude of unseen and dangerous consequences in long term. This would lead to a plethora of unmanageable and non-sustaining living conditions that haunts to wipe out our very chance of existence on this beautiful planet. This chapter brings out insights to such alarming changes with an emphasis to awaken the population to develop in healthier and self-sustaining knowledge-based systems.

Introduction

With a strong contemplation of culture and civilization that dates far back in history, ours is a most sacred, accounted and documented. The evolution of various traditional practices is based upon simple, yet most sustainable conditions. Having recorded numerous events and happenings in the past and its relevance and observations carried out in these modern times, it has made a distinct impression in the minds of Indians to promulgate and adhere to such a rich heritage.

The traditional India is the very origin and source of the India of today. It is a living reality, even now. At the existential level it is still the backbone of India. In the philosophic plane it is verily its soul. It does not call for any meticulous search or research to uncover this. It is visible to the naked eye, unless the 'modern' Indian, blinded by aggressive modernity, dismisses all traditions as backward and therefore and thereby misses their impact. India's philosophic and spiritual quests manifest explicitly and involve and bring the ordinary people of India together in millions time and again and connect them to their geography as a sacred idea in a manner unknown to any other civilization. In fact the capacity of this ancient nation to bring together the people and link them to their geography, in which their faith was physically and spiritually rooted, constituted the very basis of Indian nationhood. Therefore the geography-linked faith of the Indian people constituted their identity as a nation.

Thus, the nation in India is a sacred confluence of mass faith of the Indian people with geography of India. This is what Mahatma Gandhi too perceived, in his dialogue in Hind Swaraj, faith as the basis of India as one living organic entity, that is, in the modern idiom, one nation[1]. It needs no social scientist or demographer to offer proof for this explicit phenomenon in this country. A mere look at the mass power of a 'Maha Kumbh' or a Pushkar' in the North of India or their equivalent, a 'Mahamakam' or a 'Pushkaram' in the South of India and how these and other festivals and mass rituals in hundreds unite the people of India and link them to their geography will bring out the importance of tradition in the national life of India and also in integrating it as a nation. It is traditions like these in thousands, at the national, regional and local levels, that unite the people of India and integrate India more than all that the social contract based polity enforced by constitution and law, and penalised by courts and police for breach of contract and law, can accomplish. In fact, traditional India has effectively and emotionally twined the people of this ancient nation into one rainbow like unified society with linked diversities like the colours of the rainbow. This bond has survived the over-bearing and hostile attitude of modernity that had at the start questioned the very relevance of ancient and traditional India.

This takes us to the question how 'modern' is India in this sense today despite over half a century of efforts to modernize it. It is no secret that even now the idea of modernity in India is more a superficial veneer that masks the real India, fakes the true one which is basically traditional in nature and psyche. The privately lived India is, utterly and by conviction, traditional in varying degrees. While, in contrast, the publicly projected India is feigning to appear 'modern'—read Western—by driving underground and to obscurity all privately held traditions. The modern India is catchy and glamorous in appearance but within itself suffers alienation, and is confused and disturbed, its heart being neither here nor there. As a consequence it is utterly superficial in thinking and is influenced by exogamous drives and not by endogamous self-evaluation. Consequently, it lacks depth and understanding of traditional India's inner soul which is inextricably mixed with India's ancient traditions and religion.

With the result the 'modern' India is virtually cut off from its roots connecting it to the ancient Indian civilisational moorings. To make matters worse, 'modern' India, by compulsion of its definition, has had to openly abandon the ancient and traditional Indian tastes, lifestyle and appearances in the public domain only to be regarded and get certified as 'modern'. In fact it has not only to abandon, it has also to trivialise, the ancient and traditional India as un-modern and even as anti-modern. It is being successfully operated by the English speaking elites who have been apologetic about the traditional India and are shy of owing it and by Left thinkers most of whom negate the traditions of India as anti-progressive. Both of them, who otherwise disagree on almost everything else, converge on this. This superficially defined and even more superficially presented modernity represent the veneer that masks the real India which is intimately linked to traditions.

An effort is made through this paper presentation in highlighting the metamorphosis of methods and practices in carrying out age-old traditions. A prominent festival in South India—***Pushkaram***—is discussed in this chapter for a better and clear understanding of the changes that are witnessed within the practices in recent times. A case study of 'Pushkaram' is taken up for observing and relating the incidence of the changes that has brought a completely different look to this festival. The research was carried out by collecting information through different reference books, informative sites from the internet and actual life-experiences from people who are witnessing this event since a very long time.

Pushkaram—The Changing Scenario

The rivers of India have been closely associated with our history and civilization. Entwined with spirituality and philosophy, they have always been worshipped as personifications of divinity. The places located at the course of rivers are treated as sacred. Since time immemorial river worship is known as Pushkaram to make the people realise the importance of water, the life-sustaining force.

Pushkaram is a festival in India which occurs in any particular year with respect to one of twelve important rivers; the river for each year's festival is based on which zodiacal sign Jupiter is in at that time. The table below shows the association between rivers and signs.

River	Sign
Ganges	Aries
Reva river	Taurus
Saraswati	Gemini
Yamuna	Cancer
Godavari	Leo
Krishna	Virgo
Kaveri	Libra
Bhima River	Scorpio
Radhya Saga	Sagittarius
Tungabhadra	Capricorn
Indus	Aquarius
Pranahitha	Pisces

The Pushkaram for each river comes once every twelve years and lasts so long as the Jupiter remains in the corresponding Zodiac sign (generally, for one year). The first twelve days of *Pushkaram* are known as *Adi Pushkaram*, and the last twelve days are called *Anthya Pushkaram*. It is believed that during the above period of twenty-four days, 'Pushkar' the person, who is imbued with the power to make any river holy, will travel with Jupiter as Jupiter moves from one Zodiac house to another.

In Andhra Pradesh, Pushkaram is observed at Rajahmundry for Godavari Pushkaram, Vijayawada for Krishna Pushkaram and Kovur town in Nellore District for Pennar Pushkaram. It is considered sacred to have a holy dip in these rivers and so people gather in large numbers on the banks of these rivers, when the Pushkaram is held. Various rituals are performed and it is believed that a holy dip washes away all the sins.

In ancient times, sages used to sow the seeds and can get the yield on the very day for their meal due to their strength of 'Tapasya'(deep meditation). On one such day, when the sage Gautama sowed the seeds and sat for 'tapasya', the other sages thought that if they can create a trouble for him, he will bring the Ganga to earth and it will be good for mankind. Thinking so, they prepared a Cow and Calf with Dharbhas, infused life in them and led them into the field of the Gautama. Gautama who was performing Anushtana, drived them with the Dharbhas in his hand. Immediately the cow became dead. As it is very big sin to kill a cow, all the other sages advised Gautama to bring the Ganga to earth and take holy bath in it so as to penance the sin. So Gautama performed 'tapasya' and pleased the Lord Shiva and brought the Ganga to earth. That is Godavari. That Ganga water became the river Godavari. Because it gave life to a cow, the river got the name Godavari, '*Go*' means cow and '*da*' means giving. As Gautama is the sage who is responsible for its origin, it is named after him as Gautami.

This festival was celebrated during earlier period in complete accordance with nature and the procedures and methods employed were simpler and fitted well in the surroundings without any significant alterations/ disturbances to the environment. As per ritual even before sunrise people take the sacred bath and offer prayers to the Lord. Simple cultural programmes were organised. All that was performed as ritual, like:

- praying by reciting mantras;
- offering 'pind'—food in form of rice balls wrapped in banana / lotus leaves, thus, feeding the fishes and aquatic life forms, which in turn maintain the waters with natural life-sustaining powers;
- taking simple holy dips in the waters;
- usage of locally available natural elements, which assimilated in the environment easily without disturbing the nature was the key to sustainable progression in the society.

Small congregation organising dance and plays along with few temporary shops used to come up in the nearby area to cater to the festive mood of the people signifying the spirit of festival.

Over the years with growing population, the festival too grew considerably accounting a remarkable change in methods and practices in almost every single activity associated with the festivity. With increased number of devotees, constrained with time and schedules, the mode of performing the rituals in the right manner has remarkably modified to convenience sort of practices.

- The basic form of offering to the holy waters now is conveniently wrapped in plastics and deposited in the water body;
- the holy dips are now-a-days been enhanced to bathing using all sorts of chemical-laded soaps and detergents;
- original and complete verses chanting of mantras too are modified and distorted;

- playing of loud-speakers with 'devotional' songs that are laced with heavy music and remixes of songs from popular films are played loudly from the main area;
- Permanent structures and shops have thronged in the vicinity since few years that sell artificial jewellery, sweets, decorative items; and
- items of convenience, like disposable plastic containers, plates, polythene sheets that cover every corner to provide shelter from scorching heat and sunlight.

The diminishing water levels in the rivers is adding to the woes as people rush towards the water and those left behind take a short-cut to the ritual by throwing the 'important' offerings along with plastics wrapped securely into waters from a bridge or a river bank, thereby endangering fishes and other aquatic life forms as these get lured to the food within the plastics wrap and thus choke to death due to plastic consumption.

These are few commonly observed changes seen in these times. The changes are attributed to many logical factors too as:

- the growing number of pilgrims
- people management issues
- law and order situations
- transportation and travel matters
- extensive use of communication medias
- depletion of certain natural resources changes a usage pattern thus introducing a new element to the environment

This brief compilation of a single episode of Pushkaram can be replicated with many other activities, festivities, events and practices that can be related with the changes one experiences with those practiced in past.

REFERENCES

1. Hind Swaraj is reprinted in the Collected Works of Mahatma Gandhi, Vol. 10, New Delhi, p. 245-315.

Other relevant websites encountered for specific information

http://hinduism.about.com/cs/festivals/a/aa081603a.htm

http://www.telugupeople.com/pushkaralu/History.asp

http://pib.nic.in/feature/feyr2003/faug2003/f120820032.html

http://www.telugupeople.com/pushkaralu/aboutgodavari.asp

http://www.hinduonnet.com/fr/2003/08/08/stories/2003080801950800.htm

18

Involvement of Local Communities in the Conservation of Forest Resources

Issues in the Design of a Sustainable Model Framework

— Mr. Bhaskar Sarmah

ABSTRACT

For centuries and prior to the British rule, all sections of the Indian society enjoyed a fair share of the forest resources. Researchers argue that prior to the British period the practices of the state machinery aimed at fair distribution of returns, and acknowledged the importance of communal forest regimes. During the British period, the administrators dismantled prevailing concepts of social utility and social welfare, including those that ensured a fair distribution of returns from forest resources. The sole purpose of forest management sought to redistribute economic gains in favour of the empire. Thus, during this period, forest management was converted from a community-based regime to one of central control.

After independence, the Government of India tried to redefine the social-utility and social-welfare functions; but the emphasis of forest management regimes continued to be on commercial timber exploitation and exclusion of local people from forest. This approach led to the emergence of many socio-economic problems. In the late 1970s and early 1980s, across India, there was a sudden emergence of forest protection initiatives in response to growing forest product scarcities and threats of exploitation by outside groups. These community actions indicated the conflicts between formal and informal institutions, and inefficiencies in the existing forest regimes. The Government of India realized the failure of forest regimes based on exclusion of local people in the National Forest Policy 1988; and sought people's participation as a means for conserving existing forestlands and regenerating wastelands.

This changing approach has resulted in the new approach known as Joint Forest Management (JFM). This approach is however, not a special case of India. For the conservation of forest resources, other countries have adopted similar participatory approach as well. This chapter discusses the important achievement, failures of the above JFM approach and has tried to discuss the issues that need to be tackled in building a sustainable participatory model.

Introduction

In the modern history of forest management in India, the British period draws a special consideration. During the British period, the administrators dismantled prevailing concepts of social utility and social welfare, including those that ensured a fair distribution of returns from forest resources. The sole purpose of forest management sought to redistribute economic gains in favour of the empire. Thus, during this period, forest management was converted from a community-based regime to one of central control (Tiwari, M 2004).

Just after the independence, India passed the National Forest Policy (NFP) of 1952. The policy classified forests into four functional types: protection forests, national forests, village forests and tree-lands. In reality, this new classification was in no way much different from the British provision as was laid in the Indian Forest Act of 1927. The only difference was the introduction of last category as a new functional category (Balooni, K 2002). It was therefore evident that the NFP of 1952 did not serve any purpose other than the exploitation of forest resources for the benefit of a few private industries. Evidences suggest that during the 1950s, the paper industry was procuring bamboo at a price of Re 1 (One Rupee) per ton against the prevailing market price of over Rs 2000 (Rs. two thousand) per ton. This huge provision of state subsidy induced 'profitability of forest-based industries' and resulted in the 'explosive growth in industrial capacity and a non-sustainable use of forest stocks' (Gadgil & Guha 1992, in Balooni, K 2002).

Such huge subsidies had serious repercussions. On the one hand, it affected forest-dependent communities to the adverse; while on the other led to the further degradation of forests. Such circumstances led to several people's movements in protest against state policy, especially between the 1970s and the 1980s. In what became world known as the Chipko Movement (Chipko meaning 'to cling to' or 'to hug tight'), village women hugged the trees, interposing their bodies between the trees and the contractors' axes, to prevent them from being cut. This movement started in the Himalayan state of Uttaranchal in March 1974, later replicated in other states in India in an organized manner (Balooni, K 2002; Rajagopalan, R 2005; Sundar, N et al,

2001). The Chipko Movement achieved a major victory in 1980, when the government of Uttar Pradesh placed a 15-year ban on tree felling in Himalayan forests. This movement also encouraged many of the peoples' movement to save their environment in the later period. It is true that peoples' emotional and/or rational involvement to protect forests has led to formulation of policy measures to involve people in forest management.

This concept of Community Based Forest Management (CBFM) has been given different names in different countries. It is true that many of the forests in India have, at different points in the nation's history, been managed under a set of rules and regulations developed by different communities. Even today, some of these so-called self-initiated forest protection groups have survived or have been re-invented in response to the need of the hour to conserve community forests (Balooni, K 2002). Thus, it can be argued that participatory/joint forest management is not a 'new' concept to India; it is rather a re-invention of the erstwhile successful forest management practices. The changing approach of Government of India in the framework of Joint Forest Management (JFM) basically aims at promoting sustainable forest resource management. This chapter discusses about the issues involved in this framework of JFM. To what extent JFM has been successful and what are the areas that need to be taken care of? This chapter specifically tries to tackle the important policy issues in the design of a sustainable model framework (especially in the context of JFM) that stems from the involvement of local communities in the conservation of forest resources. The remaining discussion of this chapter has been divided into five parts. The *second* section discusses about the methodology of the paper. The *third* section discusses about some of the important basic concepts viz., the concept of sustainable forest management and the related concepts of CBFM in India. The *fourth* section discusses about the important macro issues in the design of a sustainable model framework (especially in the context of JFM) that stems from the involvement of local communities in the conservation of forest resources. The *fifth* section discusses about the policy recommendations and this chapter concludes with discussion of model framework in section *sixth*.

Methodology

This chapter is basically based on review of earlier literature in the field. It also utilises relevant secondary data from reliable sources. Relevant studies, especially based on Nepal have also been reviewed to make comparative analysis. This has been done keeping in view close socio-economic, geographic and other cultural proximities between these two countries. Remarkable achievements achieved by Nepal in CBFM (called as collaborative forest management (CFM)) is another motivating factor in this regard.

Important Basic Concepts

Sustainable Forest Management

Rajagopalan, R (2005) has described sustainable forest management (SFM) as *"the sustainable use of the world's forest resources in such a way that they continue to provide resources in the present, without depriving the future generations of their use."* It includes all the three components of sustainability, viz. ecological, economic and socio-cultural well-being. The International Tropical Timber Organization (ITTO) defines SFM as:

> 'the process of managing permanent forest land to achieve one or more clearly specified objectives of forest management with regard to the production of a continuous flow of desirable forest products and services without undue reduction of its inherent values and future productivity and without undue undesirable effects on the physical and social environment'. (Quoted in: Rawat et al., 2008).

One of the principles of SFM is the full involvement of the local community in the forest management process. This has been difficult in some cases, especially when the forest departments (FDs) are reluctant to lose their control over forest resources. In recent times, SFM has become important in climate change negotiations as well. This is because as per Kyoto Protocol, countries reap benefit if their forest environmental benefit to the world. The industrialized countries today therefore have come forward to finance SFM activities in the developing countries (Rajagopalan, R 2005).

Community-based Forest Management

Loosely speaking, community based forest management (CBFM) means involving the local communities in the management of the forest resources. In India, forest protection movement has experienced three distinct types of CBFM (Sinha, H 2006). The *first* type of CBFM has emerged out of local initiatives as a reaction to growing stress owing to rapid degradation of forest. The Chipko movement and other such movements we have already mentioned fall under this category. This has been termed as indigenous community forest management (ICFM). The *second* type of CBFM has emerged as a result of active sponsorship of local government and NGOs. During the last two decades in India, such types of CBFM units have increased significantly. This type of forest management is popularly known as crafted community forest management (CCFM). Forest department (FD) of our country promoted the *third* type of CBFM. In this type, forest cooperative societies were formed (also known as *Van Panchayat*). This type facilitated high involvement of local people, but often deprived them of their economic benefit.

Joint Forest Management (JFM) that we see today may be called as a culmination of all the above types. Researchers (Mukhopadhyay, D et al (2007) therefore, rightly argues that JFM in India has served twin objectives: *first*, to reverse the process of forest degradation and *secondly*, to meet people's need in an equitable manner. It is a device to bring together the Forest Department (FD) and the resource users—the forest community people (FC) through formation of Joint Forest Management Committee (JFMC). JFM is a unique approach and includes both the scientific management techniques and the age old indigenous practices to conserve forest on sustainable basis.

Key Macro Issues in the Design of a Model Framework for the Promotion of Sustainable Forest Management in India (Especially in the Context of JFM)

The Historicity of JFM

Before discussing about the macro issues relating to the design of a model framework for the promotion of sustainable forest management (especially in the context of JFM, India), it will be better to briefly discuss the historicity of the context that led to the introduction of JFM in the country and the progress it has recorded so far.

The initial strategy to combat forest degradation and to increase forest productivity as suggested by the National Commission on Agriculture (NCA) of 1976 included the strategies like: management of government forest lands for the production of industrial inputs and at the same time adoption of massive social forestry programme. The primary objective of the social forestry programme was reduction of pressure on government forests. But contrary to this objective it was realized that *first*, the Forest Department was unable to control forest degradation as the local communities continued to depend on forests for their needs; and *secondly*, conflicts between the communities and the Forest Department were on the rise (Saigal, Sushi n.d.; Taneja, B 2001). Apart from all these, the fact has also been India occupies only 2.5% of the world's geographic area and 1.85% of the world's forest area. But contrary to this, the country owns 17% of the world's population and 18% of livestock population (Rawat et al, 2008). In such contexts, it had become imperative to preserve manage forests on a sustainable basis, so as to ensure secure livelihood of the forest-dependent communities as well as conserving bio-diversity as well. This led to the introduction of a new forest policy in 1988. This new policy was a complete departure from the earlier ones because of the fact that it stressed on management of forests for conservation and meeting local communities' needs and made commercial exploitation and revenue generation secondary objectives (Saigal, S n.d.; Khawas, V 2003; Balooni, K 2002).

The essential difference between social forestry and JFM is that while the former sought to keep people out of forests, the latter seeks to involve them in the management of *forest* lands. JFM also emphasises *joint* management by the community and the Forest Deparment.

Trend and Experiences of JFM

Data on the following table shows the number of JFMCs in different states and the respective areas of their coverage.

Table 18.1: Selected State-wise Progress of Joint Forest Management in India (As on March, 2006)

Sl. No.	State	JFM Committeee (Number)	Membership by Social Groups (Number)			
			Total	SC	ST	Others
1	2	3	4	5	6	7
1.	Andhra Pradesh	8498	1538784	322954	464685	751145
2.	Arunachal Pradesh	362	24588	24588	Nil	Nil
3.	Assam	700	217973	NA	NA	NA
4.	Bihar	615	46893	16694	9541	20658
5.	Chhattsgarh	7820	2763100	1436278	1326822	Nil
6.	Goa	26	207	125	72	10
7.	Gujarat	2124	1045714	113904	451973	479837
8.	Haryana	1075	167300	31600	Nil	135700
9.	Himachal Pradesh	1749	254350	63046	36878	154426
10.	Jammu & Kashmir	4861	268360	19626	70750	177984
11.	Jharkhand	10903	218000	119900		98100
12.	Karnataka	2254	295646	47628	30051	217967
13.	Kerala	561	66022	7365	21952	36705
14.	Madhya Pradesh	14428	8984000	1540000	4080000	3364000
15.	Maharashtra	11799	2441245	248298	553686	1639261
16.	Manipur	283	23958	57	21106	2795
17.	Meghalaya	73	7083	Nil	7083	Nil
18.	Mizoram	505	181681	110	181571	Nil
19.	Nagaland	335	121064	Nil	121064	Nil
20.	Orissa	9905	2365404	401986	855466	1107952
21.	Punjab	1378	183145	53280	28	129837

(Contd...)

1	2	3	4	5	6	7
22.	Rajasthan	4691	509346	59177	244730	205439
23.	Sikkim	204	338257	3619[1]	20640[1]	60204[2]
24.	Tamil Nadu	2642	793369	219713	53843	519813
25.	Tripura	399	39644	9535	23018	7091
26.	Uttar Pradesh	2096	155692	29946	5006	20740
27.	Uttarakhand	12089	108801	24178	Nil	84623
28.	West Bengal	4107	558086	174993	132276	250817
	Total	**106,482**	**23717712**	**4848700[2]**	**8712241[2]**	**9465104[2]**

Source: State Forest Department. Available from Ministry of Environment and Forests, GOI.
[1] Figures represent number of families; [2] excluding data from Assam & Jharkhand

It is true that the number of JFMCs is necessarily not an indicator of any success of JFM. Researchers has termed the participatory forest management approach of India to be a mix of successes and challenges.

Major Achievements

Various studies (Saigal, n.d.; Danwar K et al, 2007; Sundar, N et al, 2001) have pointed out the following major achievement of JFM in India:

Change in Attitude and Relationship—JFM programme has been able to change the attitudes of local communities and forest officials towards each other and forests. Certain studies conducted in Himachal Pradesh, Andhra Pradesh and Rajasthan confirm this achievement. Such achievements may be attributed to the large number of training and orientation exercises carried out across different states in the country.

Improvement in the Condition of Forest—Scientific studies and other more general studies on JFM confirm that the programme has resulted in the improvement in the condition of the forests. This has been experience especially in certain areas of Andhra Pradesh, Rajasthan and Gujarat.

Reduction in Encroachment—In several areas, introduction of JFM has also been able to reduce the area under encroachment and decrease the rate of fresh encroachment. Significant achievements have been recorded in the states of Andhra Pradesh and Maharashtra in this regard.

Increase in Income—It is true that economic issues are the root of problems in forest resource exploitation and management. It is difficult to achieve sound forest resource management without developing the economy of local communities (A.P.Y Djogo in Brown A.G. Ed, 2001). It is easily understood that the local communities are unlikely to participate in any joint action unless they see some economic benefits. Sharing of economic benefits therefore becomes instrumental in sustaining the achievement of any participatory approach.

Implementation of JFM programme has increased the income of participating communities at several instances. In fact, several externally assisted projects laid emphasis on employment generation and creation of productive community assets as a part of the project. Such achievements in this regard have been recorded in the states, viz. Andhra Pradesh, Madhya Pradesh, Gujarat, West Bengal (Saigal, n.d.) and South district of Tripura (Danwar, K et al, 2007).

Role Assigned to Panchayat and NGOs—It is a fact that *Panchayats* are traditional village institutions that have a statutory status, several financial and administrative powers, and have been asked to play a supervisory role for the forest protection committees (FPCs). However, the exact nature of involvement has not been made clear. This has been the case with NGOs as well. In fact, at the outset of launch of JFM programmes in the country, the Forest Department was skeptical about the role of NGOs. The conflicts arose because the FD was reluctant to relinquish power and/or were also dis-motivated owing to their short-lived, patronizing attitude (Balooni, K 2002; Tiwari, M 2004). However, as time passed, considerable involvement of NGOs in the forestry sector of various states has been recorded (Saigal, n.d).

Major Challenges

Against the above achievements, several key issues have also emerged.

Conflicts—At several places, JFM has resulted in increased inter and intra-community conflicts, which often result in physical violence. Intra-community conflicts mainly emanate from inequitable distribution of costs and benefits of JFM among different subgroups (class, caste, gender etc.) within the community. Inter-community conflicts, on the other hand results from debates relating to boundaries and access rights.

Transparency—There is an urgent need to increase transparency at the field level, especially in areas where large amounts of funds are being provided for JFM through special projects. Some innovative mechanisms to promote transparency such as writing of expenditure and microplan details on village walls have been reported from Uttar Pradesh (Shukla 2001).

Traditional/Existing Institutions—Recognition of thousands of community groups engaged in self-motivated protection/management of forests is also a felt necessity especially in Orissa and Jharkhand. The new JFM guidelines issued by the MoEF in 2000 do emphasise on the need for "identifying, recognising and registering" these groups but do not offer any practical tips as to how to go about it.

Specific problems relating to specific geographic localities/region have also been experienced. It has been argued that owing to specific socio-economic set-up, the north-eastern states of India require a different JFM approach as compared to other parts of the country (NERFRP, 2001 and Yadav, 2001 in Saigal, n.d.).

Sharing of Benefits from NTFPs: Sharing of benefits from NTFPs is also an important issue. While NTFPs contribute to household income in many places, this contribution is socially and geographically uneven. In India as a whole, NTFP production contributes about 40 per cent of total official forest revenues and 55% of forest-based employment. It is true that the nationalisation of NTFPs and the recent JFM management system in the country provide considerable tenurial security to poor populations in accessing the usufructs. However, due to the lack of value addition to the collected NTFPs and fair marketing system, the collectors benefit little in actual fact (*Ibid, 2004*).

Other important issues that have come up relate to experiences in dense forests and protected forest areas (Saigal, n.d.). Apart from this, project specific issues have also been experienced (Saigal, n.d.).

This chapter basically tries to discuss the issues relating to the framework of design of a sustainable forest conservation model based on involvement of local communities. Specific to the issue of involvement of local communities, Sinha, H (2006) has pointed out that apart from the economic factor; peoples' participation in the forest management process is affected by the following ones:

- Formation of forest committee with heterogeneous interest groups;
- Absence of favourable socio-political environment that promotes participation;
- Incompatibility of governing rules with the local socio-cultural concept;
- Absence of participatory leadership with idealised behaviour in forest management;
- Inappropriate inter and intra-community conflict resolution mechanism;
- Lack of awareness regarding environmental protection leading towards incongruent; value system between leaders and other users.
- Tiwari, M (2004) has pointed out that the state machinery continues to follow the 'top-down approaches'. The senior bureaucrats have

continued to exercise a top-down approach to managing the JFM programmes. Again, due to lack of explicit instructions, the lower-level officers make several departures from JFM provisions in their day-to-day functions. Many of their formal work styles, such as patrol duties, the manner in which they interact with the villagers and book-keeping, are replete with methods that have been in existence since the colonial period.

Comparative Analysis: India and Nepal—Issues

Before discussing how to tackle the above factors, we shall discuss the experiences of JFM in the neighbouring country Nepal, which have adopted a similar model of forest conservation akin to India (Kothari, A 2003) called as collaborative forest management (CFM).

Studies conducted by Chakravarti, M et al (n.d.), Kothari, A (2003), Brown, A G (2001) and Tiwari, M (2004) have the following observations:

- User-groups in Nepal receive a greater share of the return from successful management in land held as common village property than those in India.
- As compared to India, the performance of Nepal has been quite remarkable. With very little investment by government, community forest management capacity has been enhanced, some of the mid-hills forests are now richer, and wildlife has significantly increased.
- The Master Plan also attempted to gain higher participation of Nepalese women. It stated that, 'one third of members of the users' committees should be women'. Mention about such guidelines in case of India, however was not found.

Comparative Analysis: India and Nepal—Policies and Provisions

In this section, we shall discuss some of the policy measures of the JFM set-up in India and Nepal. This is however, not a comprehensive discussion on policy issues. Only those policy issues have been discussed, which stem from our review of literature.

- Nepal has given more autonomy to its communities as compared to India. In recent years, the country has handed over rights (though not ownership) to some 400,000 ha of national forest to more than 7,000 community forest user groups (FUGs). This has been accompanied by progressive changes in forest-related policy.
- It is also a fact that communities in Nepal get more share of benefit return as compared to India (Chakravarti, M et al, n.d.). In India, this share of benefits varies from state to state and ranges from

20 per cent to 100 per cent. The provision in Nepal however proposes 100 per cent benefit to its forest user communities (FUCs) (Tiwar, M 2004).

- The remarkable success in Nepal can also be attribute to the several supportive programmes designed to support the SFM initiative. The legislation was updated and programmes designed to allow and encourage people to accept full responsibility for the development, management, and protection of community forests.
- One remarkable fact here however is that Nepal has initiated CFM programmes only in its hills districts. Researcher however points our that certain reluctance from the state machinery has been observed to hand over its 'valuable forests' in the CFM framework.

Recommendations

Based on the above discussion, the following measures have been suggested:

- The approach of JFM should be made more participatory in nature. It should be bottom-up approach, rather than a top-down approach. This is because each of the areas in the country has their own socio-cultural set up. Such issues should be duly considered with the involvement of local communities in each of the phases of JFM initiative viz.: policy diagnosis, design, evaluation and implementation.
- Addressing the gender issue is also important. We should not forget that the forest protection movement like Chipko was started by women. Due participation of women in the process should be taken care of and policy provisions should be made accordingly.
- The issue of upper caste dominance should also be properly dealt with. Involvement of weaker section of the society should be efficiently monitored.
- Geographic issues should be adequately considered. What is applicable in a forest in Madhya Pradesh may not be applicable in a forest of Mizoram.
- Benefit sharing should be made more reasonable. While, a certain percentage from it (say 20%) may be utilized for the development of the locality, the remaining should be shared equal (50-50) between the two major stakeholders: the community and the FD. A minimum of 50 per cent benefit to the participating community should be made mandatory.
- Policy statements regarding NTFPs should be made clear. It is true that the 1990 GOI order on Joint Forest Management has no specific

provisions for management and trading of bamboo and it continues to be clubbed with other NTFPs. The bamboo can be very instrumental in providing a reasonable income to the rural poor people. This has been done in China. Through recent policy changes, it has linked rural poor individuals with markets. This has turned the bamboo sector into an efficient competitive business enterprise with holds on important national and international markets, and has resulted in higher profits to stakeholders.

- 'Code of conduct' regarding forest harvesting and reduced impact logging (RIL) in tropical forest areas should be developed and followed. Study (Brown A.G, 2001) has shown that following of proper codes may be instrumental for the proper conservation and management of forest resources.
- The forest staff should be made more powerful to face any external challenges from smugglers and others accompanied by intra and inter community conflicts.
- Programmes for communal harmony should be made a part of JFM initiatives, especially in areas having presence of heterogeneous groups.
- In order to support institutional development, many forestry sector policies need to be redesigned. This has become necessary not only to improve their technical and legal aspects, but also to be equip them with clear objectives, instruments and rules to implement the instruments. This should be made a participatory approach.
- Promote institutional collaboration between the private sector, the local community, the government and civil society through sound collective action in forest resource management.
- Improve the capacity of local governments and local organisations such as NGOs and *Panchayat*, empowering local communities in legal aspects and raising their awareness about conservation and forest restoration.

A Model Framework

Criteria of the Model Framework

- Sustainable forest is the centre-stage of all activities.
- JFM is a participatory in all its phases: policy diagnosis, design, evaluation and implementation.
- JFM is a process of two major stakeholders: the local community and the forest department. While facilitating organization are also present in the entire process. They may include: NGOs and/or

Panchayat. However, the facilitating organization are not entitled to any benefit sharing.

- Of the total benefit, 20% goes to the development of the socio-economic environment. This may include: plantation programmed, development of roads, schools, water facility in the locality. The remaining benefit is shared equally between the community and the FD.
- Local community consists of representation from women and weaker section of the community in all the phases of JFM.

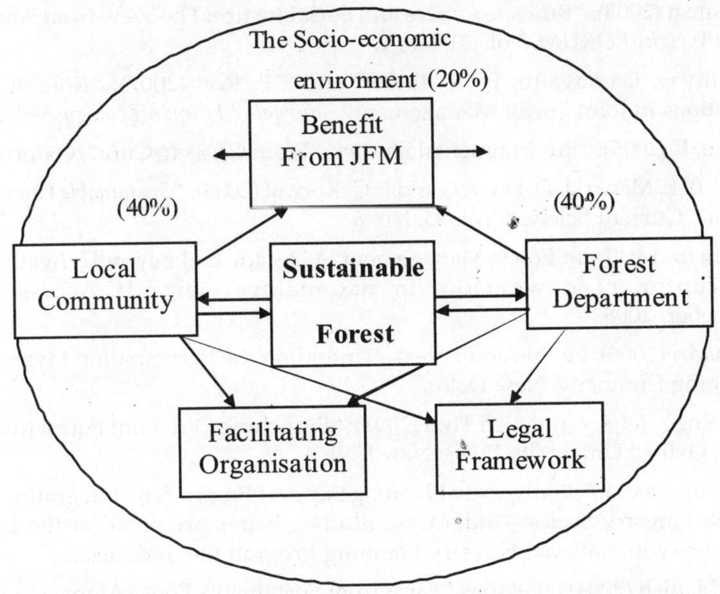

REFERENCES

Balooni, Kulbhushan (2002): Participatory Forest Management in India: An Analysis of Policy Trends amid 'Management Change'.

Brown, A G Ed. (2001): "Pathways to Sustainable Forest Management: Proceedings of the Second Hermon Slade International Workshop", held at Bali.

Camino V., Ronnie de (1999): Sustainable Forest Management in Latin America: Relevant Actors and Policies

Charkravarti, M, Samar K Datta, E L Howe and J B. Nugent (n.d.): *"Joint Forest Management: Experience and Modelling"*. Available at: http://www.iser.uaa.alaska.edu/iser/people/elhowe/research/edited_JFM_7_18.pdf. Accessed on 06th of December, 2008.

Danwar, K; R Srinivasulu and Mahesh (2007): *"The Role of JFM in Enhancing the Productive Capacity of Household: A Case Study on Tripura State, India"*, paper presented at the 43rd Annual Conference of the Indian Econometric Society (TIES).

Djogo, A.P.Y. (2001): "Decentralisation and Forest Resources in Indonesia: Removing Institutional Constraints and Redesigning Policies for a Better Future" in Brown, A.G. (2001) Ed: *Pathways to Sustainable Forest Management Proceedings of the Second Hermon Slade International Workshop*, held at Ubud, Bali.

Elias (2001): "Codes of Forest Harvesting and Reduced Impact Logging in Asia" in Brown, A.G. (2001) Ed: *Pathways to Sustainable Forest Management Proceedings of the Second Hermon Slade International Workshop*, held at Ubud, Bali.

Ferguson, Ian (2001): "Introduction and Context" in *Ibid.*

Khawas, Vimal (2003): Joint Forest Management in India with Special Reference to Darjeeling Himalaya

Kothari, Asihsh (2003): "Protected Areas and Social Justice: The View from South Asia", *The George Wright FORUM*, Vol. 20, No. 1.

Mukhopadhyay, Damayanti; H. R. Tewari and S.B. Roy (2007): "Role of Community Institutions in Joint Forest Management", *Journal of Human Ecology*, Vol. 21 No. 1

Rajagopalan, R (2005): "Environmental Studies – From Crisis to Cure", Oxford, New Delhi.

Rawat, T. S., B. L. Menaria, D. Dugaya and P. C. Kotwal (2008): "*Sustainable Forest Management in India*", Current Science, Vol. 95, No. 8.

Saigal, Sushi (n.d.): "Joint Forest Management: A Decade and Beyond". Available at: http:/www.rupfor.org/downloadq/jfm-nationaloverview.pdf. Accessed on 6th of Decemeber, 2008

Sinha, Himadri (2006): People and Forest – Unfolding the Participation Mystique, Concept Publishing Company, New Delhi.

Sundar, N; Roger Jeffery and Neil Thin (2001): "Branching Out: Joint Forest Management in India", Oxford University Press, New Delhi.

Taneja, Bansuri (2001): "Biodiversity Planning Support Programme Integrating Biodiversity into the Forestry Sector—India Case Study", Paper presented at the Integration of Biodiversity in National Forestry Planning Programme, Indonesia.

Tiwari, Dr. Manish (2004): "Lessons Learnt from Sustainable Forest Management Initiatives in Asia", New Delhi.

19

Conservation of Natural Resources and Impact of Its Depletion in Arunachal Pradesh, India

A Case Study

— Dr. Ram Krishna Mandal

Introductory Statement

As far as Arunachal Pradesh is concerned, the forests are the most important renewable natural resource. It not only constitutes the major land use and two-third share of the territory revenue but also sustain the life through direct and indirect benefits. Any type of development which affects the forests adversely will only mean that water and soil, which sustain the life, will also be affected adversely and the development process will be self-defeating. The economy of tribal people in the district is traditionally based on shifting cultivation. 90% tribals are engaged in such practices. Majority of the agriculture land are hilly and non-irrigated. The rotation period of farming is reduced to 3/4 years. But gradually by transferring the technical knowledge to the tribals, the land use pattern has been changed. The people have also been aware of the evil effects of shifting cultivation mainly depletion of the forests and land. Due to high slopes and lack of conservation measures, soil erosion is very high. The productivity of land and soil fertility has declined over the years. Shifting cultivation is highly labour-intensive, starting from slash and burn in February-March to harvest of crops in December-January. Massive weed infestation, protection of crops from grazing of animals and wildlife, rats are causing a lot of problems. However, due to non-availability of low land, the dependency continues. Gradually, people are switching over to other practices. Now besides their traditional subsistence crops, the tribals have taken cultivation of fruit production and lives stock rearing both regarded as high earning source with an income of about Rs. 10,000 to Rs. 12,000 per year.

Agriculture being an important livelihood option for a significant proportion of the families, living in the hill slopes the project places emphasis on the needs of small and marginal farmers as well as landless families who are often the most sufferers. It believes that this could be done through participatory processes aimed at improving and diversifying crop species and varieties, cultural practices, and associated technologies.

The physical environment that sustains the livelihood of the tribal people in the district compel to reduce their dependence on natural environment, further increase in rural population has pushed the man-land ratio to below sustainable level. The larger demand for foodgrains is tackled with institutional changes and unproved farming techniques, which could enhance the degradation more towards uncertainty in livelihood, though government and non-government plans keep the hope to sustain tribal ecology and economy through the advancement of overall physical environment of the district. While saying so, there is no gainsaying the fact that the tribes to be drawn into the vortex of development, encounters with development, modernization and globalization have produced devastating results on the tribal society not only in the district but all over the state.

Conservation of biodiversity and other natural resources over a long period of time has been possible because of the cultural, spiritual and other social institutions that have guided the relationship of local communities with resources. The community knowledge holds potential not only for preserving biodiversity and ecological function, but also for cultural diversity. Even in a context where deforestation is high, there are forests, streams, old trees and lakes, which have been conserved by the people extremely well. It is not just resources but also the knowledge about these resources, which have been conserved through practice and innovations. Community knowledge is rooted in tradition, contemporary in nature and is constantly evolving as individual and community responses to the challenges posed by their environment. Biodiversity provides a foundation for ecologically sustainable development and food security. The unknown potential of unexploited genes, species and ecosystem is of inestimable but certainly high value. The cultural value of biological diversity conservation for present and future generations is another reason for conserving today. It is important to build up indigenous knowledge on which resource; poor farmers including tribes have conserved many crops and ethno botanical species based on years of informal experimentation and understanding of a particular production system and ecosystem. Rapid changes in the way of life of local communities and consequent loss of community knowledge coupled with the increasing awareness that indigenous knowledge/community knowledge can play an important role in enhancing development, have led developmental workers in both Governmental and non-Governmental organizations to collect and incorporate these resources in process of sustainable development (Singh, *et. al.* 2006).

Methodology: Both conventional and participatory methods have been adopted complementarily to document community knowledge. Looking to the nature of study, participant observations complemented by anthropological approach have been used to explore the information.

In the first step rapport building was established with the village Goan Burha, Primary and Middle school teachers, extension workers and village priests. After this, 10 outstanding wise men having wide knowledge of natural resources from selected villages were selected for conducting the focus group discussions to reach at the consensus result of community practices associated with them.

Degradation of Surrounding Environment: Degradation of surrounding forests, trees and CPRs and rigid forest laws have adversely affected food accessibility, livelihood options and quality of life of local (including indigenous) communities in many areas. Such degradation has often caused periodic phases of hunger and malnutrition in absence of supportive means of livelihood for acquiring basic essentials of life. Forest plantations of eucalyptus and other species no longer provide the rich bio-diversity available earlier in natural forests. CPRs, in which groups of local people have co-equal use rights, such as community pastures, community forests, waste lands, village ponds, rivers etc., have declined at a rapid pace. In a study of 82 villages (Jodha: 1991), such resources declined since 1950-52 by at least 30 per cent and in some cases more than 50 per cent leading to immense hardship of those communities dependent on them. Such phenomena has led to diminished role of local natural resources which have traditionally constituted invaluable asset-base for meeting basic needs and livelihood requirements of local communities.

What Kinds of Forest are in Question?: The local communities are associated with natural forests, woody landscape, community forests and of recent original social plantations or social forestry, where each kind has a differcntial slant with regard to its role and importance. FAO defines a natural forest in tropical countries as either a closed forest or an open forest. A closed forest is one where trees cover a high proportion of the ground and where grass does not form a continuous layer on the forest floor (this includes broadleaved forests, coniferous forests and bamboo forests). An open forest is defined by FAO as mixed forest/grasslands with at least 10 per cent tree cover and a continuous grass layer on the forest floor. A tropical forest includes all stands except plantations. A forest may be described as primary, that is relatively undisturbed, old growth forest or it may be 'secondary' which has re-generated following natural or human disturbances A natural forest is a combination of 'primary' and 'secondary' states. Human disturbances to natural forests through small communities of indigenous people living in and around them can be considered a part of natural disturbances, such as the practice of shifting cultivation. Such small disturbances do not obstruct the functioning of forest eco-systems for nutrient re-cycling, temperature and water regulation, preventing wind and water erosion, regulating rainfall etc.

Human disturbances of higher intensity such as commercial exploitation of forests lead to breakdown of forest eco-systems beyond a point where it becomes difficult for bio-diversity to regenerate itself. Planted trees lead to simplification of the complex system of natural forests and vegetation and become increasingly unstable. Such plantation can hardly substitute for natural forests of diverse species, each with genetically complex population and better chances or survival. The loss of species diversity and of genetic variability within species can lower the resilience to rapid change in both environmental conditions and human demands upon forests (Sargent and Bass: 1992). Today, we have both natural forests, considerably reduced in size over the years, residual forests, and also large areas and patches of planted trees, which may or may not form habitats of local communities/groups.

With drastic fall in forest cover, local communities/groups, in many areas, are also associated with tree/grass plantation for restoration of degraded forests. A new concept of social forestry (also known as community forestry/agro-forestry) has been introduced to influence people's behaviour towards trees. Defining a need for trees, communities are directly involved in tree planting and management. The concept of social forestry is a broad term covering roadside strip planting, community woodlots, farm forestry, and tree planting on marginal lands by the landless. The concept of social forestry recognizes that if such programmes are designed appropriately to motivate people to plant trees, they promote such trees which provide essentials like fuel wood, small timber and income to the small producers and lead to increased benefit to poorer sections of the society (Guggenheim and Spears: 1991). A variant of social forests is Joint Forest Management (JFM) in which local forests is protected by local communities in collaboration with forest department.

For the purpose of this study, forests as natural resources include those areas falling under natural forests, reserve forests, protected areas, community forests and those forests which are under social forestry plantations.

Conceptual Models for Sustainable and Integrated Management of Natural Resources

The Integrated Management of Natural Resources is a well-accepted concept, which has been adopted in principle as part of Agenda-21.

Integrated Management of Natural Resources in India: The following conceptual models have been practiced for moving towards Integrated Management of Natural Resources in India.

(i) Village Based Management Model: This conceptual model has its origin when there was monarchy in India. Traditionally, village was a basic unit of production and self-governance aimed at achieving self-sufficiency. The system was operational on the basis of co-operation and joint action as per the needs. Each village had an elected panchayat with executive as well as judicial powers. The village community in these villages had rights and obligations, which were determined and protected by strong customary law and established conventions. The village community used and managed its natural resources in an equitable and sustainable manner.

(ii) Micro Watershed Concept Model: The National Delineation and Land Use Board in the Ministry of Agriculture in Govt. of India has divided the hilly and semi-hilly areas in the country into watersheds, sub-watersheds and micro-watersheds. The development of water and land resources including agriculture, horticulture, forestry and pasture development is practiced and developed on a micro-watershed basis by funding from Government of India, from the funds of the state government and in some cases from external bilateral and multilateral agencies. In some states separate watershed management departments have been created.

(iii) Eco-system Concept Model: According to the World Conservation Strategy (1980) essential ecological processes are those that are governed supported or strongly moderated by the ecosystems and are essential for food production, health and other aspects of human survival and sustainable development. Life support system is the shorthand for the main ecosystem involved—for example watershed forests or coastal wetlands. According to this concept the maintenance of such processes and systems is vital for all societies regardless of their stage of development.

Although this conceptual model takes into account all the five natural resources but aims about treating them in isolation and not integration at the river basin/watershed level. For example the maintenance of forest eco-system will although help in productive agricultural eco-systems but these are not proposed to be treated simultaneously and integrally and can collapse at any moment if not done that way.

(iv) Watershed Approach: The lacunae in the above mentioned models are taken care of by the watershed approach model. A watershed is defined as any spatial area or a geo-hydrological unit from which rain, snow or irrigation water is collected and drained through a common point. A small watershed of few hectares draining into a small stream may form part of larger watershed, which in turn may form a much larger watershed. These may be referred to as a micro-watershed and a sub-watershed. All the combined watersheds may form a major river basin draining a large area of landmass. The term watershed strikingly refers to divide separating one river basin from the other and over the years it has been identified with a river basin or catchment area. There is no definite size for a watershed as it may vary from a few hectares to several hundred hectares. The 73rd constitutional amendment has placed watershed management in the schedule of subjects to be handled by panchayat. This clause has to be made use of by integrating the natural resource management of five natural resources mentioned above with institutions at grass root level to achieve their sustainable management.

Impact of Deforestation

Environmental and Socio-cultural Problems: The recent debates and developments with regard to the draft National Environment Policy (NEP), 2004 and the Scheduled Tribes (Recognition of Forest Rights) Bill (STB), 2005 are illustrative in different ways of the manner in which social concerns are dealt with in environmental policy and legislation in India. Yet, while the pros and cons of specific policies and legislations have been central to the academic debates on the environment, very little attempt has been made to trace the changes in environmental policy-making and the way social concerns have been problematised.

The ecological balance favouring the complete hydrological cycle has been seriously upset over vast areas due to ignorance or lack of appreciation of methods of conserving and managing natural vegetation (whether a forest, grass land or mixed type) and of clearing the vegetation for cultivation. This misuse and destruction of plants cover combined with great increase in human and livestock population has created intense competition for natural resources, in many cases residual, as between forestry, grazing and crop production. In the continued absence of conservation and correctly integrated land use system, overall habitat deterioration has become very widespread.

Our specific focus with regard to social concerns is a community right to resources—a concern that is central to many of the debates on natural resource management. Three arguments are put forth: (*i*) that while the environment has at one level assumed a non-negotiable presence in policy, social concerns are only highlighted to the extent that they are deemed not to be environmentally destructive; (*ii*) that the discursive terrain through which social concerns are deemed harmful is overly simplistic and in need of re-examination; and (*iii*) that the changing nature of environmental discourse can only be understood within the wider shifts in development policy. Although there are many who would claim that the environment itself receives an inadequate attention in development policy, a contention that is at least partly true, we are concerned here with how emerging policies and legislations tackle social concerns given the socially constructed nature of the environment.

The environment assumed a central role in India, to a large extent, as a result of the first major international conference on the environment, namely, the United Nations Conference on the Human Environment (UNICHE) held in Stockholm in 1972. In preparation for this meeting, each member country was asked to prepare a report on the state of the environment. India setup a committee on the human environment under the chairmanship of Pitambar Pant, a Planning Commission member. The outcome was three reports, one on the state of the environment, one on the problems of human settlement and one on the possible strategies to manage resources. Environmental goals were subsequently incorporate in the Fifth Five-Year Plan onwards. Legislations such as Wildlife Protection Act, 1972 and the Water (Prevention and Control of Pollution) Act, 1974 were passed soon after as well.

While the discursive thrust of much of environmental policy-making in the late 1970s and early 1980s was on incorporating environmental principles in sectoral planning, something that was matched with legislative intervention, the latter part of the 1980s saw the focus shift towards sustainable development. The importance of this shift was that the link between social and environmental concerns was more forcefully articulated.

The 1988 National Forest Policy (NFP) was the first 'environmental' policy document in India that explicitly recognized the linkages between environmental and social concerns in terms of community rights to natural resources. Unlike the previous forest acts that privileged revenue and commercial interests, the NFP was strikingly different section different. Section 4.6 of the policy highlighted the symbiotic relationship between tribals and forests and the need to involve tribal communities in the management of forests. It also emphasized that domestic requirements of firewood, fodder and minor forest produce should be the first priority of forest management, not commercial or industrial needs.

The 1990 government order on joint forest management (JFM), while giving communities adjacent to reserved forest usufruct rights, was also aimed at improving the protection of forest. As Kolavalli (1995) has argued, citing a number of state-level government orders, JFM was the forest department's way to involve communities in the management of forests as it was incapable of doing it on its own.

But JFM has remained a policy and has not been incorporated into the forest act. Thus, while the NFP recognized the symbiocity of forest dependent (tribal) communities with forest, rights afforded to these communities have been limited and often no more (sometimes less) than existing settlement rights.

It has been undisputedly accepted that shifting cultivation creates environment and socio-cultural problems. The growth in the number of members per jhumia family and in the number of jhumia families cannot be absorbed in settled and jhum cultivation, as a result a consumption gap develops in the hills. The greater food requirements cannot be met out of dwindling yields from smaller plots of land devoted to jhuming with smaller and smaller fallowing periods. The over exploitation of forests of jhuming and for commercial purposes also lead to a deterioration of the condition of the forests. The misuse and destruction of plants cover combined with great increase in human and livestock population has aggravated the problem of eco-system. Ecological damage in the hills, widespread poverty among hill-dwelling tribal, social discontent and the growth of extension has been the fall-out of the development of the hill economy. P.R. Kyndiah, Minister of Tribal Affairs and Development of NER "underlined the strong association of jhum with community life and traditions as well as with the unique mountain eco-system."

2. *Soil Erosion:* High rainfall and undulated topography is always associated with problem of severe soil erosion, which affects the environment adversely. The excessive deforestation caused by excessive cutting down of trees for commercial purpose as well as shifting cultivation are resulting in alarming and frightening signals for human survival. Estimates reveal that nearly 181 M.T. of soil is lost annually as a result of shifting cultivation from north eastern hill region (Task Force Report on shifting cultivation, 1983). Developments in the hills and its fall out on the ecology have caused soil erosion, landslides, floods and droughts in the plains.

3. *Soil Fertility:* Burning of vegetation in the process of shifting cultivation chemically alters the plant nutrient supply from organic form to a mineral form in ash, major portion of which is often lost in course of run off. The shorter the jhum cycle preserves the lower level of soil fertility. Five year jhum *cycle* generates very low level of soil fertility. Thus, jhum cultivation becomes uneconomic progressively. This necessitates switching over to settled cultivation.

4. *Loss of Flora and Fauna:* The extent of deforestation of tropical forest has caused world wide alarm as tropical forests provide more than 50 per cent of modern medicine. Tropical forests are living museums and laboratories that have yielded only a tiny fraction of their treasures to scientific study.

Arunachal Pradesh is, as if, a natural garden of more than 20,000 identified species of medicinal plants and so many still remain unidentified. In course of shifting cultivation remarkable varieties of flora and fauna are disappearing, which need immediate attention for extensive and intensive studies.

The type of vegetations destroyed depends upon the length of jhum cycle. A dense forest of long cycle has more tree species than grasses, whereas a forest of short cycle has more number of grasses. About 300 plant species out of native flora in North-Eastern India are used for edible purpose. Of these, over 25 provide tubers/rhizomes etc., which are eaten raw or boiled. Over 50 are consumed as green with their leaves/tender shoots cooked as vegetable; about 170 ripe fruits, which are pulpy and sweet/sub-sweet are eaten raw and many of these are used for pickles/vegetables, when unripe; about 15 have edible seeds are eaten raw or roasted.

Wildlife in the natural situation constitutes the most important component of the ecosystem, which participates affectively in the energy flow and bio-geo-chemical cycling. Animal-plant, plant—plant and animal-animal interactions are the basic milestone of the success of an ecosystem and its productivity. As such, the richness of the ecosystem means the capacity of hold high species diversity but deforestation has threatened the very fabric of the survival of wildlife and the ecosystem in the region. This area is the habitat of as many as 55 major mammalian species of which 17 are rare or extremely rare. 21 rare species of extremely rare birds are found in this region and there are innumerable species of insects. As such, there are different species of wild lives found in this region. Almost all of them are dared as protected species under the protection Act of 1972. Like flora, other forest resources are also disappearing and become rare.

Arunachal Pradesh is a home to myriad life forms coexisting in diverse ecological situations in their pristine glory. The state is today known for its rich bio-diversity. Floristically, there are more than 5000 species of flowering plants, 600 species of orchids, 89 species of bamboos, 18 species of canes, 400 species of ferns, 24 species of gymnosperms and an equally high number of unexplored algae, fungi, lichens, bryophytes, and micro-organisms inhabiting the state. Faunis-tically, the state is also rich in having more than 100 species of mammals, 650 birds, 83 reptiles, 130 fishes and 7 non-human primates and innumerable species of insects, micro-organisms and other life forms. The rich bio-diversity both of flora and fauna have contributed to its recognition as one of the 25 'Bio-diversity Hotspots' in the world. The human pursuit for development has led to environmental degradation to such an extent that it has become almost irreversible loss of forests and other natural resources thereby threatening the very survival of mankind. A number of plant and animal species have either become extinct or come under rare, threatened or endangered category (Arunachal Times, 5th June, 2010).

Man inhabits two worlds: one is the natural world of plants and animals, soil, air and water which preceded him by billions of years and of which he is a part. The other is the world of social institutions and artifacts he builds for himself, using his tools and engines, his science and dreams to fashion the environment obedient to human purpose and directions. It is absolutely necessary that there should be a complete harmony and balance between the two worlds of man (Arunachal Times, 5th June, 2010).

5. ***Water Resources:*** There is ample of water resources in North-Eastern Hill Region. Almost 10 per cent of the total rainfall of the country is received in this region. Soil erosion and deforestation favour in less retention of water under ground and more run off water causing flood in the plains. This causes great loss to human and animal lives as well as crops. Now -a-days, supply of drinking water has become serious problem in every town in the hill region.

Socio-economic and Ecological Impacts

The human disturbances mentioned above lead to socio-economic and ecological impacts on local communities of which the major ones arc listed below:

- — Loss of habitat and local eco-system adversely affected
- — Food, fuel, fodder, wood crises with no alternative in sight
- — Deprived socio-economic and legal status in an exploitative framework
- — Reduced accessibility and increased deprivation

Loss of Habitat

Loss of habitat due to drastic reduction in forest areas have led to increased socio-economic problems of local communities; diverse functions of forest eco-systems such as watershed properties and micro-climatic regulations have been affected, thereby affecting lives and livelihood of local communities.

Forest communities are losing their habitat. Data on habitat defined as 'wild land', 'natural vegetation', 'degree of naturalness' etc. can provide a broad idea of its extent and loss, and, thereby, in absence of actual measure, provide a surrogate measure for loss of habitat of indigenous people who share the same natural habitat as that of bio-diversity.

Basic Needs Crises

Forests are sources of living and livelihood. The diverse functions of a forest are critical to many local communities in traditional economies. Accelerated deforestation has affected livelihoods of local people. The local women are also required to walk longer distances for collection of fuel, fodder, food etc.

Deprived Status

Exploitation, expropriation and threats from outside agencies have increased where some local communities have been forced to forfeit their lands and join the ranks of the landless. In case of constitutional right, of local people they get violated most often and, in practice, they stand to lose in the existing socio-economic and political set-ups, which arc repressive, and, most often, work to their disadvantage.

Reduced Accessibility

Large areas of forests have been formally kept virtually out of reach of forest people who may be in a position to manage forests sustainably for subsistence and income (Douglas: 1983). Such action/policies have led to tensions in social control of forests and have become acute. Increased pressure on forests is making for low resilience of forests systems leading to fuelwood and fodder problems for local communities. Social and economic problems of local people are increasing and so also are the areas of conflict. As an illustration, let us consider the case of India. The colonial laws have led to state-ownership of nearly 97 per cent of India's forest land (Source: World Resources, 1994-95, p.103) which limits people's accessibility to forests. Local communitics having limitcd access to forests without ownership rights face increased pressure of livelihood. This leads to tension and conflict between foresters and local communities where the latter's need for forest resources is overlooked and not acknowledged in practice. Such a state of affair in natural resource management calls for better management by redefining access to forest resources and clarifying roles and responsibilities of local communities.

Meeting the Challenge of Resource Depletion

For local communities, depletion of forests and CPRs through human intervention, have resulted in disturbance or breakdown of their support-base and has led to immense hardship especially because of limited substitution possibilities available for alternative sources of livelihoods. There are also those local communities, whose traditional access and rights have been denied to such local resources thus paving way for their increased impoverishment. However, on the brighter side, there are many cases where local communities have accepted the challenge of natural resources depletion and are participating at local levels, either by themselves, or in collaboration with developmental agencies, to organize themselves for regenerating trees, forests and water bodies while conserving and preserving the existing ones.

Human Interventions, Natural Lands and Local Communities

The benefits flowing from forests, trees and CPRs to local communities have been adversely affected by human interventions in natural resources. The following is an outline of the impact of human interventions at the global level which directly or indirectly impact on lives of local communities. There are different kinds of interventions/policies/actions bringing about changes in the nature of natural lands, particularly forests and in the ultimate analysis, posing disturbances to the harmonious relationship of local communities with nature.

Major human interventions in forests are deforestation, commercial logging, setting up of protected area, partial closure of forests etc. which are described below:

- — There is increasing deforestation due to commercial exploitation, building of dams, mining and construction activities (Litvinoff: 1990). During 1981-90, tropical forests were lost at the rate of 0.8 per cent (15.4 million hectares) in a year. Net annual deforestation during 1981-90 exceeded 2 per cent in 10 tropical countries of Asia and Africa.
- — Commercial logging for industrial activities is increasing rapidly. Eighty-four per cent of such logging took place in closed tropical broadleaf forests in primary (undisturbed forests) during 1980s. Logging activity is a causal factor for forest degradation and is reflected in rough wood production which increased by 19 per cent between 1979-81 to 1989-91. Globally, almost 50 per cent of such rough wood was used for industrial purposes, rest for heating and cooking.
- — Setting up of protected areas for conservation purposes has led to complication and conflict-situation with local communities and also denial of many of their rights and privileges.
- — Closure of parts of forests for setting up of industries or agro--based activities for private, semi-private lands, construction of railways, roads and new settlements has led to shrinkage of forest cover and increased hardship for local communities in their day-to-day existence.
- — Interventions for adhering to international agreements have also alienated many local communities and some of their practices for example, tribal hunting of wild animals which goes against bio-diversity agreements.
- — Policies of economic liberalization, privatization and globalization have both, directly and indirectly, led to reduction of forest cover and cuts in subsidies and grants affecting food subsidies and other welfare schemes involving poor and marginalized communities.

Forests and Road Network

The inadequacy of road is the most important constraint. In the accelerated economic development of remote areas, roads are a precursor of development and are required for all sections of the economy including agriculture, animal husbandry, forestry, power generation, spread of literacy etc. With the extension of roads rapid communication, the people living in remote localities develop need for consumption goods which in turn creates additional demand thereby creating a multiplier effect. Thus, the extension of road network eventually results in a change in outlook and induction of new values. Due to development of road connectivity, forest dweller's movement will increase in finding the alternative way of livelihood. As road connectivity is poor in the district, the people have to search forest based livelihood. So far road connectivity has developed only after the Chinese aggravation, 1962. Till now road connectivity in the remote villages are so poor, people leads their livelihood only depending on forest based agriculture. With the development of road connectivity, horticulture and other alternative way of livelihood may develop and thereby human pressure on forest will be reduced.

Awareness for Conservation

The observations revealed that local farmers are quite aware about the importance of biodiversity and natural resource management. Monpa tribe has developed their location specific indigenous strategy for sustainable biodiversity conservation and overall natural resource management at community level. They follow many practices for conserving the indigenous forest trees and thereby agro-biodiversity. Maize is a staple food crop, managed, produced and conserved with the natural dynamics of indigenous species of Paisang. Leaves of Paisang, a deciduous woody perennial tree found in the sloppy hilly terrains, fall from last week of January and continue up to last week of February. This is the peak period when women folk make the group called Mila to collect and carry the dry leaves of Paisang from community based groves/forest and private land (Singh, et.al. 2006).

For the effort of informal in-situ indigenous agro-biodiversity conservation, Monpa deserves reward and honour. The agro-ecosystem is rainfed and most of the farmers are economically poor. Besides these factors, the biophysical condition of this area does not allow them to apply the inorganic fertilizers, thereby making them dependent on the dry leaves of Paisang and Pine. During the study of exploring the dynamics of community knowledge associated with Paisang tree and its conservation, most of Monpa tribe felt that the Paisang conserved on the village community land should remain. This land should not be allowed to convert into orchards of temperate fruits, showing their interest in protection and preservation of

Paisang tree than the commercial benefit obtained from temperate fruits. Majority of Monpa tribe are interested in either expanding or preserving their Paisang tree land.

Factors Aggravating Damage

Such interventions/policies/actions adversely affect the lives and livelihoods of local communities. Their ability to participate fully in sustainable development practices on their lands becomes limited as a result of multiple factors which are of economic, social and historical nature. Their position is aggravated by the following factors, such as:

- Lack of effective communication between intervening agencies and local communities/groups
- Lack of awareness about their rights and privileges
- Inadequate compensation received and rehabilitation problems
- Denial of forest rights
- Falling production, payment and nationalization of minor forest produce (MFPs)
- Diversion of MFPs to industries
- Exploitation by government agencies and contractors in marketing of MFPs
- Lack of programmes to regenerate sources of MFPs (Chambers, Saxena and Shah: 1991)

Source: Discussion with the villagers in the surveyed area

Local Communities and Opportunities for Participation

The experience and knowledge of local communities is a living inventory containing a wealth of information on their 'know how' about local natural resources and their intricate relationship with them. Such local communities have traditionally preserved and conserved natural resources such as forests through their1sustainable use and it is their participation which needs to be solicited to re-establish the weakened linkages and also for protecting and enriching natural wealth. Agenda-2l (UNCED:1992), while describing the basis of action for conserving of biological diversity emphasizes 'participation and support of local communities' as elements essential to the success of such an approach. Their ideas, knowledge, experience and stakes in local natural resources provide the much needed links for regenerating degraded resources with their active cooperation, involvement and endeavour.

After tracing the relationship of local communities with natural resources, human disturbances in such relationship, their impacts on local communities, and opportunities for community participation. These are very necessary to look into this matter so as to keep sustainability of natural resources.

Findings

Community knowledge plays an important role in food security, resource management, and environmental and biodiversity conservation. The study and research concerning indigenous knowledge/community knowledge need not be restricted to medicinal plants or other forest resources that are potentially profitable to the society and thereby to the state. Instead, research should also focus on other ecological implications, which would prevent the misuse and abuse of forest resources.

Presently, tribal indigenous lifestyle, including mode of economy, societal status, culture, polity as well, are intrinsically linked with and transformed according to the overall changes in the ecological base of their present habitats. Though no less impressive is the pattern of their spatial distribution. In addition, unprecedented increased in population among tribes also generates environmental degradation in such tribal habitats of the district. So, increasing tribal population results into a tremendous stress on the natural environment of the tribes in those areas which again reduces the capacities of local environment to provide adequate support to the tribal people and the others. Thus the problem of physical survival of the tribal people of the district under such circumstances crops up inviting attention of the authority by and large.

It is evident that, tribal assimilation into peasant mode of production is a very slow process though its consequences may be detrimental due to the fact that slow rate of change in tribal economy, leading to the transformation of tribal mode of production again led to the destruction of physical environment in the end.

Conclusion

Due to the productive, protective, scientific, strategic, aes-thetic, recreational and other uses, the forest resources of Arunachal Pradesh have a key role to play in the economic development of this territory and environmental conservation of the entire north-eastern region. However, encroachments, jhuming, forest fires, indiscriminate grazing, illicit felling, faulty road construction, faulty methods of extraction of forest produce and various other factors pose a grave danger to the forests of this territory. In addition to the problem of difficult terrain and climate as well as lack of infrastructure including roads, accelerated development of the study area as well as in the territory is a very challenging task.

In order to harness the natural resources viz. forests, soil and water to the best advantage, it would be necessary to conduct detailed land capability surveys for determining the best land use pattern, to carry out land settlement operation for finalizing the ownership pattern to rationalize the industrial policy framework, to nationalize forest working, to harmonize the competing claims of sectoral development and above all to evolve an integrated development strategy. The task is formidable. Yet a beginning should be made as early as possible. Location specific integrated development approach could also be tried on the pattern of Mandi Project in Himachal Pradesh with suitable modifications.

The aim of an integrated development plan would be to develop an ecologically and economically viable development plan for the mountain eco system of the territory based on the best land use pattern. A sound plan for forest management could be developed to fit into the overall plan so that the forests can play their due role in the development and welfare of the territory.

Formation and strengthening of self-help groups provide the critical social infrastructure to involve everyone in the community to initiate intensive Natural Resource Management. Awareness building about conservation-livelihood synergy, entrepreneurship motivation training, visioning exercises, NRM planning exercises etc. is undertaken with adequate training and exposure for acquiring the know-how.

Indigenous knowledge/community knowledge is the areas where there is need to cultivate a bottom-up approach to development building upon the resources and strength of indigenous people, their experiences and diversified knowledge systems. Self help groups of the local farmers can be formed and need based training should be imparted to them for strengthening resource management, and environmental and biodiversity conservation.

REFERENCES

Janssen, M A, J M Anderies and E Ostrom (2007): "Robustness of Social-ecological Systems to Spatial and Temporal Variability", Society and Natural Resources, 20: 307-22.

Jodha. N.S. (1991), Common Property Resources—A Growing Crisis, Gatekeeper Series, Sustainable Agriculture Programme, IIED. London.

Johns, M. (2000): Ovenbird (Raleigh: North Carolina Wildlife Resources Commission), available at http://www.ncwildlife.org/ pg07_Wildlife Species Con/ Profiles/ ovenbird.pdf.

Mandal, R.K. (2008): "Herbs and Their Sustainability in Arunachal Pradesh", *Kurukshetra*: A Journal on Rural Development, Vol. 56, No. 5, March, Ministry of Rural Development, New Delhi

Mandal, R.K. (2007): "Herbs in Arunachal Pradesh:Economic Viability and Sustainability', *Resarun*: Journal of the Directorate of Research, Vol.33, Govt. of Arunachal Pradesh, Itanagar

Mandal, R.K. (2008): "Forest and Its Sustainability in Arunachal Pradesh" in Joseph, T.M.(ed), New Governance Paradigm: Issues in Development, Kalpaz Publications, New Delhi

Mandal, R.K. (2009): "Forest in Arunachal Pradesh: What is Its Future?", *Arunachal Review*, Vol.-I, No.5, IPR, Govt. of Arunachal Pradesh, Itanagar

Mandal, R.K. (2006): "Control of Jhum Cultivation in Arunachal Pradesh: Retrospect and Prospect", *Kurukshetra*: A Journal on Rural Development, Vol. 55 No. 02, December, Ministry of Rural Development, New Delhi

Mukherjee, Neela, (1993), Participatory Rural Appraisal: Methodology and Applications, Concept Publishing Co., Delhi.

Sangal, P.M. (1977) "Forestry and Integrated Development" in Pandey, B.B.(ed) "Patterns of Change and Potential for Development in Arunachal Pradesh" Himalayan Publishers, Itanagar, New Delhi.

Singh, R.K. et.al. (2006): "Community Knowledge and Biodiversity Conservation by Monpa Tribe", Indian Journal of Traditional Knowledge, Vol. 5 (4), October, pp. 513-518.

Vasudeva, S.P. (2010): "Integrated and Sustainable Management of Natural Resources", *Kurukshetra*, March, Vol. 58, No. 5, pp. 8-12.

Index